FAIRFAX

Also by John Wilson

C.B.: A Life of Sir Henry Campbell-Bannerman

FAIRFAX

*A Life of Thomas, Lord Fairfax,
Captain-General of all the Parliament's forces
in the English Civil War,
Creator & Commander
of the New Model Army*

JOHN WILSON

Franklin Watts

NEW YORK

1985

First published in England in 1985
by John Murray Ltd
First published in the United States in 1985
by Franklin Watts, Inc.,
387 Park Avenue South, New York NY10016
ISBN 0-531-09709-9
Printed in Great Britain

Contents

Illustrations

SOURCES

1, dustjacket and 7, Leeds Castle Foundation; 2, 5, City Art Gallery, York; 3, 6, Joshua Sprigge's *Anglia Rediviva*, 1647; 8, private collection; 9, British Library; 10, from the collection at Broadlands, Hants; 11, Buccleuch Recreational Enterprises, Bowhill; 12, Fitzwilliam Museum, Cambridge.

Maps

To the county of Yorkshire,
which gave me my wife
and from which both my parents came,
this account of one of the most notable
of her sons

'It hath pleased the Lord of Hosts, who was called upon to decide the controversy of this nation, to write His name upon your sword in very legible characters.'

The men of Pride's Foot in a petition to Fairfax as they marched to Westminster. From *The Moderate Intelligencer* for 14 December 1648.

'As the Honour of these Actions, under God, is Yours; so all that they enjoy by these successes, is also Yours: And . . . when this Generation have exhausted themselves, and done their part, they must commend it to their Posterity, to pay the Remainder to your Name.'

Joshua Sprigge's 'Apologie to His Excellencie Sir Thomas Fairfax,' prefixed to his *Anglia Rediviva; Englands Recovery*, 1647.

Preface

OVER THE YEARS, a great many books have been written about Oliver Cromwell. He has been studied at length by writers so various as Thomas Carlyle, Theodore Roosevelt, Samuel Gardiner, Sir Charles Firth, John Morley, John Buchan, Isaac Foot, C. V. Wedgwood, Christopher Hill and Antonia Fraser. But very little has been written about his comrade-in-arms, Thomas Fairfax, the General of the Parliamentary forces in the English Civil War. There have been only two biographies, one published a hundred and fifteen and one forty-seven years ago, and a book for children, Rosemary Sutcliffe's *The Rider of the White Horse*. Except in Yorkshire, he has been largely forgotten. Yet 'Black Tom's' life was extraordinary enough and he is the most notable member of a great Yorkshire family which has made its mark on both sides of the Atlantic.

In his early twenties he was an immensely dashing cavalry officer, of the Jeb Stuart or Joachim Murat type, who was repeatedly wounded and performed all sorts of spectacular feats — so that reading about them sometimes seems like looking at the script of an early Douglas Fairbanks film. Not many soldiers have broken out of a besieged town — Bradford — with half-a-dozen companions, cut their way through one body of three hundred enemy cavalry, defeated another, been shot in the wrist, stayed forty hours in the saddle in a fighting retreat, seen their wife captured in the process (to be returned a few days later in the enemy general's coach) and at the same time dumped and later rescued a baby daughter (later to be a duchess) on the way. In our day he would have earned a VC or DSO several times over.

He organised and led one of the finest English armies ever to take the field — the New Model — confronted and defeated his Sovereign in a pitched battle — Naseby — had both Houses of Parliament wait on him to give him their thanks at his London house, captured — and released — Prince Rupert twice, besieged and captured Oxford, Bristol, Bridgwater and Exeter. He was spoken of as a possible king, and played a key part in the long struggle between Parliament and the Army after the first Civil War. His wife made a scene, twice, at the trial of Charles I, and at the pinnacle of his fame he threw it all over and retired to his house in Yorkshire, where he appointed as tutor to his daughter the poet Andrew Marvell. He played an important part in the restoration of Charles II.

He himself was a modest man, whose brilliance as a soldier was not matched by equal talents for political intrigue. He was a moderate Puritan, a true representative of the English seventeenth-century country gentleman, who in the political struggle after the Civil War found himself caught between militant extremists on either side — on the one hand an obstinate and devious King and conservative Presbyterians in Parliament altogether lacking in common sense, and on the other the republican fanatics. His middle-of-the-road views were brushed aside by both parties, but he was still essentially right and moreover represented what most people in England really wanted. He was also an attractive figure, a strange mixture of dash and diffidence, adored by his soldiers.

It seems timely to attempt a reassessment of this man.

I am once again grateful for the help given me by my wife, who originally suggested this biography. My thanks are due to Sonia, Lady Fairfax, who was kind enough to allow me to look through her collection of Tom Fairfax's letters and to see her portraits of the Fairfax family, to Mr and Mrs Gavin Fairfax and Miss Fiona Fairfax, and to Miss Joan Dawson, who allowed us to visit Nun Appleton. Others who were most helpful were Mr D. S. Porter of the Bodleian Library, the Librarians of the North Yorkshire County Library, York, the London Library, the Edinburgh University Library, the Minster Library at York, the Central Library of Leeds City Council, the Brotherton Library at Leeds, the Department of Manuscripts of the British Library, Mr W. J. Connor of the Archives Department of Leeds City Council and the Director of the Borthwick Institute of Historical Research at York. Mr and Mrs C. P. Wykeham-Martin were kind enough to show us their paintings and relics relating to Fairfax, Mr Nigel Yates, ancient Cistercian nunnery of Nun Appleton. Not to be put off, he scaled the wall at night, abducted the heiress and married her in the local church of Bolton Percy before the prioress could find them. This judicious move, in 1518, brought the Fairfaxes a whole port-folio of properties, including the manor of Denton and two great houses in York, Davy Hall and Bishophill. When the monasteries and nunneries were dissolved twenty years later the family acquired the nunnery lands at Nun Appleton, demolished the old buildings and built a new manor house on the property. Isabel left Denton, Bilbrough and Nun Appleton to her son Thomas, while the younger son Gabriel, to whom his father left lands at Steeton and Bolton Percy, founded a separate branch of the family there.

Thomas, founder of the Denton and Nun Appleton branch of the Fairfaxes, had a number of sons. One lost his life at the siege of Ostend when a marshal of France was killed beside him by a cannon ball and a chunk of the marshal's skull struck him in the face. Another was a poet, translator of Tasso, and demonologist, whose daughters insisted that they had been bewitched. But the eldest, another Thomas Fairfax, was a tough, shrewd and success-ful Elizabethan gentleman. He fought in the Low Countries under the professional soldier Sir Francis Vere and later under the Earl of Essex, and was knighted before the walls of Rouen. He was sent by Elizabeth on diplomatic missions to James VI of Scotland, who offered him a title which, knowing Elizabeth's views about other people's collars for her dogs, he wisely declined. But he was one of the first to swear allegiance to the new king when he succeeded Elizabeth as James I.

As an important public man in Yorkshire, and a member of the Council of the North, he lived in some style at Denton with his wife Ellen, whose father, Robert Aske, had led the Pilgrimage of Grace in 1536 and had been executed in York by Henry VIII. His orders for the house, which survive, describe a large staff with a porter, butler, yeoman of the chamber, steward and chaplain. It was run with military precision, for example:

Morning . . . the Clark of the Kitchen must appoint the Cooks what must be for Breakfast for the Ladies in the Chambers, and likewise for the Gentlemen in the Hall or Parlour, which must be served by Eight of the Clock, and not after. Dinner must be ready by Eleven of the Clock. Prayers tenne . . .

For the Ushers . . . If any unworthy Fellow do sitt himself down before his betters, he must take him up and place him lower . . . Let the best fashioned and apparelled servants attend above the Salt, the rest below. If one servant have occasion to speak to another . . . let him whisper, for noyse is uncivil . . . the cupber-keep . . . must know which be for Bear and which for Wine for it were a foul thinge to mix them together . . .

The patriarch of this establishment had twelve children. Two of his sons were killed in 1621 fighting for the Protestant Elector Palatine at Frankenthal in the Thirty Years' War. Another was killed taking part in the first Duke of Buckingham's disastrous expedition to La Rochelle. A fourth perished mysteriously in Turkey. All were brave but unsuccessful. More prosaic and more fortunate was the eldest son, Ferdinando, of whom his father said sourly, but unfairly, 'I sent him into the Netherlands to train him up a soldier, and he makes a tolerable county justice.'

Ferdinando, as the eldest son of an important Yorkshire gentleman, was married to Mary, daughter of the president of the Council of the North, Lord Sheffield. He became quite a prominent member of the House of Commons, sitting for Boroughbridge in the last three parliaments of James I and the first four of Charles I. He had two sons and six daughters. His elder son, yet another Thomas Fairfax, the future general, was born at Denton at 1612, just after the publication of the Authorised Version of the Bible. He grew up at Denton and at another house nearby, Skow Hall, living the life of a country boy in Yorkshire.

He was eight when the *Mayflower* sailed for America and the Protestant cause was crushed at the battle of the White Mountain outside Prague, leading to the flight of the Winter Queen, Elizabeth of Bohemia, sister of Charles I, with the infant Prince Rupert. He was still a child when his four uncles were killed overseas and in his early teens when King Charles came to the throne. In 1626 he went at 14, the usual age in those days, to St John's, Cambridge, like many of his friends, for Yorkshire links were with Cambridge, not Oxford. His grandfather had written to Ferdinando, 'I purpose, God willing, to go shortly to London, and to bring your son up with me, and to dispose him into this or some other course for his education as I shall be advised there.'

In London the young King Charles was becoming exasperated with the cloud of French priests and hangers-on who had come over

with his French Catholic wife, Henriette Marie, and finally, in a
cri de coeur which rings down the years, wrote to Buckingham:

Steenie,

   . . . I command you to send all the French away to-morrow out of the
town. If you can, by fair means, but stick not long in disputing, otherwise
force them away, driving them like so many wild beasts, until ye have
shipped:– and so, the devil go with them. Let me hear no answer, but of the
performance of my command.

   So I rest

     Your faithful, constant, living friend

              C.R.

But Charles had other difficulties too, above all money difficulties,
and as one of many devices to raise funds he reduced the price of
peerages, which in his father's time had cost some £6000. Titles
became as easy to buy as they were to be much later in the days of
Lloyd George and Maundy Gregory. The elder Thomas Fairfax,
alert to a chance to consolidate his position, bought a relatively
inexpensive Scottish peerage for a down-payment of £1500, and so
became Lord Fairfax. It was still a rarish distinction — there were
under one hundred peers in England.

The younger Thomas Fairfax studied at Cambridge and spent
his holidays in Yorkshire, where he and his grandfather shared a
passion for horses. Both of them were to write treatises on the horse.
His grandfather is alleged to have once said to him, 'Tom! Tom!
mind thou the battle; thy father is a good man, but a mere coward;
all the good I expect is from thee!' The young student was 16 when
Oliver Cromwell was first elected to the House of Commons and
when Thomas Wentworth, newly appointed Lord President of the
Council of the North, offered the Vice-Presidency to his grandfather. The following year, 1629, King Charles dismissed his third
parliament and began his eleven years of personal rule, during which
time no parliament met and the King was constantly short of money.

Like many of his contemporaries Thomas went on from Cambridge to an Inn of Court, in his case Gray's Inn, for some grounding
in the law, useful in preserving one's estates in a hard world. But he
did not stay there long and was never called to the Bar. He had
more of a mind to see the world and try his hand at a little fighting.
In February 1628 his father wrote to his grandfather 'from Watson's, a Tailor's house, in Woolstable':

My lord of Clare adviseth to send my son to my Lord Vere's company, at Dort; he saith he may there practice arms, fencing, dancing and study the mathematics; and my Lord Houghton promises his best care over him whilst he is there . . . I could not resolve anything herein until I knew your Lordship's pleasure . . .

So Thomas, together with another Yorkshire boy, John Hotham from Scarborough, went over to the Low Countries to join the English forces and the Prince of Orange, where he found crowds of other volunteers whose names were to become famous fifteen years later — men like Philip Skippon, Thomas Glemham and Jacob Astley. The army marched from Arnhem to Nijmegen, crossed the Maas and laid siege to the Spanish forces holding Bois-le-Duc (or 's-Hertogenbosch) in Brabant.

In a letter to his grandfather, written in May 1629, Thomas showed his first interest in military affairs:

Sir, we are now before Busse, a town of great strength; all the one side of it is marsh ground, which makes it very strong. We have entrenched ourselves with a running trench round the town . . . and have raised seven batteries; there are three schooners belonging to the town, which we must take before we do any good; and we are making mills to draw the water before we can approach the town . . . they have great want of corn, so that we think we shall not be long about it . . .

But, though the historian Ranke maintains that the siege riveted the attention of Europe, soldiering and fencing, and even dancing, do not seem to have detained Tom for long. He moved to France and spent a year there, saying, 'I only learned the language, and knew war only by an uncertain relation.' He ran short of funds there, a correspondent telling his grandfather that 'his present means only keeps him in meat and lodging, with (scarce) an addition of clothes' and that if his allowance was not increased 'he can but be a wandering prisoner, debarred the enjoyment of the best of manners'. Another described him as 'in health, and with some gentleman at Meuse'. He caught smallpox there but recovered. His grandfather clearly did not approve of his stay in France. He may have felt like Sir Henry Slingsby, who warned the tutor who was taking his son to France that he should 'take heed what companie he keeps . . . for the frenche are of an ill conversation and full of many loathsome deseases'. 'Many letters have I written unto you,' wrote young Thomas, 'to gain your good will, but as yet received no answer.'

Now 20, he came back to England but stayed in London, writing to his grandfather to say that it was his 'earnest desire to see the army of Sweden'. His grandfather did not take kindly to this idea. He looked on young Tom as a flibbertigibbet. An effort to intercede on behalf of the erring youth was made by Lord Fauconberg, formerly Sir Thomas Bellasis, who had married old Sir Thomas's sister:

> give me leave to interpose my opinion concerning my cousin, your grandchild, whose sweet condition begets him love of all that know him . . . it were a great pity this condition should be altered with discontent, or the spirit dejected with want . . . it being nothing that he hath exceeded his allowance as the times are now. This much I write because I think he is oppressed with melancholy, which may do him hurt, if it be not purged by heart's ease and liberty.

Another was made by Ferdinando's father-in-law, now Lord Mulgrave, who wrote to Lord Fairfax to 'intimate to you . . . the reasons that moved him to abide in these parts . . .' namely his 'desire . . . to employ some further time in those famous actions now abroad with the King of Sweden'. Lord Mulgrave, a veteran of the Armada and a Knight of the Garter, added, 'mine eyes have been upon him and his carriage hath given me such good satisfaction, as I am confident (God blessing him) he will be a comfort to us both, and a joy to his friends . . .'

With these great men pouring oil on the waters, Thomas was able to go and see his grandfather, but the prospective jaunt with the Swedish army was vetoed. So ended Thomas's education. He now began to live at Denton and Nun Appleton as a young country gentleman.

The Yorkshire gentry in the seventeenth century were an important, influential, wealthy and much intermarried group, who were largely responsible for the administration of the county, collecting the taxes, enforcing the law and controlling the militia. It has been calculated that there were 679 gentry families in Yorkshire at the time. Yorkshire had not been exempt from the great movement for the reform of the Church, led by Luther and Calvin, which had swept Europe since the end of the fifteenth century. The county had rebelled against the drastic changes introduced by Henry VIII and Thomas Cromwell but its revolt had been ruthlessly crushed. It had experienced the religious revolution led in England by Tyndale, Latimer and Cranmer and the reaction under Mary which, unlike the Counter-Reformation on the continent, had failed to reimpose the authority of the Catholic church. The county was left divided between adherents of the new Protestant beliefs and those who clung to the old Catholic religion. Now about a quarter of the gentry families were Catholics and about the same number, including the Fairfaxes, Puritans. Many, like the Fairfaxes, were old-established families, but a quarter of all the gentry families, again including the Fairfaxes, owned property which had belonged to the monasteries. This, and a threefold increase in farm prices since the accession of Elizabeth, had made many of them wealthy, though others of course had failed to prosper or had withered away. Many had built themselves large, usually E-shaped, manor houses, each with its hall, richly decorated great chamber, and sometimes a long gallery. They often had swarms of servants — Sir Richard Cholmley had fifty or sixty menservants and never went to London without taking thirty or forty with him. The manor houses like Denton were largely self-sufficient, making their own bread and beer and living on their own farm produce. Yorkshire has always produced men of an independent cast of mind, but life on these self-contained estates, each a little world of its own, produced a particularly proud type of gentleman, who liked to make up his mind for himself. Those who, like the Fairfaxes, had become Protestants, were reinforced in this by a faith that left a man alone and unsupported with his God.

This independence of spirit extended to resistance to taxation, although it was not really at all onerous. The elder Thomas Fairfax had loyally co-operated in helping to collect Charles's forced loan or 'free gift' of 1627. But other Justices of the Peace reported that in the West Riding, they had read the King's letters, and 'after some silence of the people . . . they did all . . . agree in the negative, pleading their poverties and alleging the occasion of their wants, which is by the late dearth of corn, the present dearth of cattle and the want of trade in this poor part of the country . . . yet all, with much alacrity, expressing in their words their forwardness to defend his majesty with their lives, and with their goods when God shall enable them'. Even future royalists like Sir Marmaduke

Langdale and Sir Hugh Cholmley incurred severe censure from the King and Wentworth for opposing the levy of Ship-Money in 1634.

The historian of the Yorkshire gentry says that 'it was customary for a marriage to be arranged between the respective families without too much attention being paid to the wishes of the young couple'. This was indeed the nature of the negotiation which started in 1635 for a marriage between Thomas and Anne Vere, the fourth daughter of the celebrated soldier, Lord Vere, under whom Thomas had briefly served at Bois-le-Duc.

Sir William Constable, staying at Sheer's Court without Aldersgate, conducted the bargaining on behalf of Thomas's father, Sir Ferdinando. He used an intermediary, Dr Gouge, who reported that the general's widow, Lady Vere, intended to give each of her daughters a portion of £3000 or £4000 'according as she shall like of the party: and that there is no haste on her part of having them bestowed, since the longer they stay, the better she shall be able to do for them'. Sir William then tried to arrange that he and his wife 'might have had a sight of these two young gentlewomen'. Two months later he sent a progress report. Lady Vere, he said, 'could not enlarge her offer' but a Mrs Barrow 'seemed to think that her lady might be wound up to some few hundreds above £4000'. He disclosed that another offer was being considered and thought himself that the best prospect might be to accept 'part of the portion in land and part in money'.

A month later Thomas himself took a dutiful but far from enthusiastic hand, writing to his father from the *Three Black Birds* in Fleet Street:

> Sir,
>   Since my coming to London I have studied to do my best in effecting the business I came up about; but whether my lady Vere disliked me, the conditions, or us both, I cannot tell; but she put me off with an unwillingness to marry her daughter in a time of such perplexity as she pretends to be in . . . whether I should proceed farther in this business or no, I refer it to you . . .

This sounds to our ears almost painfully subservient but we must remember that in the seventeenth century parental authority was absolute. John Aubrey indeed wrote, 'Gentlemen of thirty and forty years old were to stand like mutes and fools bareheaded before their parents.' While not carrying matters to these lengths, Thomas always treated his father with great deference and respect, even after he himself became one of the most important men in England. Constable thought that Thomas had been too easily discouraged — 'It seems that he, in a desire to bring it to a short point . . . met with an answer which, perhaps, he apprehends more absolute and positive than was intended.' Three months later Lord Fairfax himself wrote to Ferdinando: 'We are free in our offers, and I hope my lady will consider it; if not, she hath her monies, and we our wares . . .' The person thus described as 'wares' was still however expected to correspond regularly — 'Your son hath forgotten to write unto me . . .'

At last the settlement was made. Lord Fairfax wrote urging that the young couple should come up to Yorkshire and saying, 'I would have Tom put into the commission of peace . . . I would have my name left out.' The marriage took place at Hackney parish church on 20 June 1637. Ferdinando, who described Lady Vere as 'very tender of this child and affectionate to my son', wrote to Lord Fairfax that 'The marriage that my lady intended private, was made too public; a very great feast made and many at it. I hope she will prove a good wife; her affection to her husband, and her demeanour in these few hours promiseth well.' Anne Vere seems to have been no great beauty but, like her two parents, a strong personality. Contemporaries considered that she exercised considerable influence on her husband. Tom and Anne appear to have become very fond of one another.

Things did not start well, for almost immediately Tom, still at Hackney, was stricken by the ill health that plagued him all his life. Lady Vere wrote to Ferdinando:

> Within two or three days after your going down, my son, after a fit of the stone, fell into an ague, which hath held him ever since with somewhat long fits each other day . . . My daughter, with watching and cold she got, is fallen into a fever, which is the more to her, because she hath never had any sickness.

A week later she wrote that Tom was much better, 'his fits come now to be but very little. He is, with his ague and spare diet, brought low.' But soon he was worse again and Lady Vere said that the stray fits

> seize so upon his spirits. I perceive he hath but a weak body, and the more care and circumspection for the preservation of his health will be required, especially against melancholy, which is, I think, the ground of all . . . I

cannot much blame my daughter in case of so much fear and danger of a husband so dear to her . . . though she somewhat exceeds in giving way to her affections.

Lady Vere was the second person to remark upon Tom's melancholy. The same observation was made about Cromwell as a young man by his doctor. But Tom recovered and was soon writing to 'The Right Honourable My Very Good Grandfather' with the news from London — of Lady Townsend's baby, the siege of Breda, the imprisonment in the Tower of the Bishop of Lincoln ('the fate of this Bishop is much lamented . . . in the lowest ebb of fortune did he show the treasures of a rich mind') and the imprisonment of Prynne and Bastwick.

The young couple went to live in Yorkshire and the following year their daughter Mary was born at Bishophill in York. They began their married life with Lord Fairfax at Denton, but life with the difficult old man, now nearly eighty, proved to be disagreeable and they soon moved to Nun Appleton, which from then on became their home.

Tom was now caught up in public events, for Charles I was raising troops in Yorkshire to punish the Scots for repudiating his prayer book, abolishing bishops and adopting the National Covenant. This reaffirmed the Calvinist profession of faith of 1580, condemned many Catholic doctrines, protested against the Popish tendencies of the King and Archbishop Laud and bound signatories to maintain the sovereign, the true religion, and the laws and liberties of Scotland. Ferdinando was made colonel of a regiment of the Yorkshire trained bands and Tom raised a troop of 160 dragoons from the villages on the family estates — the 'Yorkshire redcaps' as they were called — so assuming his first small command.

In his correspondence with his grandfather, discussion of the horses they both loved took priority over the military preparations. Tom wrote:

I intended to have returned your bald horse this day, but because I thought your lordship would not use the other yet, and having some delight in his going, I thought to keep him till I received your lordship's commands, which I now have, and as ready do observe. I fear he will want something of what is required in a good stallion; his age is much, and his body but small, yet he is of a good race and well spirited, and, as I hear, hath got both larger and handsomer horses than himself . . .

His grandfather replied, 'I have by this messenger sent the bay gelding to the Honourable Mr Percy . . .' But the scratch expeditionary force which was being assembled received some attention. Tom told his grandfather that: 'the army is not yet got together; it will fare the worse when it doth, for provisions are very scant . . . yet, if it please God, He can do it by this or weaker means . . .' The old man took up his pen to write proudly to 'My very loving grandchild, Thomas Fairfax, captain of a troop of horse in His Majesty's service': 'Tom, I desire you to be mindful to serve God with all your soul, and the King with all your heart . . . Avoid private quarrels as much as you can . . . My prayers shall always be for the King and the good success of the army . . .'

He was fond of his grandson, but doubted whether he had the worldly prudence and sharpness necessary to survive and flourish in a competitive world, and perhaps he still brooded over the row which had led Tom and Anne to leave Denton for Nun Appleton. Tom's uncle Charles recorded a conversation he had with the old man a few months before his death in 1640:

> He was walking in his great parlour at Denton, I only then present, did seem much perplexed and troubled in his mind, but, after a few turns, broke out . . . 'Charles, I am thinking what will become of my family when I am gone; I have added a title to the heir-male of my house, and shall leave a competent estate to support it. Ferdinando will keep it, and leave it to his son; but such is Tom's pride, led much by his wife, that he, not contented to live in our rank, will destroy his house.'

Having said this, the old man instructed Charles to make his prophecy known 'when I saw a probability that it might so turn out'. What did happen was that Tom and Anne failed to produce a son and heir. This year of 1640 Anne had a second daughter, but she died in infancy and they had no more children, so they were left only with the two-year-old Mary.

Training and exercising their newly-raised troops was a novel experience for most of the Yorkshire gentry: 'These are strange, strange spectacles to this nation in this age,' wrote Sir Henry Slingsby, 'that have liv'd thus long peacably, without noice of shot or drum & after we have stood newtrals & in peace with all ye world . . . it is I say a thing most horrible that we should engage our self in a war one with another.'

Tom Fairfax, known from his dark looks as 'Black Tom', rode

north with the army to Berwick and took part in cavalry skirmishes against a much more effective Scottish army. He was knighted by the King at the age of 28 in January 1640. Whether he took part in the second Scottish war that year is uncertain, though Bishop Burnet claimed that he was with the army that was defeated at Newburn 'and did not stick to own that till he passed the Tees his legs trembled under him'.

In May his grandfather died, leaving Tom 'my best arms, my best horse, my gilt plate, with all my household stuff now at Denton, provided that his father have the use of them during his life'. Ferdinando became Lord Fairfax. In November the King was at last forced to summon Parliament and the struggle between them began in earnest. Possession of a Scottish peerage did not prevent Ferdinando from sitting in the House of Commons and he became an active member of the radical party led by Pym. He voted for the attainder of his fellow Yorkshireman Thomas Wentworth, now Lord Strafford. The views of the Fairfaxes had changed since old Sir Thomas had been invited by Wentworth to join the Council of the North thirteen years before. It has been pointed out that 'the new Yorkshire families, the Saviles, Hothams, Fairfaxes, Vanes, who had replaced the Percies, Eures, Constables and Ellerkers as the leading men of the county, were all hostile to Wentworth.' Ferdinando shared the views of a correspondent, Thomas Stockdale, that 'that great engine the Lord Strafford . . . hath . . . battered down their laws and liberties, and levelled them with the most servile nations.' He served on the committee which brought in the Grand Remonstrance in November 1641. It was probably because he objected to the arbitrary rule of the King and Strafford that he came out so strongly against the King. But he may too have been influenced, as a Protestant, by the appalling reports from Ireland at the beginning of 1641. The same Thomas Stockdale wrote to him saying,

I had a letter the last week from my brother Dick Parsons now at Chester; wherein he writes, that by general reports and by the calculation of judicious and knowing men, the papists have murdered and destroyed in Ulster, fifty thousand Protestants, men, women, and children . . . it concerns us all to endeavour the prevention of the like in this Kingdom.

Although the reports may have been exaggerated, nevertheless, throughout the next ten years, Protestants in England, like the

Fairfaxes and their friends, never forgot this massacre of their
fellow Protestants in Ireland, the harbinger of many troubles to
come.

1641 was the last year of peace before the outbreak of the Civil
War. There has been prolonged controversy among professional
historians about the causes of that war, and one of them, Professor
Kenyon, has written that 'Instead of striding along a brightly
illuminated high road, the historian now shuffles uneasily in a thick
fog.' When professional historians are fogbound, it would be pre-
sumptuous for anyone else to be dogmatic about why the war
broke out when it did. The Yorkshire Fairfaxes were, it appears,
nostalgic for Queen Elizabeth. One of old Sir Thomas's friends
reminded him that she 'had raised them from a pea to a nation'.
They found Charles I, in Rushworth's words, 'excessively in love
with his darling prerogative' and seeking to establish that absolute
monarchy which he had seen when he went to Madrid as a young
man to seek a wife. They were incensed by the high-handedness in
Yorkshire of the King's agent, Strafford, and by the exactions of a
King who had tried to dispense with Parliament and was desperate
for money. They resented the King's actions against Parliament —
a body largely composed of country gentlemen like themselves —
from the death of Sir John Eliot in the Tower in 1632 to the attempt
to arrest the five members ten years later. They suspected that the
King, influenced by his Catholic wife and by an archbishop thought
to have Roman tendencies, was altogether too well disposed to
'popery'. They found the King himself 'conscientious and untrustworthy'. They wanted a King, but a King firmly subjected to
the will of Parliament. They certainly did not want a war, but
while the political struggle continued, and opinion polarised, the
two sides drifted unwittingly nearer the edge of the precipice, while
tension increased with every month that passed.

The Eve of War

I N J A N U A R Y 1642 Parliament decided that some of the Yorkshire trained bands under Sir John Hotham should secure
Hull, where an important stock of arms and ammunition was
kept. Other magazines were put under guard and the houses of
Catholic recusants searched for arms. A letter from Thomas Stockdale in February told the new Lord Fairfax that 'the malignant
party is not confined within the bounds and number of the recusants', and that he was keeping Sir Thomas Fairfax privately
informed of the information that came from his father at Westminster.

Thomas Fairfax, with other leading Yorkshiremen, including his
cousin Sir William Fairfax, the Lord Mayor of York 'and others of
quality', now signed petitions to the King, Lords and Commons,
drawn up by Stockdale. These expressed thankfulness for the purging 'the House of Peers of the prelates' votes', called for 'guards
over the houses of Papists and popishly affected persons', for the
laws against priests and Jesuits to be fully executed and for the
King's 'evil councillors' to be discovered and punished. The
signatories undertook to maintain 300 horse and 3000 foot to be in
readiness. In York there were clashes between Royalist 'blues' and
Parliamentarian 'oranges', when the latter smashed church windows
and 'took away superstitious pictures'. The supporters of the
petition were referred to as Roundheads or Gadarenes.

The King came to York in March 1642. On 23 April he tried to
enter Hull but Sir John Hotham shut the gates in his face. Shortly
thereafter five parliamentary commissioners, one of them Ferdinando, came to York and had fruitless discussions with the King.
Charles demanded that the Yorkshire gentry should raise a guard
for his person, a demand to which there was only a limited response,

Sir Henry Slingsby writing, 'I perceiv'd a great backwardness in them, & upon Summons few or none appear'd.' The King then issued a proclamation summoning the 'ministers, freeholders, farmers, and substantial copyholders' to meet him on 3 June on Heworth Moor, just outside York, beyond Monk Bridge over the river Foss.

A vast concourse met at Heworth — 'the like . . . was hardly ever seen in Yorkshire'. The King rode among the crowds and he and his supporters explained his determination to uphold the law and the Protestant religion and his desire for a personal guard. The opposition had prepared a petition complaining about the King's stay in Yorkshire, away from the Parliament, about his collecting horse and foot and 'cavaliers from other parts' and interrupting the clothing trade, and begging the King to refrain from warlike preparations and to come to terms with Parliament. They chose Thomas Fairfax to hand it over. The King refused to accept it. Fairfax was a determined young man, so, on foot, he followed the King about, pushed his way through to him and finally thrust the petition in front of Charles on the pommel of his saddle. Either the great horse was frightened or the King impatiently spurred him on. The horse plunged forward and it seemed as though the King was trying to trample Fairfax underfoot. Even if you are a King of England, it is unwise to try to ride down a Yorkshireman. The two men were not to see each other again until, just three years later, they met commanding the two armies at Naseby.

Men were now being forced to take sides. Those in England north of York, in Wales, the country around Oxford, and Cornwall — in general the poorer and more conservative rural areas — supported the King; while those in London, the Midlands, the southern counties, East Anglia, the seaports, and the clothing towns in Yorkshire — the richer, urban and commercial part of the country — were for Parliament. Most, but by no means all, of the great magnates and their dependents and nearly all Catholics were for the King, the majority of Puritans for the Parliament. Fairfax later wrote, 'I must needs say, my Judgment was for the Parliament, as the King and Kingdom's great and safest Councell . . .' He went on:

my father being yett att his House att Denton, where I then waited upon him, though he had Notice from his Freinds that it was resolved that he should be sent for as a Prisoner to York, yet resolved not to stirr from his own house, not knowinge any Thinge by himself to deserve itt; but (the

Country sufferinge daily more, and more) many were forced to come and intreat him to joyne with them in Defence of themselves and Country . . . and (much importund by those that were about him) was resolved (seeinge his Country in this great Distress) to runne the same Hazard with them in the just Preservation of itt.

Clarendon wrote:

There were very few Gentlemen, or Men of any Quality, in that large County, who were actively or factiously dissaffected to his Majesty; and of those the Lord Fairfax, and his son, Sir Thomas Fairfax, were the chief: who were govern'd by two or three, of inferior Quality, more conversant with the People, who were as well known as They. All these were in the county, at their Houses, within few miles of York; and the King resolv'd, at his going away, to have taken them all Prisoners . . . But the Gentlemen of the County . . . hearing of this Design, besought his Majesty 'not to do it;' alledging that he would, thereby, leave them in a worse condition . . . many really believing, that neither Father nor Son were transported with over-vehement inclinations to the Parliament; but would willingly sit still, without being Active on either side . . . And so his Majesty left York . . .

Fairfax signed the protest of leading Yorkshiremen on 29 August — Mr Rushworth writing from London to tell Ferdinando that the 'House is much contented with Sir Thomas Fairfax's noble carriage of Thursday last' — but did not rush to arms when the King raised his standard at Nottingham. Indeed, when it came to the point, many of the Yorkshire gentry felt at first that the quarrel could be settled elsewhere and that they could stay out of it. There was a peaceable spirit abroad, what Clarendon called the 'drowsy and unactive genius of the Kingdom (contracted by long ease and quiet)'. Sir Robert Poyntz was later to say, 'my countrymen love their pudding at home better than a musket or pike abroad, and if they could have peace, care not what side had the better'. Tom Fairfax was one of those who negotiated a local treaty of neutrality between Ferdinando and Henry Bellasis, the two knights who had sat in Parliament for Yorkshire and who now took opposite sides. But his father made this agreement subject to Parliamentary approval, and an outraged Parliament speedily disavowed it.

The Royalists were making active preparations, and Henry Slingsby recorded:

Sr Tho. Fairfax . . . being at York & seing me, as I was riding one evening to my own house, sends his man after me in ye street, for he desir'd to speak with me; & it was to let me know he took notice that ye gentlemen held their meeting in York, for raising monys & men by ye commission of array, which was against law & caus'd ye country to be in fear . . . I told him that I conceived that neither himself nor any of his had any cause of fear, seeing as that he had [not] appear'd in Armes . . .

Fairfax himself later wrote that the 'many honest people' who opposed the King were 'a very considerable pt of ye Country' and defined them, significantly, as 'beinge for Religion, Estats and Interests'.

In September Ferdinando, described by Essex as 'a great patriarch of your country', was chosen by the Yorkshire parliamentarians to command their forces in the county; Tom, now 30, 'having a Commission under him to bee Generall of ye Horse'. The Fairfaxes based themselves in Leeds and Bradford, where they could recruit among the clothing workers, nearly all of whom supported the Parliament. But they were handicapped by having no money to pay the soldiers they collected. They were both proclaimed traitors by the Earl of Newcastle (who was himself proscribed by Parliament).

In the 1640s warfare was still a primitive affair. The basic infantry weapon was the pike — a 15- or 16-foot ash pole shod with an iron spike. Although this was described by the Spaniards as the noblest of weapons — 'la señora y reyna de las armas' — and to 'trail a pike' was thought an honourable role, it was in reality little better than an Iron-Age spear. It was primarily a defensive weapon, used with the butt on the ground to resist a cavalry charge, by a pikeman wearing an armoured cap and a corslet or 'back and breast'. The pikemen, who might also use halberds, were intermingled with and protected the musketeers. These used heavy, three to four foot long, unreliable and inaccurate matchlock muskets, aimed with the help of a rest and firing bullets weighing an ounce and a quarter, of which most were carried in a pouch but one for ready use in the musketeer's mouth. The charge of powder in the musket was ignited by a 'link' of match — two or three yards of cord boiled in vinegar or the dregs of wine. The rate of fire was extremely slow and very often the piece failed to go off. It was also dangerous. When it rained, as Fairfax himself later wrote, it 'made our firearms little useful either for assault or defence'. But when it did go off the musket 'spoyles horse and man thirty score off', meaning that it could be effective at something over 400 yards.

In the cavalry the heavily armoured cuirassiers, needing a very strong horse to carry the weight, were obsolescent at the beginning of the Civil War, only Sir Arthur Hazelrig's 'lobsters' in the south surviving for a time, and lances were seldom used except by the Scots. The cavalry of the Civil War, organised in troops, each of some seventy sabres, were technically known as harquebusiers. They wore a light helmet, known as a 'pot', and a 'back and breast' over a buff leather coat. They were usually armed with a straight sword and a pair of firelock pistols, while the officers sometimes carried carbines. Cavalry tactics, as evolved by the German *reiters*, had been to ride up to the infantry line, fire their pistols and retire, but Fairfax and Rupert preferred to charge home, using the tremendous weight of massed men and horses — the troopers riding knee to knee — to create a shock effect.

Dragoons were musketeers mounted on cheap 'nags', who in action were sent ahead to hold bridges or line hedges or to act as outposts and fought dismounted, while every eleventh man held the horses of ten of his comrades.

Artillery consisted of inefficient guns with picturesque names, from the ponderous culverin, which needed eight horses to pull it, through the demiculverin, saker, minion and drake to the tiny falconet. These had little value in battles but were effective in battering down walls in sieges of cities or castles or fortified houses.

Throughout the Civil War there was a tendency for weapons to grow lighter and for armour to be discarded. Infantrymen cut down their pikes and musketeers discarded the musket rest. Colonel Hutchinson, who held Nottingham Castle for Parliament, made a typical move when he 'put off a very good suite of armor . . . which being muskett proof, was so heavie that it heated him, and so he would not be persuaded by his friends to weare aniething but his buffe coate'. By the time of Marlborough's campaigns, fifty-five years after the Civil War, armour was abandoned altogether, the matchlock had been replaced by the flintlock and the pike by the bayonet.

Many engagements in the Civil War were casual hit-and-run affairs, minor raids or skirmishes. But in a set-piece battle like

Marston Moor or Naseby the troops were drawn up formally in what was called 'battalia'. Usually the foot was in the middle, the horse on either flank, with guns disposed between them, the baggage wagons collected behind, and dragoons lining any convenient hedges. Normally the horse began by charging the horse opposite them. Rupert and Fairfax fought with the dash of fighter pilots but found it difficult to stop and reform. It was the singular merit of the older Cromwell, commanding his disciplined heavy cavalry, and with more of the steadiness of a bomber pilot, that he was able to keep his men in hand after a charge and therefore to attack again.

If a charge was not successful in routing the opposition at the first shock, the issue had to be fought out with swords and pistols. When the pistols had been fired they were often hurled at the enemies' heads.

Meanwhile the foot would engage each other 'at push of pike'. If a regiment of horse was victorious on its wing it might then attack the enemy's foot. It could not charge a solid array of pikes, so musketeers or dragoons had first to open a gap by firing into one section of the foot. Once the horsemen could get in through such a gap they usually made short work of the enemy pikemen and musketeers.

Each army had a 'scoutmaster' responsible for reconnaissance and intelligence, who needed to be 'a good Cosmographer' but to beware 'of Rashnesse and Credulitie'. Summonses to the enemy were delivered by a 'trumpet'. It was considered very bad form to shoot or molest the 'trumpet'. The armies could travel at the rate of about ten miles a day. An advance body, or vanguard, was usually referred to as a 'forlorn hope' or simply as a 'forlorn'.

The Rider of the White Horse

> 'When I was a child (and so before the Civill Warres)
> the fashion was for old women and mayds to tell
> fabulous stories nightimes, of sprights and walking of
> ghosts . . . When the warres came, and with them
> Liberty of Conscience . . . the phantoms vanished.'
>
> Aubrey *Brief Lives*

THE FAIRFAXES' first action was at Bradford, where their little force of some 300 was attacked by a Royalist force of 700–800 with two guns. But the attackers were beaten off. A few days after this, the Fairfaxes and Captain Hotham, who had joined them with three troops of horse, tried to surprise the Royalists at Leeds but 'ye Enemy having Notice of itt quitt ye Towne'. Royalist intelligence was good.

Throughout November Tom Fairfax was in the West Riding, helping his father to assemble and train troops, while a net was being drawn round the Royalists in York. Soon they had collected 1000 men and Ferdinando made his base at Tadcaster, 'that wee might have more Roome, and bee less burdensome to our Friends', as Tom put it. Ferdinando appointed Captain Hotham Lieutenant-General of his army. At the end of the month Tom was at Wetherby with 40 horse and 300 foot to cover the West Riding, 'whence our chiefest Supplyes came'. But Parliamentary intelligence was bad — 'our Scouts could gett no Notice of them' — and, as Fairfax later wrote, 'ye Guards were all asleep in Houses; (for in ye Beginninge of ye War, Men were as impatient of Dutys as ignorant of them)'. So at six one morning he was surprised by Sir Thomas Glemham with 800 men. According to his own account he was himself just riding out of the other end of the town to go to Tadcaster to report to his father. According to Slingsby he was 'draughing on his Boots'.

He at once galloped over to the guard house but could find there only two foot serjeants and two pikemen. Undeterred he faced Glemham with this miniature force, and after a 'sharp Incounter' in which a Royalist major was killed and in which, Slingsby says, 'every one had his shot at him, he only making out at them with his sword', drove them off, while other pikemen turned out of bed and reinforced the five. He was lucky to survive but this was a notable personal success. The Royalists promptly attacked again, but at this point Fairfax's magazine blew up. This struck terror into the attackers, who fled. Fairfax's few horsemen pursued them and took a number of prisoners. It was a tiny action — Fairfax lost only eight or ten men — but was carried out with dash and spirit and total success. Nevertheless it had been a near thing. Fortunately Glemham's officers were poor shots. The author of *Northern Intelligence* records that 'Sir Thomas Fairfax, that did the gallantist on our side doth utterly abhor it; and yet it were a diminution of God's glory not to have the same in some measure acknowledged.' Fairfax was always modest; and he and his men had had a lesson to keep a sharper look out.

The Earl of Newcastle, a Cavendish and a grandee in the Spanish style, described by Clarendon as 'a very fine gentleman . . . most accomplished in those qualities of horsemanship, dancing and fencing, which accompany a good breeding . . .' and as 'amourous in poetry and music', was now advancing from the north with a substantial force of 6000 men. Parliament insisted on regarding it as composed of subversive Catholic shock troops. Speaker Lenthall described it as 'that Popish army' and a declaration of both Houses asserted that it consisted of 'thousands of Papists (whose Principles engage 'em to spill the Blood of Protestants . . . cut the Throats of all Men of Estates, and ravish their Wives and Daughters)'. In actual fact it behaved impeccably.

At the beginning of December Newcastle crossed the Tees, defeated the younger Hotham at Pierce Bridge, disarmed the parliamentary levies in the North Riding and relieved York. On the 7th he had his first clash with the Fairfaxes at Tadcaster. Although they had only 900 men, they beat off a determined attack by a force of some 4000 on the bridge over the Wharfe and drove Newcastle's men out of the part of the town they had occupied, but then, their ammunition having run out, they retreated to Cawood

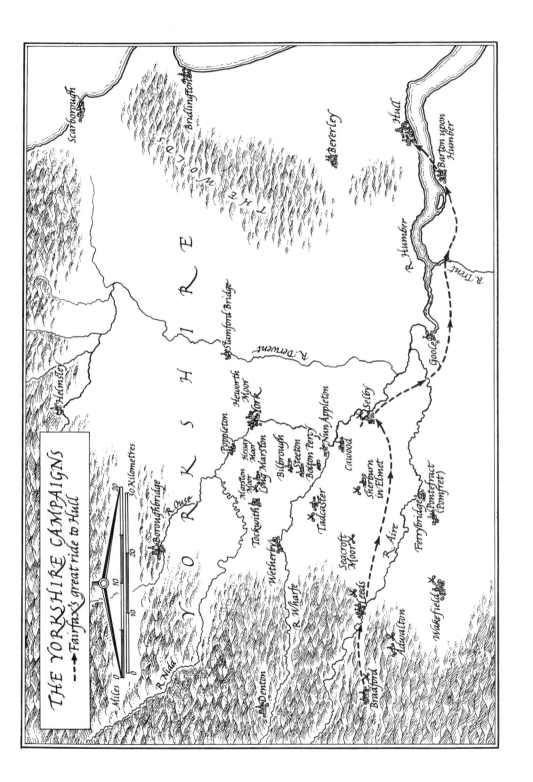

THE YORKSHIRE CAMPAIGNS
— Fairfax's great ride to Hull

Miles 0   10   20
        0   10   20   30 Kilometres

R. Nidd
R. Ouse
Boroughbridge
Denton
R. Wharfe
Wetherby
Tockwith
Marston Moor
Long Marston
Hessay Moor
Poppleton
Heworth Moor
York
Stamford Bridge
R. Derwent
Helmsley
THE WOLDS
Scarborough
Bridlington
Beverley
Hull
Barton upon Humber
R. Humber
R. Trent
Goole
Selby
Cawood
Nun Appleton
Bolton Percy
Steeton
Bilbrough
Tadcaster
Sherburn in Elmet
Ferrybridge
Pontefract (Pomfret)
Wakefield
R. Aire
Seacroft Moor
Leeds
Adwalton
Bradford

and Selby to avoid being overwhelmed by numbers. Newcastle established himself at Pontefract, or Pomfret as it was then often called, so cutting Yorkshire into two. The King was delighted and wrote to him saying, 'The business in Yorkshire I account almost done.' The Fairfaxes were now fighting against heavy odds, and it seemed unlikely that they could keep going.

On 10 December Ferdinando reported to the Committee of Lords and Commons for the Safety of the Kingdom:

> . . . yesterday I sent my son, Sir Thomas Fairfax, with five companies of foot and two of horse towards Leeds, intending he should continue there, to secure that place and the other clothing towns against the Earl of Newcastle's forces, if it were possible. But the enemy's forces were laid so strong in the way as he could not pass; so he only beat up a quarter of the enemy's in a small village, took five prisoners and retreated to Selby.

Tom was to have gone to Bradford by way of Ferrybridge but once again Roundhead intelligence had been bad. He was however determined not to be cooped up in Selby, believing that 'our Men must either have more Roome, or more Action', so he and Captain Hotham decided to 'beat up' an enemy quarter at Church Fenton, but finding the enemy gone they went on to Sherburn-in-Elmet, 'intending only to give them an Alarme'.

They could not easily surprise Sherburn, as on the flat, open country they could be seen a mile or two off, and the Royalists sent out twenty or thirty horse to guard a position nearby. Fairfax told Hotham that 'if he would second mee I would charge those Horse, and if they did fly I would pursue them soe close as to gett into the Towne with them'. Hotham agreed so Fairfax charged. The Royalist party of horse fled back to Sherburn and closed the barricade. Fairfax was hot on their heels and his horse was shot in the breast. He and his cavalry were in a narrow lane, retreat seemed likely to cause confusion, 'so wee stood to itt, and stormed the Works with Pistol and Sword'. He led his men in through a small gap, where a Royalist troop of horse fled. Now his horse fell down dead but he mounted another and then made his way out of the town with some prisoners, the Royalist general, Goring, following them out.

Slingsby wrote,

> . . . we had thought ye enemy to be disheartn'd as that he would not dare to look upon us any more; but it prov'd otherwise to our cost, for just that day

7 night [that] we beat them from Tadcaster, cometh Sir Tho. Fairfax with a party of 300 horse, & it seems hearing that ye horse in Sherburn were to have a feast, comes at noon day, beats up their Quarters, takes commissary Windham, Sir Wm. Reddall, & many others prisoners, & having ransackt their quarters takes away their best horses & returns back to Cawood with ye prize.

Tom Fairfax, with the younger Hotham, had carried out an almost perfect cavalry raid, galloping in across the fields, achieving complete surprise against a 'well-guarded barricado' holding 800 horsemen and getting clean away. He was already showing two of his special qualities as a soldier which he was to demonstrate time after time — speed of movement, and resilience, the ability to bounce back undiscouraged after a reverse. And he was operating in his home territory. Tadcaster and Sherburn are both only five miles from Nun Appleton and Cawood is only two.

In December Newcastle ordered Sir William Savile, a nephew of Strafford and the father of Halifax the Trimmer, to subjugate the clothing towns. Savile took Leeds and Wakefield without opposition but the militant Puritans of Bradford, men who were prepared to listen to a preacher for six or seven hours with 'tears and groans', offered a determined resistance. They were men who took a simplistic view of the causes of the war, one of them writing,

King Charles the first . . . to say nothing of his own wicked disposition, did by the constant solicitation of the bloody Queen, together with the swarms of Jesuits and evil affected Councellors, Bishops, and men of great estate . . . all put their heads together to destroy Christ's interest in the nation . . . and so have enslaved this land to Rome, the mother of harlots; whose kingdom is established by blood.

They put the few musketeers they had in the steeple of the church and hung woolpacks round it to protect it. The rest of them fought with 'clubs, scythes, spits, flails, halberds, sickles . . . and such like rustic weapons'. Against all odds they drove out the Royalist forces. Such a town could hardly be left unsupported. Tom Fairfax called it 'a Towne very intenable, but, for their good Affections, deserving all we could hazard for them'. He rode over by night from Selby to stiffen the defences with three troops of horse and 300 foot, and at once began building up his strength by recruiting in the district.

On 9 January 1643 he wrote to the 'Right Honourable my honoured Father' to tell him that:

> These parts grow very impatient of our delay in beating them out of leeds and Wakefield for by them al traid & provisions are stopt so that the people in these clothing townes are not able to subsist . . . I am sure I shall have above six hundred muskets, if I summons the country to come in, besides 3000 and more with other weapons, that would rise with us. If your lordship please to give me power to join with the readiness of the people, I doubt not, by God's assistance, to give your lordship a good account of what we do.

He did so 'summons the country', built up his infantry to the number of some 800 and was joined by some Yorkshire gentlemen, including his cousin, Sir William Fairfax. Soon he had 1200 or 1300 men and was able to capture Lord Savile's house at Howley. (Thomas, Lord Savile was a different person to Sir William Savile of Thornhill. Thomas was also a Royalist, but a wobbly one.)

It was still a small force and his soldiers were only 'unexperienced fresh-water Souldiers' but he then decided to attack Sir William Savile at Leeds. He crossed the Aire, suddenly appeared on Woodhouse Moor outside Leeds and sent in a trumpet to demand its surrender. When this was rejected, the Royalists saying that 'Itt was not civilly done to come soe neare before I sent the Summons,' he launched his attack in a snowstorm. The defenders had built breastworks and dug trenches and had two drakes, but in two hours Fairfax's assault succeeded at all points. Savile and the Royalist vicar swam the river on their horses but a major was drowned. Fairfax lost only 20 men, took 600 prisoners, the two guns and many muskets. It was a timely success, and caused the Royalists to abandon Wakefield as well and Newcastle to retreat from Pontefract to York, 'leaving once more a free Intercourse betwixt my Father and us, which he had soe long Time cutt off'. It was then that a contemporary tract described him as 'The Rider of the White Horse'. And it was Fairfax's first successful storming of a town. He enforced strict discipline and prevented much pillaging by his men. He promptly garrisoned Wakefield and the town of Pontefract (the Royalists still holding the castle).

He began now to have doubts about the reliability of Captain Hotham, his companion on the Sherburn raid and the attack on Leeds, who, though a good soldier, was, he noted, of 'a peevish humour'. He warned his father that 'no order will be observed by him but what he please'. The fact was that the Hothams, father and son, were intensely jealous of the Fairfaxes and did not like serving under them. They were perhaps already thinking of changing sides, and within three or four months were corresponding secretly with Newcastle, suggesting that £20,000 and a couple of peerages might help them to reach a decision.

The Queen had been for a year in Holland, first taking her daughter Mary to join her husband William of Orange, and then selling or pawning her own jewellery, some of the Crown Jewels, and even the King's pearl buttons, to buy arms and gunpowder. With this and some experienced soldiers, she now landed at Bridlington on 22 February, being ungallantly cannonaded by Admiral Batten after she disembarked, and reached York on 9 March. Ferdinando's offer to escort her on her way south to join the King, if she travelled alone, without troops, money or arms, was of course rejected. It was probably an offer made primarily for propaganda reasons. She was immediately successful in seducing some of the Yorkshire Parliamentarians from their allegiance to the Roundhead cause. Sir Hugh Cholmley, governor of Scarborough, was the first to go over. But the two Hothams began to wobble more and more and could not now be depended on to back up the Fairfaxes from Hull. As Clarendon wrote, 'Sir John Hotham's . . . pride, and contempt of the Lord Fairfax, upon whom the Country chiefly depended, hinder'd him from seconding and assisting his Lordship.'

Ferdinando had chosen the Selby/Tadcaster area as his base, not simply because it was his own country, but because it was midway between the port of Hull, with its access to seaborne supplies, and the West Riding — the area round Leeds and Bradford, where Parliamentary supporters predominated. But the lack of support from Hotham made it too risky to stay in the low country, so he decided to move west to Leeds. His journey, with 1500 men, guns and ammunition, was inevitably slow and Tom Fairfax came down from the West Riding to cover his retreat. Once more, he noted ruefully, the Royalists had 'perfect intelligence of our March'. But he placed his force between the Royalists and his father and 'to amuse them the more' drove the Royalist garrison out of Tadcaster and destroyed its defences. Captain Hodgson, in his memoirs, criticised him for losing time doing this, claiming that he 'exceeded his commission' and 'there trifles out time so long' that the enemy were able to catch them. For Newcastle had sent George Goring to engage him. This was to be the second of many encounters between them.

Goring was four years older than Fairfax. They could not have been more different. Goring had been the most rip-roaring of young court gallants, a reckless spender, a gambler and heavy drinker, ambitious, unscrupulous and immoral. He had been one of a group of officers who in 1641 had planned to march on London, free Strafford and break the power of Parliament. But Goring had betrayed this plot to the Parliament, who thought of making him Lieutenant General of the Horse under Essex. He then deceived the House of Commons and went back to the Royalists. He was lame from an old leg wound at Breda. But he was a very capable man and a first class soldier, and he and Fairfax were well matched as cavalry leaders. He had just returned from the Continent and been made general of Newcastle's horse. On this occasion he had twenty troops of horse and dragoons. Fairfax had only three. Fairfax sent his foot ahead to retreat over Bramham Moor while he covered them with the cavalry, doing what he could to delay Goring's advance. But the infantry moved only slowly or not at all and broke ranks to go into some houses in search of drink, for it was a very hot day, and on 30 March, on the edge of Seacroft Moor, part of Whin Moor, five miles from Leeds, Goring caught them and charged the disorganised force in flank and rear. Both Fairfax's foot, who were short of pikes, and his horse broke, and many of them were killed or taken prisoner, he himself escaping to Leeds. 'This,' he wrote, 'was one of the greatest Losses we ever received.' Two months after his great success at Leeds he had suffered his first defeat, on almost the same ground. But at any rate the main objective of his covering operation had been achieved — at a price — as his father's force had reached Leeds unscathed.

Nothing daunted by this reverse — his ability to bounce back must have been maddening to Newcastle — he at once set about the job of building up his strength again, though news came that Newcastle's forces had ranged southward and taken Rotherham and Sheffield. A month later he was at Bradford, asking his father to send an engineer and noting that one Captain Rutliffe 'is retretted to the enemy & most of his Company if not al'. He added, 'The enemy lies strong at Wakefield, but I shal have an eye of them . . .' The still very defective Parliamentary intelligence reported that there were 800 or 900 Cavaliers in Wakefield, six miles away. The Fairfaxes were under pressure from the 'continual Cryes, Teares and Importunityes' of the families of the men taken prisoner at Seacroft Moor. Tom Fairfax must have felt personally responsible. So he persuaded his father to let him 'attempt' Wakefield with his cousin William and 1100 men.

On Whit Sunday of 1643 he led this force to Wakefield. As usual the Cavaliers 'had Notice of our cominge, and had manned all their Works, and sett about five hundred Muskiteers to line the Hedges without the Towne which made us now doubt our Intelligence, which was too late'. Fairfax began to realise that the town was much more strongly held than he had believed. But it was too late to turn back and he stormed the town in three places. After an hour's fighting the foot opened a gap and Fairfax led the way in with his own troop, two others following. The street they got into was full of foot 'which we charged through and rooted'. Goring, who was in command, was in bed with a fever but he got up and led his cavalry to charge Fairfax's. There was 'a hott Incounter' but Fairfax's men prevailed. Goring himself was taken prisoner.

At this period of his life Fairfax's exploits as a cavalry leader, as they have come down to us, sound almost impossibly dashing. On this occasion he charged recklessly forward, and having captured two enemy colonels, found that he had got right ahead of his own men and was facing an entire regiment of Royalist foot in the market place. He was surrounded by enemy troops. Some officers came up to the two captured colonels who were with Fairfax, having no idea who he was, and asked them for instructions. The two had given Fairfax their word 'to be my true Prisoners' and so said nothing. But clearly in another minute Fairfax's identity would have been discovered and he would have been killed. 'Soe beinge well mounted . . . I rushed from them . . . & made my Horse leape over the Worke and soe (by a good Providence) gott to my Men againe.' By this time Fairfax's men had brought up a gun, the streets were being cleared and the day was theirs. It had been an immense success. Fairfax had attacked a garrison of 3000 men with 1100. He took 1400 prisoners who could now be exchanged with his men who had been captured at Seacroft Moor, 8 officers, 28 colours, a great deal of ammunition and Goring himself, who spent the next nine months in the Tower. The Duchess of Newcastle recorded that it 'was a very great loss and hinderance to my Lords designs, it being the Moity of his own Army, and most of his Ammunition . . .' Rushworth wrote that Ferdinando 'rather accounts it a Miracle than Victory'. And Tom Fairfax knew that he owed his life to a well chosen horse. But within six weeks, as he put it, 'itt pleased God to mix Water with our Wine'.

The Queen left York for the south on 4 June, and Newcastle now determined to deal once and for all with the Fairfaxes. He advanced against them at Bradford with 10,000 or 12,000 men. In London the Venetian Secretary, who had reported Fairfax's success at Wakefield to the Doge and Senate, had added that to 'reinforce Fairfax junior Cramuel, a parliamentary leader, is now advancing with 1000 foot and 1000 horse'. This detail was erroneous. In fact from Nottingham the leaders of the Eastern Association, including Cromwell, had all signed a letter to Ferdinando, drafted by the younger Hotham, saying that they would like to help but thought it best to stay where they were as they had 'certain intelligence' that Newcastle's army was 'weak and distracted'. They were badly misinformed.

The Fairfaxes were on their own. They had only 3000 tired men but Ferdinando, who was hardly the poltroon described by his father, decided nevertheless to risk a battle. He marched south-eastwards out of Bradford along the ridge leading to Adwalton five miles away, and here he found Newcastle's army, outnumbering his own nearly four to one, drawn up in battle order awaiting him. He organised his own force, putting General Gifford, whom Tom subsequently denounced as incompetent and possibly treasonable, in charge of the left, and Tom in command of about 1000 foot and 5 troops of horse on the right, where he was over the top of the ridge on the southern side and out of sight of the rest of the army.

It was cultivated ground: Fairfax held some enclosures and lined the hedges with musketeers. Here they were repeatedly attacked by Royalist cavalry coming in over the open moor, once by 13 or 14 troops (not far short of 1000 sabres), numbers that the Fairfaxes could not begin to match. But they beat them off after some stiff fighting and two of the Royalist commanders, Colonels Howard and Heron, were killed in succession.

Four of Fairfax's troopers stripped Colonel Heron's body, much to Fairfax's disgust. A stray cannon ball killed two of them and wounded the others. Fairfax regarded this as 'a remarkable Passage of Divine Justice' on 'these Villains' and seized the opportunity to point the moral — 'Wee had not yet Martial Law amongst us, which gave mee a good Occasion to improve itt, by shewinge the Souldjers the Sinfulness of the Act, and how God would punish when Men wanted Power to doe itt.'

Unaccountably, the outnumbered Parliamentary forces began to prevail. Fairfax pursued the retiring Royalist cavalry to their guns and the left advanced too. Newcastle began to think of retreating. But at this moment, a Colonel Skirton, described by Fairfax as 'a wild and desperat man' carried out that rare thing, the charge of a stand of pikes. It was successful and the tide of battle suddenly turned. Gifford's left crumbled and in no time at all the retreat on the left turned into a rout. If Ferdinando gave Tom orders to retire they never got through, and he, out of sight over the ridge, was left isolated and facing yet another cavalry attack. His retreat towards Bradford was cut off but he got his men away without great loss down a lane on the southern slopes leading to Halifax, eight miles away. He marched them there, but learning that Bradford had not been overrun he promptly marched there 'despite the fact that his Foot had marched fifteen miles that day and fought a battle. Only a General who had a tight hold of his troops and an iron will could have accomplished this.' Such is the admiring comment of Brigadier Young and Richard Holmes in their military history of the Civil War.

Newcastle was made a Marquis after the victory. For the Royalists a splendid prospect now opened up. Hitherto fighting in the south had been indecisive. The King had twice advanced on London in the autumn of 1642 but had been stopped by the London Trained Bands at Turnham Green. He had occupied Oxford and made it his main base. The Parliamentarians had taken Winchester, Chichester, Bristol, Hereford, and Reading, while the Royalists had taken Lichfield and Cirencester. Edgehill had been a drawn battle. If the Fairfaxes could now be eliminated, Newcastle would be free to march south, perhaps to take part with the King in a new and much stronger drive on London, and in any event to help tilt the balance in the King's favour. Victory now became for the King a real possibility.

Fairfax and his father reviewed the situation. Their position was grim. They had suffered a total defeat, Newcastle confronted them with vastly superior forces, their men were dispirited, and they had learnt that Sir John Hotham had finally declared for the King and had said that if they tried to come to Hull he would shut the gates in their faces. The outlook was wholly dark, and they must have felt something like despair. It was certainly, for Tom, the blackest moment of the war.

Yet if ever any soldier was imbued with the spirit of 'never give in' it was Tom Fairfax. Not for nothing did the actions of father and son wring this tribute from the Royalist Clarendon:

> . . . it must be confessed, the enemy in those parts, with whom the earl of Newcastle was to contend, in courage, vigilence and insuperable industry, was not inferior to any who disquieted his Majesty in any part of his dominions, and who pursued any advantage he got farther, and recovered any loss he underwent sooner, than any other in the kingdom: So that there were more sharp skirmishes and more notable battles in that one county of York, than in all the Kingdom besides . . . the Lord Fairfax and his son with incredible activity reducing towns when they had an army, and when they were defeated in the field, out of small towns recovering new armies.

Disaster and Recovery

A T THIS NADIR of his fortunes there came news which Tom not unreasonably regarded as 'a great Providence & Mercy of God'. A messenger rode in from Hull, saying that its citizens had risen against and arrested Sir John Hotham and his son, and that the Fairfaxes would be welcome there. Immediately the situation was transformed. The Fairfaxes had an objective, and if they could only get there they would possess an immensely strong fortress with access to the sea. But Hull was sixty miles away and the Royalists now controlled all the country in between.

Ferdinando started at once for Leeds where, however, the Royalist prisoners broke out and seized the magazine, so that he had to push on towards Selby and Hull. Tom was left in command at Bradford with 800 foot and 60 horse. He also had with him in the town — for Nun Appleton was now in enemy territory — his wife Anne and his little daughter Moll, just under five years old. Newcastle wasted no time in investing the town and his guns opened on it. Fairfax's stocks of powder — 'not above five and twenty or thirty Barrels' — began to run low. Newcastle offered conditions which Fairfax was realistically prepared to accept, 'soe they were honourable for us to take, and safe for the Inhabitants'. But the Royalists broke the truce while negotiations were going on and, in the middle of the talks, began to storm the town. They were twice repulsed, but Fairfax was now down to his last barrel of powder and had no more match for his musketeers, so it was clear that the town could not hold out any longer. He and his officers decided at a midnight council of war to try to break out. Bradford had to be left to its fate. In fact Newcastle treated the people well. They were so surprised that they attributed this to the fact that 'something came on the Lord's Day night, and pulled the clothes off his bed . . . and cried out . . . "pity poor Bradford!" ' This 'something' clearly belongs in the ghost stories of M. R. James.

The breakout now took place in the small hours. The foot were sent through narrow lanes to attack the Royalist dragoons. They broke into their quarters but, through what Fairfax called the 'cowardly Feare' of their commander, retreated again and were all taken prisoner except for eighty bold spirits who seized horses from the dragoons and rode off to Leeds. Fairfax himself, a handful of officers and about fifty troopers set out to ride the sixty miles to Hull. Anne Fairfax was mounted behind one of the officers, and a nursemaid (an early example of the redoubtable race of British nannies) carried the infant Moll on the saddle in front of her.

Just as dawn began to break, Fairfax looked up and saw about 300 Royalist cavalry drawn up on a hill above him, blocking the way east. As always, he didn't hesitate, but charged straight at them with twelve others. A Captain Mudd was killed but the rest of them broke clean through. Scattered by the charge, the little group rode on to Leeds while Fairfax alone drew rein to look back. The rest of his company had been overwhelmed and mostly taken prisoner, and among those rounded up was the officer with Anne mounted behind. 'I saw this Disaster,' he wrote, 'but could give no Reliefe.' So, sadly, he turned away and rode on to Leeds, arriving 'having broke his stirrop and lost his Pistoles'.

He found 'all in great Distraction'. He rallied his men and held another council of war at which they agreed to try and ride through to Hull, dodging the enemy cavalry. Everything depended on speed, for Newcastle would clearly strain every nerve to round up both Fairfaxes before they got there. Tom Fairfax and his men got through to Selby unscathed, after twenty hours' non-stop hard riding, and as they rode in, word came that Ferdinando was just ahead of them, about to cross the Ouse by the Selby ferry, and that Royalists from the Cawood garrison, very near Nun Appleton, were out to capture him.

Tom, pausing only to drink a cup of ale given him by 'a good Wife' as he drew rein, dashed ahead with forty troopers and found his father embarking in the boat as the Royalist cavalry rode into the town. He drew up his men in the market place while the enemy entered it and turned right handed. Then he charged them in the flank, split their force and chased them 'downe the longe Strett that goes to Brampton', finally catching them bottled up in a lane leading to Cawood. Here there was hand-to-hand fighting, and Fairfax was shot through the left wrist, 'which made the Bridle fall out of my Hand, which beinge amongst the Nerves and Veines, suddenly lett out such a Quantity of Bloud as (that) I was ready to fall from my Horse'. The Royalists however, were now intent only on escape and, bleeding profusely, Fairfax took the bridle in his right hand, in which he already held his sword. He pulled his horse out of the mêlée, though barely able to keep in the saddle. His men laid him on the ground 'almost Senceless'. Now, surprisingly, came timely help, for 'my Chyrurgean came seasonably, and bound upp ye wound'. Fairfax doesn't say whether this surgeon had ridden with him from Bradford or Leeds or had come over from Nun Appleton, or where he had sprung from. But he did an excellent job and staunched the flow of blood. After fifteen minutes Fairfax was in the saddle again and was given the good news that his troopers had driven the Royalists back to Cawood. He sent some of his men over the ferry after Ferdinando to help protect him from further attacks.

But he decided to take a different route and turned south to ride through the levels — the marshlands south-east of Goole — so keeping to the south of the Ouse and Humber. It was a difficult passage, continuously interrupted by skirmishes with enemy cavalry, during one of which his plate was captured. By the time they had fought their way across the Trent, near where it flows north into the Humber, Fairfax and his men — and the redoubtable British nanny — had been forty hours continuously in the saddle, twenty of them since he had been wounded. But forty hours' ride in a skirmishing retreat is hard on a five-year-old, and little Moll was at the limit of her endurance. So Fairfax sent her and her nanny to a house nearby — perhaps somewhere near Burton Stather or Thealby, 'with little Hopes of seeinge her any more alive'. He pushed on to Barton upon Humber with a hundred troopers sending word over to Hull that he was there. Then he snatched another quarter of an hour's rest, battered but with his spirits 'nothinge at all discouraged'. Here again the Royalists came up but the ship sent over from Hull kept them off with her guns and so on 4 July he and his men went over to Hull, he himself exhausted, bloodstained but alive and free.

Next day he sent a ship over for little Moll who arrived, still with her admirable nanny, 'pritty well recovered'. She clearly inherited her father's resilience. A few days later there appeared a coach, with a cavalry escort, carrying Anne, returned by the chivalrous Newcastle. More and more of their men trickled into Hull and the Fairfaxes began to raise new forces. Soon they had 1500 foot and 700 horse. Ferdinando was appointed by Parliament to be Governor of Hull and Speaker Lenthall wrote to him saying that the House of Commons 'have been frequently informed of the carriage and deportment of your son, Sir Thomas Fairfax, in his command, so full of valour and honour, for which this House will be ever ready to give to him . . . all due encouragement'.

Fairfax took all the horse and 600 of the foot north to Beverley, while Newcastle moved south and captured Gainsborough and Lincoln. But the irrepressible Fairfaxes went out to launch an attack on Stamford Bridge and Newcastle soon found that his own Yorkshire troops refused to march south while their houses were at risk from Fairfax raids. So Newcastle had to bring his army back and lay siege to Hull. In forcing him to abandon his move south, the Fairfaxes had already performed a valuable service.

As soon as Newcastle's 16,000 men began to move against Hull, Tom Fairfax realised that he and his little force would have to abandon Beverley, but the local Parliamentary committee, whose 'want of Military Skill' disgusted him, at first vetoed his withdrawal, so he had to conduct a risky but successful fighting retreat, holding Beverley itself briefly, covering the retiring foot with his cavalry, and giving Newcastle's advance guard a last volley at a bridge two miles from Hull.

The siege of Hull began on 2 September, but the Fairfaxes opened the sluices and flooded the land for two miles round and the governor took prompt measures to extinguish the 'fyery Bulletts' shot into the town. But in a regular siege of this sort Tom Fairfax's cavalry were useless. He kept them outside under the walls but there was little food for the horses and many of them began to die. On the 18th some of Cromwell's forces appeared on the southern bank of the Humber, and Fairfax began shipping over his troopers and their horses. Four days later, Cromwell himself was in Hull, buying some muskets and powder. He and Fairfax now met for the first time.

For the next seven years these two men were to work very closely together. Cromwell, now in his mid-forties, was thirteen years older than Fairfax, a complex man of undoubted genius. In some ways he was a quintessential Englishman, yet in fact he was partly Welsh. Indeed if his great grandfather had not changed his name he would have been called Oliver Williams. As is so often the case, the English strain only flourishes when there is an admixture of Scottish, Welsh or Irish blood. The two men, though very different, seem always to have got on very well together.

In the last days of September, Fairfax crossed the Humber with the rest of his cavalry — twenty-one troops of horse and dragoons, but most of them new levies, to give a hand to the leaders of the Eastern Association, based on East Anglia. Sir John Henderson, Governor of Newark, was there with 5000 men to prevent Fairfax joining Cromwell but he failed to act. The Parliamentarians were unaware of his presence. Fairfax found that Cromwell's intelligence was no better than his own, but 'I altogether trusted to the Care of our new Freinds beinge a Stranger in those Parts.'

At Boston Fairfax and Cromwell met the Earl of Manchester, overall Commander of the Eastern Association, who had captured Lynn and was now besieging Bolingbroke Castle, fifteen miles north of Boston. The Royalists sent a force to relieve it under Sir William Widdrington. Fairfax was despatched by Manchester to provide a protective cavalry screen in the west, falling back as they advanced, with some desultory skirmishing.

On 11 October Manchester formed up his troops on a ridge near the village of Winceby on the southern edge of the Lincolnshire Wolds, between Horncastle and Bolingbroke. The Royalists formed up on the next ridge 600 yards away with what Fairfax described as 'a little Plaine' between them. Cromwell was put in charge of the van, Fairfax of the reserve of horse and Manchester himself took charge of the foot. But in fact Winceby fight was a purely cavalry action.

It began with an exchange of fire between the dragoons of each side (the advanced troops described by Fairfax as 'the Forlorne Hops'). Then the main cavalry on both sides moved against each other. As Cromwell led on his two regiments the Royalist dragoons fired two volleys. Cromwell's horse was killed and when he got up he was promptly knocked down by Sir Ingram Hopton, who was himself killed a moment or two later. Cromwell was in due course remounted on a 'poore horse'. Nothing is recorded of Cromwell's part in the rest of the battle. But the shock of the charge had driven the Royalist cavalry back on their reserves.

Fairfax now led his own cavalry reserve away to the right and then swung back so as to take the Royalists in the flank. As a contemporary account describes it, 'Sir Thomas Fairfax . . . fell in towards the flank of the enemy's body, which they perceiving, the enemy's body broke, and so Sir Thomas had the chase and execution of them a great way . . .' The pursuit through and beyond Horncastle was relentless and at one point the demoralised Royalists were trapped against a gate and cut down. The place is still known as Slash Hollow. Two hundred Royalists were killed and two thousand taken prisoners. Others drowned in Horncastle river and twenty-six colours were taken. The defeated commander sadly told Newcastle, 'Their horse are very good.' The victorious Manchester told Parliament that 'Sir Tho. Fairefaix (who is a Person that exceeds any Expressions as a Commendation of his Resolution and Valour) . . . performed what he was commanded with Readiness and Success.'

On the same day Tom heard distant guns in the north. Ferdinando had sallied out of Hull and, after severe fighting, had captured the besiegers' great guns and turned them on Newcastle's troops. Newcastle abandoned the siege and retired to York. October 11 had been a great day for the Fairfaxes: yet it was only just over a hundred days since the disaster of Adwalton Moor.

It was perhaps now that Fairfax, according to Mrs Lucy Hutchinson, 'came with those horse, that were left him, into the Vale of Belvoir, and so visited Nottingham Castle', urging the governor and the local committee to raise more troops, 'offering arms and commissions for them', and subsequently sending a commission from Ferdinando for Colonel Hutchinson to command both the town and the castle of Nottingham.

Fairfax took part in the recapture of Lincoln, and on 20 December stormed Gainsborough. He hoped then to be able to settle into winter quarters. But he was not to have long to rest his men.

In mid-winter, he was ordered by Parliament to relieve Nantwich in Cheshire, where Sir William Brereton's men were being besieged by Lord Byron (an ancestor of the poet). Byron had been sent north to form a new Royalist army there, his objective being to reconquer Lancashire and then join Newcastle in crushing the Fairfaxes. Byron had been reinforced by five regiments of infantry from Ireland.

Fairfax regarded Parliament's instructions as unreasonable. He had just had a letter from his officers professing 'hearty affection to your person' but pointing out their 'extreme wants' and lack of clothes, shoes and harness for their horses. He complained that his men were 'ever the worst payed . . . sickly and almost naked' and he asked Parliament to supply their wants first. It was not then, or later, a characteristic of Parliament to be reasonable. They ordered him peremptorily to march, which was, Fairfax thought, 'to make Brick without Straw'. He realised that if his men were to have any clothes he would have to find them himself so, on his own credit, he bought cloth for 1500 men. He asked the Committee at Stansford for some briefing: 'My desire is, that I may by your means receive information which way from thence I may most safely march: what your intelligence is concerning the interposition of the enemy's forces . . . If you shall think fit thus to send us any further light, the messenger may either meet with or hear of us at Leicester . . .'

So on the 29 December, he set out from Falkingham in Lincoln-shire with 1800 horse, 500 dragoons and power to call in the Lancashire and Cheshire regiments. He marched through Derby-shire and Staffordshire but found the local colonels disaffected and quarrelsome. Mrs Hutchinson records that he sent for some arms from Nottingham Castle, and asked for all the cavalry in the garri-son, but they refused to go, 'not out of cowardize, for the men were very stout . . . but only had the generall fault of all the parliament partie, that they were not obedient to commands, except they knew and approv'd their employment . . .' But within a few days Fairfax had secured 3000 foot. Some of them, old comrades from Adwalton Moor, were apparently so ragged and in such a poor state that he burst into tears when he saw them. Other county levies were con-temptuously described by Byron as 'a rabble of cudgellers'. So Fairfax advanced to Nantwich, which was almost at its last gasp. And he learnt from an intercepted letter that on the 26th Byron had stormed some Parliamentarians in a church and 'put them all to the sword, which I find the best way to proceed with these kind of people . . .'

Fairfax's intelligence (now at last somewhat better) told him that Byron was planning to meet him. He took no chances. He knew that he was now going to face experienced soldiers accustomed to being victorious. To avoid surprise he drew up his force in fighting order and made his way slowly forward, sending Colonel Morgan and the dragoons ahead to clear a pass near the town.

The river Weaver was swollen with melting snow and this split Byron's force, but at a council of war Fairfax and his officers decided to push on to join with the town's garrison. So they advanced through the hedges but were attacked in the rear by Byron's cavalry. Fairfax sent his own regiment and two others to engage them and with the rest of his army engaged the Royalists in front of him. At first Fairfax's foot were pushed back but his cavalry — one detachment commanded by another remarkable Yorkshire soldier, John Lambert — drove out the enemy's from the lanes about the town and this so encouraged the infantry that they pushed the Royalists back from hedge to hedge. The garrison now sent out 700 or 800 musketeers to attack the Royalist rear, who were under a man with the peculiar name of Sir Fulk Hunk.

The Royalist cavalry made off in good order but their foot, 'caught as in a trap', were overwhelmed. The officers retreated into a church and were forced to surrender. These officers included Colonel Monk, of whom more would be heard. Fairfax had won what Mrs Hutchinson called 'a miraculous victory', capturing 72 officers and 1500 men, all the Royalist artillery, ammunition and baggage, 22 colours and 120 women camp followers armed with long knives (whom he later set free).

He wrote at once to his wife, addressing the letter 'For yourself, dear heart', to tell her of the 'great victory it hath pleased Him to give us over the Irish army.' He went on: 'I have endured some hardship since I parted with you, being forced to march and watch night and day this frost and snowy weather. I have much trouble to command these forces I now have, there being such divisions amongst the commanders, which doth impair my health . . . Remember my humble service to all my honourable and noble sisters, and to my sister Elizabeth and to Moll.' Clarendon described this victory as 'a new rung to the ladder which Sir Thomas Fairfax ascended to the height of his honour' and as 'the most sensible blow to the king he had yet sustained'.

The Lady of Lathom
and Marston Moor

AFTER THE VICTORY of Nantwich Fairfax spent the early months of 1644 in Cheshire and Lancashire, reducing various Royalist strongholds, such as Crewe House and Darison House, while he consolidated his hold on the clothing towns of the West Riding. Pym, in the closing months of his life, had been working to bring the Scots in on Parliament's side. The Scots' main demand was for 'unity in religion', by which they meant the adoption of Presbyterianism. As a result, on 25 September 1643, the House of Commons swore to observe the Solemn League and Covenant. In this they pledged themselves to the reformation of religion, to 'endeavour the extirpation of Popery' and prelacy, to preserve the rights of Parliaments and the King's person, to punish malignants, and to keep the two Kingdoms together 'in a firm peace and union to all posterity'.

This Covenant became the touchstone of the forces opposed to the King. It also opened the way for Scottish intervention, and on 19 January the first Scottish regiments crossed the Tweed. A month later the Committee of Both Kingdoms was set up to be a sort of joint English/Scottish Parliamentary war cabinet. Newcastle's task was to stop the Scottish advance in Durham, while at the same time resisting Ferdinando's activity in the East and North Ridings, where Sir William Constable (the negotiator of Tom's marriage) had taken Whitby for the Parliamentarians. Manchester and Cromwell threatened to come north to throw their weight into the balance. So in February the King despatched Prince Rupert to the north. Rupert rode to Chester and thence to Newark, where he crushed the Parliamentary forces and raised the siege.

Fairfax meanwhile had told the Lancashire authorities that he must have £4000, no more 'than a fortnight's pay', for his troops, also 300 more horse, and that 2000 men from the local levies should be enabled to 'move with me out of the county . . . as there shall be occasion'. This was always a difficulty, as most troops did not like moving away from home. Moreover, now that spring was at hand, one officer told Fairfax that his men had 'disbanded themselves and are following the plough'. Others refused to stir because they claimed that they needed to protect their homes against the 'uncivil' dragoons.

At the end of February Fairfax laid siege to the Earl of Derby's stronghold, Lathom House in Lancashire, a fortress on 'moorish, springy and spumous ground', with walls two yards thick, nine towers, each with six guns, a moat and a central tower, garrisoned by 300 men. It was commanded by his wife, a large and redoubtable French-born lady, Charlotte de la Trémouille, Countess of Derby. On top of the towers were Lord Derby's keepers and fowlers, experienced shots with 'birding pieces'. Lady Derby had been shut up in this fortress since May of the previous year. Fairfax decided to try to reduce it.

Remembering perhaps Newcastle's civil treatment of his own wife, he sent a courtly letter to Lady Derby asserting that the Lathom garrison was 'a receptacle of great incurragement to the Papest & inaffected parson[s] in those partes, which I cannot beleeve your Ladyship doth naturally affect', offering her 'honourable and convenient' terms, enclosing a rather dog-eared Act of Parliament, and adding 'yet Madam, I do owe you that I much Honor your Ladyship as I would use all just means that would make me capable of serving your ladyship . . . that your ladyship may make use of the clemency of the Parliament'.

Lady Derby played for time. Fairfax offered to send her in her own carriage to another house nearby. She repudiated this offer, saying that 'she remembered both her lord's honour and her own birth, conceiving it more knightly that Sir Thomas Fairfax should wait upon her than she upon him'. Eventually she declared that 'though a woman and a stranger, divorced from her friends, and robbed of her estate, she was ready to receive their utmost violence'. No doubt she succeeded in embarrassing Fairfax. Lady Derby was both brave and articulate, and the news of the gallant defence of her house by a woman naturally aroused sympathy. Fairfax had a letter from Lord Derby asking for safe passage out for his wife and children but Lady Derby refused to surrender unless she were assured that this was what her husband really wanted.

At the beginning of March Fairfax heard from John Lambert at Bradford, who said, 'We all, in these parts, exceedingly long for and desire your appearance here, which, I am confident, were enough to clear these parts, if the opportunity be not slipped.' Soon after he was ordered back to Yorkshire by Ferdinando, so (no doubt with relief) he left his cousin William and the Puritan lawyer Rigby to continue besieging Lady Derby, who held out defiantly for another three months until she was relieved by Prince Rupert, who killed 1600 of the besiegers. Fairfax himself rode back into Yorkshire with 2000 horse.

He met his father at Ferrybridge, but immediately received orders from Parliament to go north to Northumberland with his cavalry and dragoons to join with the Scots, who were short of cavalry and could not therefore make any impression on Newcastle's forces at Durham. But Ferdinando planned to attack the Royalists at Selby, so Tom decided to give him a hand before riding north.

Tom's cousin, Colonel John Bellasis, the Royalist Governor of York, had come south from the city with 1500 horse and 5000 foot to try to prevent the conjunction of the two Fairfaxes, and was now holding Selby. Here on 11 April he was attacked by Tom and his father. Ferdinando's foot made the assault in three divisions and, despite a vigorous resistance, captured the enemy's outworks but could not get further because of the Royalist cavalry. At this point, as Ferdinando's report of the action ran, 'my son with his Regiment of Horse rushed into the Town, where he was incountered by Colonell Belasyse, and the Enemies Horse, but they being beaten back, and Master Belasyse himself wounded, and taken prisoner . . . the Enemy was wholly routed'. The cavalry action took place between the houses of Selby and the river Ouse. After Fairfax's first charge half the Royalist cavalry fled over a bridge of boats towards York. The other half, led by Bellasis himself, counterattacked. Fairfax, being, as always, out in front of his men, took the brunt of this charge and his horse went down, but his cavalry fought their way forward, rescued him, wounded and captured

Bellasis and drove the Royalist cavalry out of the town, so clearing the way for Ferdinando's foot. The victory was complete and the Fairfaxes took 3000 prisoners. Parliament ordered a day of public thanksgiving.

The effect of the action at Selby was dramatic. As the Royalist Slingsby wrote: 'This proved a fatall blow to us . . . so it prov'd of consequence to ye parliament as ye very dawning of that day which brought prosperous success unto them.' Fairfax himself assessed the consequences thus: 'This good Success put them into great Distraction and Feare att York, who speedily sent to the Earle of Newcastle to hast back thither . . . leaving the Scotts who . . . were reduced to great Extremity, but now advance without Delay after him.' The Scots had really been in a bad way. Slingsby wrote that the 'Scots must be forc'd to retreat, not having Sir Tho. Fairfaxes assistance as was look'd for, if this unfortunate news had not come unto them of ye beating and routing of our Yorkshire forces.'

There was now no need for Fairfax to go north to join the Scots. Selby had helped them far more effectively. Moreover Nantwich and Selby had made people sit up and take notice of Fairfax. Clarendon wrote of Nantwich, 'Fairfax improved his reputation by a speedy, and unlook'd for march into Cheshire,' and of Selby, 'This was the first Action for which Sir Thomas Fairfax was taken Notice of.'

Now at last the Parliamentarians were able to concentrate their forces in the north. The Scots marched south and met the Fairfaxes at Wetherby so that the united army comprised 16,000 foot and 4000 horse. Fairfax rode south with Lindsay and the Earl of Crawford to ask Manchester to join them, which he and Cromwell promptly agreed to do with a further 6000 foot and 3000 horse. Ferdinando and the Scottish general, Lord Leven, proceeded to lay siege to the great city of York, in which Newcastle and his army had taken refuge, around 20 April, a day or two after the Queen at Oxford had said goodbye to the King for the last time.

Tom Fairfax did not have a great deal to do during the siege. Newcastle had sent away most of his cavalry and siege operations were essentially for infantrymen and engineers. Ferdinando held the sector east of the city from Fulford in the south to the King's Fishpool on the river Fosse in the north, taking in Foulforth and Heslington. He may have helped to mount a battery on Windmill

Hill near Heslington and to bring up cannon to batter the walls by Walmgate Bar. It must have been strange for him to be besieging what was, in many ways, his own city, with the family house of Bishophill just over the walls. Manchester and his troops arrived at the beginning of June and took over the northern sector. There was then some parleying about terms and the assault on the city began in earnest only on 16 June. Lawrence Crawford, Manchester's major-general, exploded a mine prematurely under St Mary's Tower, 'ambitious' as Fairfax says, 'to have the Honor alone of springinge the Mine'. Crawford sent his men into the breach but had done nothing to warn the other besiegers, so his assault party were unsupported and were driven out with heavy loss by Newcastle's famous Whitecoats. This, says Fairfax drily, was 'very prejuditial' but Crawford, he adds, escaped being called to account 'by reason of this Triumviral Government'. With the tower were destroyed the records of the monasteries of northern England, but an antiquary, Roger Dodsworth, had been transcribing them for Fairfax from 1635 on, being paid £40 a year. These transcripts were preserved and given by Fairfax to the Bodleian.

Meanwhile, Rupert had swept north through Lancashire, gathering reinforcements as he advanced, being joined by Goring and Lucas, and capturing in succession Stockport, Bolton and Liverpool. He was at Skipton on 26 June and three days later stayed at Denton Hall, Ferdinando's house, where Tom was born. A portrait in the house reminded him of the two Fairfaxes who had been killed in the Palatinate twenty-three years before, fighting for his parents, and he gave orders that the house was not to be touched. Next day he was at Knaresborough.

At last there was work for the cavalry to do. The three Parliamentary generals, Leven, Manchester and Ferdinando, raised the siege and took up battle positions north-west of the city. For Tom it was a new experience to be commanding a contingent in a great army of some 27,000 men, and with a major battle a probability. But while the army waited Rupert gave them the slip, dodging round to the north by Boroughbridge and crossing the Ouse by a captured bridge of boats at Poppleton. He stayed outside York but sent Goring in to relieve the city. He didn't bother to confer with the 52-year-old Newcastle, who was clearly put out at being superseded by a royal princeling of 24.

Clarendon, with the benefit of hindsight, is strongly critical of Rupert's decision to force a battle. 'If he had sat still,' he wrote, 'the enemy's great army would have mouldered to nothing' because of arguments between the English and the Scots. 'But the dismal fate of the kingdom would not permit so much sobriety of counsel.' Rupert held himself bound by a letter from the King saying that 'If Yorke be lost, I shall esteeme my Crown little lesse . . . but if Yorke be relived, & you beate the Rebelles Armies of both Kingdoms . . . then but otherwise not, I may possiblie make a shift . . . to spinn out tyme, untill you come to assist mee.' Rupert construed this as a definite order to give battle, though his forces were a good deal less than his opponents' and though Newcastle advised against an engagement.

While the Parliamentary army made its headquarters at the village of Long Marston, Fairfax and most of the cavalry spent the night on Hessay Moor. They all now knew that a battle was coming. But the minds of some ordinary Yorkshire countrymen were on other things. An officer on reconnaissance near Long Marston encountered a labourer and asked him whether he was for King or Parliament. 'Be them two fall'n out then?' was the reply. Within twenty-four hours even this yokel would have been aware that there had been a difference of opinion.

Next day it was decided that the combined army, now commanded by a committee of three, should move south towards Cawood and Tadcaster — the Fairfaxes' home country. According to Fairfax, this pointless move was made because, although 'the Englishe was for feighting', the Scots were 'for retreatinge, to gain (as they alledged) both Tyme and Place of more Advantage'. So the army set out for the south.

Fairfax, Cromwell and David Leslie with their cavalry stayed to cover the rear. Before long it became apparent to them that the Royalist cavalry to the north of them were increasing in numbers and that they were facing a whole army. They were alarmed that the Parliamentary army might be caught spread out on the march and sent urgent messages to the three commanders to come back. Some of the infantry had got as far as Tadcaster but they were marched back and began to form up south of the villages of Long Marston and Tockwith, a mile and a half apart on the road running west of York towards the valley of the Nidd. They were on high ground. In front of them a great field of rye ran down to the road and three or four hundred yards beyond it was a ditch. Beyond that was the open moor, flat country, upon which Rupert's army was formed up waiting for Newcastle's men to join them from York.

Fairfax commanded the cavalry on the right, nearest to Long Marston. It consisted of his northern cavalry — some 2000 sabres, including some newly levied, untried Lancashire troops, with John Lambert commanding his second line, and behind, as reserves, three regiments of Scottish horse, including one of lancers, under the Earls of Dalhousie and Eglinton and Lord Balgonie. Several of his old opponents were in the field on the other side. Opposite him Goring, whom he had encountered at Seacroft Moor and Wakefield, commanded the Royalist horse, with Sir Charles Lucas in charge of the second line and Sir Marmaduke Langdale among his officers. Away on the other wing, near Tockwith village, Cromwell and David Leslie (whom Fairfax calls 'Major General Lashley') faced Lord Byron (Fairfax's opponent at Nantwich). In between the Parliamentary foot, under Manchester, Ferdinando and the Scottish commanders, faced the Royalist foot. The senior general on the Parliamentary side was Alexander Leslie, Earl of Leven, an immensely experienced soldier with a European reputation, who had fought for Charles IX and Gustavus Adolphus all over Europe for thirty years against Wallenstein and the Imperialists, the architect of many victories, a little, 'crooked' and surprisingly modest man.

Apart from a few cannon shots the two armies remained facing each other as the afternoon wore on, while rain showers swept over the ground and the Parliamentary army, as Slingsby records, 'in Marston corn fields falls to singing psalms'. Uniforms being rudimentary and friend often hard to distinguish from foe, each side was, as usual, given a word of recognition — 'God and the King' for the Royalists, and 'God with us' for the Parliamentarians, who also wore a white badge or handkerchief in their hats to avoid confusion.

The Royalists expected no engagement that day. Newcastle's foot only arrived from York in the afternoon. Rupert sat down to supper and Newcastle went to smoke a pipe in his coach. But suddenly, at a time variously given as 5, 7 or 7.30 in the evening, the whole Parliamentary army began to move forward.

In the next three or four hours, beginning on that wet summer evening, and continuing into the night under a harvest moon, was fought one of the biggest and most decisive battles ever seen in England. It was also a very strange battle, which the Parliamentarians almost lost and the Royalists almost won. The contemporary records are fragmentary and frequently contradictory. And it all took place over three hundred years ago. So all accounts of the battle must necessarily be to some extent speculative. One can only fit the surviving evidence together and make the best guess about the fragments of the picture that have disappeared.

When the Parliamentary foot swept forward down the cornfield and across the Long Marston–Tockwith road they carried the ditch after brief resistance from some musketeers, and were soon engaged in a desperate struggle with the Royalist foot. Ferdinando's men gained ground at first but were then borne back by Newcastle's Whitecoats. On the left Cromwell's charge made some ground, but resistance was fierce and he was held up — 'they stood at sword's point a pretty while, hacking one another . . .' Cromwell was slightly wounded in the neck, and according to some accounts left the field and went into Tockwith to recover and have his wound dressed. His cavalry only finally prevailed when David Leslie and his Scots horse charged the enemy in flank. Rupert himself brought up cavalry reinforcements and counter-attacked vigorously but the Ironsides were too strong for them and the Royalist cavalry on that side of the field were finally routed and fled. Rupert, uncharacteristically, had to hide in a bean field.

Meanwhile on the right, when the line moved forward, Fairfax advanced at the head of his great mass of two thousand cavalry, too many of them raw and inexperienced. It was, Fairfax remembered, difficult ground, 'by reason of the Furrs and Ditches . . . which putt us into great Disorder', and, as Bowles recorded, 'was next the hedges possessed by the enemy'. Moreover Goring had musketeers interspersed with his troops of horse. Their fire was effective and caused heavy casualties among Fairfax's men.

When he was through the gorse bushes and ditches, Fairfax charged the enemy — probably their extreme left — with some four hundred troopers whom he had immediately under his hand. There was a tough fight, 'hottly disputed a longe Time at Swords Poynt', in which Fairfax's cheek was slashed by a sabre and his horse wounded by a musket shot. Cromwell's scoutmaster Watson, who did not himself see this part of the battle as he was over on the

other side, wrote that 'Sir Thomas Fairfax (wounded in the head or
face) carried himself as bravely as a man could doe, was unhorst,
lay upon the ground, and was relieved by our horse.' But this does
not seem to fit with other accounts of what happened. Fairfax
fought with his usual dash in this particularly savage engagement.
Not only was he himself wounded, but the captain of his own troop
was shot in the arm, his cornet had both his hands cut and was
maimed for life, and almost every officer was wounded. His own
brother Charles, who was deserted by his men, and another Major
Fairfax were both mortally wounded. And what remained of his
four hundred finally overcame the enemy wing he had engaged and
'pursued them a good way towards York'. However, he was now
not a mere junior commander but in charge of a large force.
Remembering this, he drew rein and rode back to see what had
become of his main body — the other 1600 men he commanded.
What he found must have come as a shock. Goring had charged his
disordered horse, and, as Fairfax admits, 'rooted them'.

One contemporary account — *A Full Relation of the late Victory* —
says, not of Fairfax's cavalry but of 'the right Wing of our Foot',
that

> betwixt them and the enemy there was no passage but a narrow Lane, where
> they could not march above 3 or 4 in front; upon the one side of the Lane
> was a Ditch, and on the other an Hedge, both whereof were lined with
> Musketiers . . . [and then goes straight on to say that] notwithstanding Sir
> *Thomas Fairfax* charged gallantly, but the enemy keeping themselves in a
> body, and receiving them by threes and fours as they marched out of the
> Lane, and (by what mistake I know not) Sir *Thomas Fairfax* his newly
> leavied regiments being in the Van, they wheeled about and being hotly
> pursued by the enemy came back upon the L. *Fairfax* Foot and the reserve
> of the Scottish Foot, broke them wholly and trod the most part of them under
> foot.

This passage has perplexed historians, but one recent researcher
has suggested that it refers to a now vanished part of Atterwith Lane,
at the extreme right of the battlefield. It is not clear whether the
account means that only the foot or the horse as well were caught in
the lane. Cavalry were sometimes confined to a narrow lane, as was
to happen later, with better success, at Langport. Possibly some of
Fairfax's front line did get bunched up in the lane and were shot
down as they emerged, and this precipitated their flight.

A Scottish commander, Sir James Lumsden, wrote of this part of the battle: 'Sir Thomas Fairfax commandit in cheiff, ane brave commander, but his horse answered not our expectatioun, nor his worth.' That may be said to sum it up.

Goring had driven the beaten cavalry pell-mell back over the road and over the hill, pursuing some of them for two miles and cutting them down as they fled. Some had been so panic-stricken that they had ridden over their own infantry, so precipitating their flight and that of their commanders, for both Leven and Ferdinando took to their heels, convinced that all was lost. Leven bolted to Leeds and Ferdinando to 'his house at Cawood' (presumably Nun Appleton) where he went to bed. It was, on Goring's part, a remarkable achievement. And Lucas, with the second Royalist cavalry line, turned to attack in flank the Scottish foot — or what remained of it after the panic flight — but was stoutly resisted. Half the Parliamentary army was now on the run, though Manchester's foot and some of the Scots held on and fought it out grimly with the Royalist foot. Of Tom Fairfax's own forces Lambert, 'who should have seconded mee (but could not gett upp to me)' and 'charged in another place', was still in the field with some well-ordered cavalry, though he had had his horse shot under him. The fugitives spread rumours that Rupert had 'utterly defeated the bonny Scots and rebels and taken prisoner that Arch-Rebel Sir Tho. Fairfax'.

Fairfax now found groups of Royalist horse all round him. 'Soe taking the Signall out of my Hatt, I passed through for one of their owne Commanders, and soe gott to my Lord of Manchester's Horse, in the other Winge . . .' The account in *A Full Relation of the late Victory* says that:

> Sir *Thomas Fairfax*, Colonell *Lambert* . . . with five or six Troopes charged through the enemy and went to the left wing of Horse, the two Squadrons of *Balgones* regiment being divided by the enemy . . . one of them being Lanciers charged a regiment of the enemies foot, and put them wholly to the rout, and after ioyned with the left wing of Horse, the other by another way went also to the left wing. The Earle of *Eglington*'s regiment maintained their ground . . .

Fairfax himself is silent about the rest of the battle. He had joined Cromwell after riding across the entire battlefield. He must have told Cromwell how matters stood on the right, where Lindsay's Scots were still holding out and had captured Lucas. Cromwell had been standing still, apparently bemused, after the grim but ultimately successful struggle with Byron's horse, though Denzil Holles's hostile account, which says that Cromwell was simply frightened and was upbraided by Crawford as a poltroon and a coward, does not ring true.

Now Cromwell's horse, Fairfax and Lambert probably with them, rode back under the moon to the right of the battlefield and turned right to face Goring's disorganised troops returning from the pursuit and from looting the Parliamentary wagons. They charged and scattered them. Then they helped Manchester's foot to overcome the resistance of the Royalist foot, including the last stand of Newcastle's heroic Whitecoats, who fought on till their ammunition was exhausted and they were cut down almost to a man where they stood. Fairfax hated this massacre of brave men. He is reported to have called out, 'Spare the poor deluded countrymen . . . who are misled and know not what they do.' But his words fell on deaf ears. So the battle ended just before midnight. Fairfax and Cromwell, both wounded, were too spent to move and for two days stayed amidst the wreckage on the battlefield, while their men collected pikes and muskets and buried the dead.

For Fairfax this, his first great battle, had been both a disaster and a triumph. He had won (at considerable cost) his own small personal bit of the battle, but the main body for which he was responsible had been defeated and scattered. As on some previous occasions, he had been too intent on dashing ahead himself. But this time it mattered much more. His part of the Parliamentary army had failed. His brother was dead and many of his men dead or wounded. But he had gone off on his own, bearing a charmed life. He had shown extraordinary courage. As one account says, 'Sir Thomas Fairfax . . . lost no honour this day, for though many of his soldiers did faint and fall back, yet his heart continued like the heart of a lion . . .' And he may have played a crucial role in bringing the Eastern Association horse over to the right wing at the exact moment when its intervention was decisive.

Certainly the defeat of the horse on the right wing did nothing to damage his reputation among contemporaries. Thomas Stockdale described how 'our broken forces were rallyed againe . . . in which service the Earle of Manchester and Lieftenant Generall Cromwell have merited most, and Sir Thomas Fairfax very much'. Independents tended to play up Cromwell's part and Presbyterians to play it down. As the historian Ranke wrote, 'The question of which of the two portions of the army had done best assumed a sort of theological importance.'

Contemporaries and some of those writing soon after couple the names of Cromwell and Fairfax as responsible for the victory, and Bulstrode Whitelocke attributes it to 'colonel Cromwell, with the brave regiment of his countrymen and sir Thomas Fairfax, having rallied some of his horse'. The modern military historian Alfred Burne concludes that 'to two men above all is the credit due; to Sir Thomas Fairfax and to Oliver Cromwell. Marston Moor should be eternally connected with these two names.'

Once the battle was over Rupert rode off with his beaten but still intact cavalry, and Newcastle, who, with his splendid infantry destroyed, had no heart for further fighting, made for the coast to take refuge on the continent.

The victors began at once to take some liberties with the truth in their accounts of the victory. Two of the Parliamentary leaders, Leven and Ferdinando, who had run away, believing that all was lost, were brought back somewhat shamefacedly with Manchester, who had also at one stage sought safety in flight but had got back earlier, to compose a suitable despatch describing how they had together won the day. Cromwell, a propagandist, as well as a soldier, of genius, claimed (not quite accurately) that 'we never charged but we routed the enemy'. He dismissed Leslie's troopers, who had played a decisive part on his wing, as 'a few Scots in our rear', and, as master of the memorable phrase, said of the enemy (not for the last time) that 'God made them as stubble to our swords'.

Fairfax and his father joined in the resumed siege of York. Honourable terms were granted to the Governor, Sir Thomas Glemham, and the Parliamentarians entered the city on 16 July. They held a service of thanksgiving in the Minster (which Fairfax's men, unlike Cromwell's elsewhere, had the strictest orders to safeguard) and the Fairfaxes were at last able to move back into their York house, Bishophill. The hospital and church of St Nicholas in

Walmgate had been badly damaged but Fairfax had the porch
preserved and later gave it to St Margaret's church. He also
rescued the ancient horn of Ulph which had been stolen in the
siege and the family returned it to the Minster. Ferdinando became
Governor of York and Tom rode off to conduct mopping-up
operations against Royalist strongholds. He took 1000 horse to
within five miles of Scarborough but, hearing that Sir Hugh
Cholmley was prepared to surrender it, rode to Helmsley and began
the siege of the Duchess of Buckingham's castle there. It was
vigorously defended and during a sortie by the garrison he was hit
and badly wounded by a musket ball which broke his shoulder and
arm. He was taken to York and cared for at Bishophill. In those days
of primitive medicine his case looked bad and he described himself
later as 'being doubtful of recovery'. The sad news came of the
death of his cousin and comrade in arms Sir William Fairfax, killed
like Nelson and Wolfe at the moment of victory, outside Mont-
gomery Castle. But he himself did recover and by Christmas he was
up and about again and, far from going off for a proper con-
valescence, began the siege of the great castle of Pontefract. Here
again he was very slightly wounded by a musket ball — the fourth
time he had been wounded in eighteen months — and, leaving
Lambert to blockade Pontefract, he returned to York.

General of the New Model Army

'Their new high-flying hawk of the North'
Arthur Trevor to the Marquess of Ormonde
9 April 1645

MARSTON MOOR effectively ended the civil war in the north. There were still some minor actions to come — indeed Ferdinando was to suffer a reverse outside Pontefract at the hands of Sir Marmaduke Langdale — and a number of castles had still to be reduced, but the main issue had been settled.

In the south it had been a different story. The fortunes of war had ebbed and flowed without any decisive result. Reading kept being taken and retaken. The two Parliamentary generals, Essex and Waller, had failed to work effectively together. Essex had wandered off into Cornwall, been trapped by the King and escaped, leaving all his infantry to surrender. Joshua Sprigge wrote: 'whatever was the matter, two Summers past over, and we were not saved: our Victories so gallantly gotten . . . were put into a bag with holes; what we wonne one time, we lost another . . . the Game, however set up at Winter, was to be new played again the next spring . . .' Fairfax himself wrote of 'Ther being some Yers spent in those Parts a lingeringe Warr betwixt ye Forces of ye Kinge and Parliament; and several Battails soe equally fought as could scarce be knowne on which side ye Business in Dispute could be determined,' and described affairs in the south as being 'then somethinge in a declininge Condition', and in a 'Distemper'.

There was a growing feeling that Essex had not enough fire in his belly, was too easy-going and not steely and ruthless enough. There was also a growing conviction in the House of Commons that Essex and Manchester wanted a compromise settlement, and were not disposed to fight to the finish. Cromwell denounced Manchester in the House in November, and in December argued that 'if the Army be not put into another method, and the War more vigorously prosecuted, the People can bear the War no longer, and will enforce you to a dishonourable Peace'. As so often in British wars, the time had come when the amiable but bumbling leaders who were in charge to begin with had to give way to tougher and more forceful men.

The instrument by which the more determined Parliamentarians sought to bring this about was the Self-Denying Ordinance, by which all Parliamentary generals who were members of either House of Parliament would be required to resign their commissions. This would remove from their commands Essex, Manchester, Waller, Ferdinando — and Cromwell. It was proposed in the Commons in December 1644 by Zouche Tate, and sent up to the Lords that month. The Lords threw it out on 13 January but the atmosphere was becoming steadily more tense. In January both the Hothams, and a few days later Archbishop Laud, were executed. The Commons then adopted the proposal for a reorganised, or New Model, army, and for the first time Fairfax's name was mentioned. He himself, convalescent at York, was being kept informed of developments by letters from John Lambert in London. On 14 January James Chaloner wrote to Ferdinando: 'There is a design to have the Militia new moulded . . . and . . . I hope . . . that no stranger, but one of our own nation, have the command in chief. It is probable Sir T. Fairfax will be called up to be general of the horse . . .' This had been proposed by a committee of the House of Commons under Tate, who had also suggested Philip Skippon as senior colonel of foot. Skippon was a man who had worked his way up from the ranks and could not read and write, but had served many years in Holland — like Fairfax, he had been at the siege of Bois-le-Duc — and was extremely competent.

In this form the proposal went to the House itself, who were concerned to elaborate the plan for a reorganised army and to out-flank the Lords, compelling them by the force of public opinion to accept the plan for a New Model Army as a preliminary to accepting the Self-Denying Ordinance. Fairfax's name gave them their solution, for he had not been involved in the quarrels among the southern leaders and he was not identified with either side in the religious argument. In this the Independents, on the one hand, rejected a national church, and believed in the independence of each congregation. They included Cromwell and Sir Harry Vane. The Presbyterians, on the other, held that the only legitimate system was a national church run by ministers who were equal among themselves. They were monarchists, though opposed to Charles I, and more conservative in politics than the Independents. No one knew for sure whether Fairfax was a Presbyterian or an Independent. As Colonel Baldock wrote in his *Cromwell as a Soldier*:

> Fairfax had shown himself a bold, determined leader, whose spirit never flagged under the most adverse conditions. A man of spotless integrity and winning manners, he was adored by his soldiers, and liked and respected by friend and foe. The son and heir of a peer, he might be expected to sympathize with the Lords . . . Yet he was a personal friend of Cromwell.

A legend has grown up that Fairfax was a mere catspaw of Cromwell's. This started early. Baxter, for example, writing in 1696, attributed the choice of the Lord General entirely to Vane and Cromwell, saying:

> For General they chose Sir *Thomas Fairfax*, Son to the Lord *Ferdinando Fairfax*, who had been in the Wars beyond Sea, and had fought valiantly in *Yorkshire* for the Parliament . . . This man was chosen because they supposed to find him a Man of no quickness of Parts, of no Elocution, of no suspicious plotting Wit, and therefore One that *Cromwell* could make use of at his pleasure. And he was acceptable to sober Men because he was Religious, Faithful, Valiant, and of a grave, sober, resolved Disposition; very fit for Execution, and neither too Great nor too Cunning to be Commanded by the Parliament.

But there does not seem to be any hard evidence that the choice of Fairfax was in fact a design by Sir Harry Vane and Cromwell to put in a man who could be used by Cromwell as he wished. The plain fact is that Fairfax was the military commander with the best reputation who was not subject to the Self-Denying Ordinance.

Indeed Sprigge says he was made General 'to which trust and honour he was preferred upon no other grounds, than the observation of his Valour, and all answerable abilities for the same, testified in many notable services done by him in the North, whilest he was yet in a lower sphere . . .' What happened was recorded by Whitacre: 'Sir Thomas Fairfax being named for the first colonel of the horse, it was afterwards upon debate resolved that he should be commander in chief over the whole Army of which the model was made and it being from thence inferred that the Lord General Essex must be laid aside.' A Venetian Ambassador, Contarini, noted that Essex and Manchester were being replaced by an individual of much lower rank — 'di molto minore consideratione'.

So on 21 January 1645, the House of Commons voted, by 101 to 69, that Fairfax should command the New Model Army. Immediately thereafter they voted that Skippon should be Major General of the Foot. Nothing was said about who should now be Lieutenant General of the Horse, the post Fairfax was to have had. On 4 February Fairfax's new appointment was accepted by the Lords, despite the fact that the colonels named to serve under him were none of them members of Parliament.

But the Lords were anxious not to let the Independents get too firm a grip on the new Army. So they stipulated that all Fairfax's officers should be selected by both Houses and that everyone in the new Army should take the Covenant and agree to church arrangements as approved by Parliament. The Commons did not want Fairfax's powers cut down and Cromwell, as a soldier, argued unsuccessfully that the commander-in-chief should have a free hand to choose his own officers. The Commons finally decided that Fairfax should choose his officers but that both Houses should approve his selections. They agreed too on the taking of the Covenant but decided that soldiers in the new Army could hardly approve a form of church government that did not yet exist. So on 17 February the arrangements for a New Model Army commanded by Fairfax were finally settled.

Fairfax was at York, as he himself said, 'not fully recovered of a dangerous Wound'. He was still only 33. He must have been flattered, but not wholly surprised, when he heard that he might be made general of the horse, for there was little more work to do in the north for a cavalry commander. But the proposal that he should become the commander-in-chief of the main Parliamentary army must have amazed him. Hitherto he had been a second-string commander in an important but secondary theatre. It is not surprising that, being a shy man, devoid of ideas of personal aggrandisement, he was nervous about being rocketed to such eminence. His inclination was to have 'hidd myself amonge the Stuff, to have avoyded soe great a Charge'. But he hesitated to disobey a call from Parliament itself and his friends persuaded him to accept, so he rode south.

Sir Thomas Widdrington was keeping Ferdinando informed of developments. On 11 February, when he still expected Tom to be in charge only of the cavalry, he wrote: 'Sir Thomas Fairfax is expected here every day. It hath not yet been moved publicly that he should bring up any of his own horse, but to so many as it hath been privately intimated, it seems very fitting and reasonable . . .' A week after this, on the 18th, Fairfax arrived in London, accompanied by Sir William Constable, Colonel Alured and Thomas Widdrington, who had ridden out to meet him. Next day he called on the Speaker. He was escorted in by four MPs, refused to use the chair put out for him, but stood bareheaded while the Speaker told him that the House 'from their great Experience and Confidence of his Valor, Conduct and Fidelity, had thought fit to make him Commander in Chief of their Armys, and would give him their Protection in the discharge of that weighty Trust the Kingdom repos'd in him'. The Speaker then made suitable references to Agamemnon. Afterwards Fairfax called on the outgoing Lord General, Essex. He now had to nominate all the officers in the army below the rank of colonel. He knew few of those who had served in the south, but he took good advice, and within a week he had a full list ready for Parliament's approval. This was not finally approved by the Lords, after some changes had been made, until 18 March. It included some men who were to make their mark — Fleetwood, Rich, Rossiter, Ireton, Whalley, Sir Hardress Waller, Rainsborough, Robert Hammond, Desborough and John Okey in charge of the dragoons.

Fairfax had so far led the straightforward life of a fighting soldier. He was now to encounter for the first time the quicksands of political conflict. His appointment was welcomed by most of the House of Commons and by the City of London, but it displeased many Presbyterians. It was a new experience for him to come across what James Chaloner called 'the designs of his maligners, either secret or professed', or to find people who were out to do him down. He later wrote:

> . . . had itt not bene in the Simplicity of my Heart, I could·not have supported myselfe under the Frownes and Displeasures those shewed mee, that

were disgusted with these Alterations, in which many of them were them-selves soe much concerned . . . these . . . sought all means to obstruct my Proceedings in this new Charge . . .

What these disgruntled opponents, 'soe viperous a Brood', as he bitterly calls them, could do was to frustrate Fairfax's requests for adequate pay and equipment for his new force, so that 'it seemed rather wee were sent to be destroyed and ruined than to doe any Service to the Kingdome'. It was a foretaste of many difficulties to come.

Fairfax had enough troubles of his own. Not only was his wound still bothering him, but he was suffering agonies from the stone (a complaint that also troubled Cromwell). He was still a young man, but he had been four times wounded and his health had never been good.

On 24 March the Commons produced his Commission. Sig-nificantly it left out the phrase which had been included in Essex's about the need to preserve the King's life. On the same date a com-mittee of the Commons produced a new version of the Self-Denying Ordinance which, unlike the first, did not permanently exclude anyone from service. A week later his commission was accepted by the Lords — by one vote. Fairfax was to be general of the new, reorganised Army in the south. He was not yet put in charge of all forces in England and Wales. That was to come, but not until July 1647. Next day Essex and the other discarded leaders resigned. These included Ferdinando, who came to London to sit in the House of Commons. A day later the Lords finally passed the revised Self-Denying Ordinance. Fairfax succeeded his father as Governor of Hull, but made John Maleverer his deputy. On 3 April he left for Windsor to organise the New Model Army.

He had been appointed to the command of what was to be one of the most celebrated, extraordinary, and, with Wellington's Penin-sular Army, one of the most successful armies in English history. It has been said of it that it was 'the most astonishing creation of the age. There had been nothing like the New Model in the history of our island, nor has it had a successor.' Yet it was originally patched together out of the materials at hand and very little about it was really new except its general. It was the result of five months' deliberation by the Committee of Both Kingdoms and a few days' debate in Parliament. It had been decided then that it should consist of 21,000 men — 12 regiments of foot, making 14,000 men, 10 regiments of horse, or 6000 sabres, and one regiment of 1000 dragoons. One more regiment of horse had been added, bringing the total to 22,000 men. The Army was to be, essentially, Parliament's own force, no longer depending on the local committees which Fairfax himself had found so unsatisfactory.

Fairfax went down to Windsor in, as Joshua Sprigge records, 'a private manner, purposely avoiding that pomp, which usually accompanies a *General* into the field'. He appointed a general rendezvous at Windsor and gave himself just a month — the month of April — to organise the new force. He reported progress to the Committee of Both Kingdoms and Parliament, which sent him letters of thanks and encouragement in reply.

Fundamentally the New Model was created out of what was left of the three southern Parliamentary Armies — those of Essex, Waller and Manchester. The two first were beginning to break up and Waller's men had been in open mutiny. But the tact of Skippon and the prospect of more regular pay produced a change, and most of those who were wanted agreed to enlist. Some serjeants and corporals even agreed to re-enlist as privates. The numbers had to be made up by large drafts of pressed men — up to half the infantrymen were obtained in this way. Fairfax's men, like Nelson's, came in good part from the press gang. Fairfax asked for Fleetwood's regiment from Lincolnshire and incorporated some other entire regiments.

The new Army was to cost around £53,000 a month, raised by county tax assessments. An infantryman and a dragoon were to be paid 18d a day — hardly more than an agricultural labourer — a cavalry trooper 2 shillings (but to provide for his own horse) and Fairfax himself £1 a day. £1000 was allowed to Fairfax for intelligence and £500 for artillery. The Army's pay was never provided in full — they received perhaps half of what they were supposed to get, so that the arrears mounted rapidly, but they did receive some pay regularly. The New Model, when it took the field, astonished the people of England by actually paying for the horses, picks, shovels and ladders it needed and acquired locally.

A volume of contracts for the supply of equipment to Fairfax's new army that spring, thrown out as waste paper by ordnance officers at the Tower of London zealously engaged in the disastrous process known as 'weeding', was miraculously rescued and has found its way to the London Museum. In it are contracts with 'John Thacker of ffanchurch Streete for 400 pikes of good ash & sixteene foote long with steele heads at 3s 10d a peece . . .' 'Elizabeth Betts for one hundred Dragoone Saddles at Seaven Shillings and six pence a peece', and 'William ffell for fifty paire of Pistolls with good holsters at Twenty six shillings p paire English, full bore and proofe'. Orders went out for 'Horseshooes at 4d ye pce' and 'Brests, Backs & Potts att 20s the sute'.

The Army had a powerful siege train of heavy guns. Even security was not neglected. A secret code of agreeable simplicity was devised. G was the King, T Parliament, X Fairfax, L Cromwell, FF the House of Commons, D the House of Lords and OO money.

Throughout April the new force took shape, with some new faces on the General's staff such as Mr John Rushworth, Secretary to the General and Council of War, Master Winter, 'Chirurgion to the General's owne Person,' Edward Bowles, chaplain, who became a close friend of Fairfax's, and Joshua Sprigge, another chaplain, who wrote the history of the New Model's campaigns. Fairfax had, as was customary, his own regiments of foot and horse, commanded for him by Captains Fortescue and Gladman.

The whole Army wore red coats, first worn by the London men in 1642, so that this Army began the tradition of the British red-coats. Fairfax's own regiment wore red with blue facings, blue being his own colour. 'Richard Downs Citizen of London' contracted 'for Sir Thomas fairfax his Army to provide . . . Two Thousand Coates and Two Thousand Breeches at seventeen shillings . . . the coates to be of a Red Colour and of Suffolke, Coventry or Gloucester-shire Cloth . . . The Breeches to be of Gray or some other good Coloure & made of Reading Cloth . . .' When they contracted with Downs 'for Two Thousand Cassacks and breeches' the Committee for the Army was careful to call for the 'cloath to bee shrunk before making'.

The policy in the new Army was that promotion should primarily be by seniority, somewhat tempered by considerations of merit — the principle of Buggins's turn is so deeply ingrained in English society that it survived even in this army. But in practice merit did play a substantial part under Fairfax and humble men could rise to high command as they could not after the Restoration.

Fairfax, helped by Skippon, carried out the organisation of the new Army swiftly and efficiently. 'Many expected a great mutiny upon this regulation of the old army; but it came off better than it was expected,' wrote Whitelocke. This was all the more remarkable as Whitelocke also noted that 'Letters from sir Thomas Fairfax gave an account of the state of his army and the cheerfulness of his soldiers, and his want of pay for them. This was very early for them to want pay . . .' It was a problem about which much more would be heard in the future.

Pay was the responsibility of Parliament and Parliament's ordinances ranged surprisingly wide. Whitelocke's diary of events records two of them:

> Power given to sir Thomas Fairfax to receive all trumpeters and other messengers from the enemy, for exchange of prisoners or other matters touching his army, and to . . . acquaint the houses with all their messages.
>
> An ordinance against such who are called *spirits*, and use to steal away and take up children, and bereave their parents of them, and convey them away: and they ordered another ordinance to be brought in to make this offence felony.

It is to be hoped that the spirits were as punctilious in respecting the Parliamentary ordinances as was Sir Thomas Fairfax.

From the beginning Fairfax enforced strict discipline, so that the Army acquired a reputation for good conduct. In this it often contrasted very favourably with its opponents. On the Royalist side Culpepper this year urged on Digby 'a severe and most strict reformation in the discipline and manners of the army', saying 'Our courage is . . . enerved by lazy licentiousness, and good men are so scandalised at the horrid unpiety of our armies that they will not believe that God can bless any cause in such hands.'

In the New Model the foot were largely uneducated men but the cavalry troopers came from a higher social stratum. Especially was this true of the horse of the Eastern Association which formed the bulk of the New Model cavalry. Cromwell's double regiment of fourteen troops — the celebrated Ironsides — was incorporated in the New Model and divided up to give Fairfax a cavalry regiment of six troops, and another to Colonel Whalley, the two remaining troops going to other regiments.

There is no hard evidence that Fairfax sought to maintain a religious balance between Presbyterians and Independents. Both points of view were represented in the Army. And in the Army, in contrast to London and the Parliamentary garrisons, they got on well together because they had a job to do and put that first. Sometimes the balance was tilted fortuitously, as when at the outset four Scottish colonels resigned, perhaps because they needed to go home to fight Montrose. Of course the New Model had its preachers — Hugh Peters and Richard Baxter being the most celebrated. Indeed, despite Parliament's disapproval, a good many New Model officers took to preaching themselves, Lieutenant Webb at Steeple Ashton interrupting a sermon in the morning and occupying the pulpit himself in the afternoon, while his colonel preached both morning and afternoon, arguing that the local parish priest was Antichrist.

One surprising aspect of the new Army was that it contained hardly anyone from the northern forces. Fairfax did not seek to bring in his old Yorkshire comrades. Perhaps he had not forgotten the poor showing of most of his northern cavalry at Marston Moor in contrast to the steadiness and determination of Cromwell's East Anglians. At any rate even Lambert was not at the outset given a command in the New Model. He was made Commissary General of the northern Army, and took charge of mopping up in the north.

Denzil Holles, the leader of the Presbyterian party in Parliament, argued, in a singularly snobbish and unpleasant passage in his memoirs, that the New Model was officered by parvenus. It was, he said,

> a mercenary Army ... all of them, from the General (except what he may have in expectation after his father's death) to the meanest centinel, not able to make a thousand pounds a year in land; — most of the Colonels and officers mean tradesmen, Brewers, Taylors, Goldsmiths, Shoemakers, and the like; a notable dung-hill, if one would rake into it, to find-out their several pedigrees.

Why he thought it necessary that its officers should be blue-blooded landowners he failed to explain. Moreover what Holles wrote also happened to be largely untrue. There were some key officers in the New Model who, to their credit, had worked their way up from humble origins. Thomas Pride, found as a baby in a church porch, had been a drayman and John Hewson a cobbler; John Okey was said to have been a stoker in a brew-house in Islington. But the majority came from the rural gentry.

Under the New Model Ordinance passed by Parliament all members of it were supposed to take the Covenant, but in practice no attempt was made to enforce this with the rank and file and only one officer excluded himself by refusing to take it, the famous radical John Lilburne. As time went on, Fairfax enlisted in the New Model a good many Royalist prisoners, and thought highly of them. Sir Philip Warwick, a Royalist, whose wife was related to Fairfax, talked to him later on in the war, and 'when complementing him with the regularity and temperance of his army, he told me, *The best common soldiers he had* (for he himself was of a rationall temper, not phanaticall) *came out of our army, and from the garrisons he had taken in. So* (sayes he) *I found you had made them good soldiers and I have made them good men.'*

Fairfax had full powers over the New Model and could choose his own officers. Indeed Sir Charles Firth wrote: 'Fairfax exercised a power to which it is difficult to find a parallel in later English history. From the beginning of his first campaign he had more authority over the New Model than Wellington ever possessed over the army in Spain and Portugal.' Firth pointed out that Fairfax could promote any man he thought fit; whereas Wellington complained that he had not the power of making even a corporal. He also noted that Fairfax, unlike Wellington, did not have incompetent officers thrust upon him by the government he served.

But there were, to begin with, severe limitations on Fairfax's freedom of decision. For the first three months there was an unsatisfactory division of control between the Committee of Both Kingdoms at Derby House, who reckoned that they were running the war, and the general in the field, and communications were inevitably slow. Moreover Fairfax always had his council of war, with whom he discussed alternatives before any engagement. At these councils there was often intense debate between the army leaders, but at the end of the day the final decision was Fairfax's own. He was not bound to take the advice of his council of war, and once he had made up his own mind that was the end of the matter. Indeed Whitelocke wrote, 'I have observed him at councils of war, that he hath said little, but hath ordered things expressly contrary to the judgement of all his council.'

The King derided 'the rebels' new brutish general' as he described him to the Queen. His contempt was premature.

Naseby

THE WORK of organising the New Model, which went on throughout April, was done entirely by Fairfax and Skippon. Cromwell had no part in it. But he was still active in the field. He had not resigned his commission as Essex and Manchester had done. The revised Self-Denying Ordinance had only been passed on 3 April, and he had forty days before he needed to do so. In the meantime he had taken the Eastern Association cavalry on a highly successful foray. On 9 April he wrote to Fairfax from Salisbury, marking the letter 'Haste, Haste', asking for reinforcements. A few days later he won an engagement at Islip and took Bletchington House — to the outrage of the King, who had Colonel Windebank shot outside Merton College for surrendering it. Soon afterwards, perhaps on the 22nd, he came to Windsor to kiss Fairfax's hand and take formal leave of the new General. But there was an element of unreality about this farewell. The post of Lieutenant-General of the Horse in the New Model was still vacant, and Fairfax had made no move to appoint anyone to it. Both men must have known very well that there was only one man who could fill it — the cavalry leader who had turned defeat into victory at Marston Moor.

But now the time for action had come. At the behest of the Committee of Both Kingdoms Cromwell was sent off again to the west with a body of horse and dragoons. On the first of May Fairfax set out with his new Army, though it was still 'far short of its intended number of 21,000' — perhaps by 4000 or so — and he himself was far from well, having had an 'ague' for some time. He knew very well that his new Army contained a large number of raw troops and pressed men, and Marston Moor had shown that such troops could be unreliable. He must have been conscious of his great responsibility: like Jellicoe in the First World War, he was the one man who could lose the war in an afternoon. But he was in good heart.

He was, however, irritated by the orders he had from the Committee, on which both Essex and Manchester sat. He himself had no doubt that his objective must be to seek out the King's main army and destroy it, but the Committee ordered him to go first to Taunton to relieve the siege there. So, marching ten miles a day, he took the road to Reading, Andover and Blandford. From the outset he insisted on rigid discipline. He hanged a deserter and a mutineer to make it clear that he would stand no nonsense, and proclaimed that plundering would also be punishable by death. He treated everyone alike and refused to give his own regiment any special privileges. Early on, when it claimed the right to march at all times in the van, he dismounted and himself marched for two miles in front of the regiment where he had placed it in the rear. Thereafter it went where it was told without argument.

News now came in that the King and Rupert had left Oxford and moved north, shadowed by Cromwell. Orders came to Fairfax from the Committee to besiege Oxford. He thought this no more sensible than the previous instruction to go to Taunton, but he did what he was told, detaching a brigade under Colonel Weldon to prevent Colonel Blake being overwhelmed in Taunton, which it effectively did, and, as he moved back towards Oxford, capturing 'three carts laden with Canary wines' besides 'forty horse and their riders'.

Cromwell's forty days now ran out, but he was given a further forty-day extension, and joined Fairfax in front of Oxford around 20 May. A few days later Cromwell was ordered by the Committee of Both Kingdoms to go off to East Anglia. By the 31st he was at Cambridge; but on that day Rupert struck a shattering blow against Parliament by successfully storming Leicester. As Sprigge wrote, 'Great was the discouragement of the Parliaments friends,' while the King soon after wrote to the Queen saying that 'since this Rebellion my affairs were never in so hopefull a way'. Cromwell meanwhile wrote to Fairfax saying that he found things in the east in 'a very ill posture'.

In the meantime the Royalists had suffered from fatally divided counsels. At a meeting at Stow on the Wold Rupert, supported by

Marmaduke Langdale, had argued for a push to the north to relieve Chester and attack the Scots. Others had been for attacking Fairfax's new Army, which the Royalists referred to contemptuously as 'The New Noddle'. The disastrous decision had been taken to try to do both, Rupert taking the main army north and Goring going to the west to face Fairfax. When Fairfax moved to Oxford, Rupert recalled Goring, but Goring liked his independent command, and found reasons for not complying with these orders. The Committee of Both Kingdoms was equally inept and ordered Fairfax to release Colonel Vermuyden with 2500 horse to meet the Scots, whom they supposed to be moving south. Gardiner comments that 'the extraordinary directions given by the Committee were the result of the not uncommon tendency of politicians to subordinate military action to political intrigue'. Fairfax himself complained to his father: 'I am very sorry we should speend our time unprofitably before a Towne whilst the King hath time to strengthen him selfe & by terror to force obedience of al places wher he comes . . . it is the earnest desire of this army to folow the King, but the endeavours of others to prevent it hath so much prevailed.'

The King and Rupert dawdled about Daventry and Langdale's northern cavalry refused for a time to move any further south. Some of their infantry disappeared with the loot they had collected at Leicester. But the loss of Leicester had shocked the men at Derby House and at last Fairfax was allowed to raise the siege of Oxford, which he did on 5 June. At Newport Pagnell he found Vermuyden, who had failed to join the Scots. Vermuyden resigned his command for personal reasons and went back to the Netherlands, but at least Fairfax had go this cavalry back. On the 8th he called a council of war. It confirmed his view — which he had held all along — that the destruction of the King's army must be their objective.

Then Fairfax proposed to them that they should ask for Cromwell to command the horse. They agreed unanimously, and Colonel Hammond posted to London with the request for Cromwell, which stressed 'the constant presence and blessing of God that have accompanied him'. It was agreed to at once by the House of Commons. The Committee of Both Kingdoms too, now gave Fairfax a free hand to conduct his operations. In future he could make his own decisions instead of having them taken for him by men miles away at Derby House.

As always, Fairfax moved fast, and on 12 June he reached Kislingbury, only five miles from the Royalist army. The Royalists were taken completely by surprise. The King was out hunting and the army's horses out at grass. Fairfax learnt this from some prisoners and learnt too from an intercepted letter that Goring could not join the King.

That night he mounted his horse and rode round the sentry posts till four in the morning, making sure himself that his Army could not be caught by a surprise attack. As he rode round in the darkness he must have known that he was about to face the supreme test of a general. He knew that his cavalry were the formidable troopers of the Eastern Association, but that his foot were mostly untried. They might panic and disappear in headlong flight if things went badly. It was with them that he must be chiefly concerned, though he knew that he had a pronounced superiority in numbers — perhaps some 13,000 against the King's 7000 or 8000.

Revolving these things in his mind he forgot the password, and when challenged by a vigilant sentry was made to wait in the wet until the Captain of the Guard could be fetched. He had the sentry rewarded for his firmness. Now in the small hours he could make out enemy horsemen moving fast over Burrow Hill, making fires, and giving indications that they were on the move. In fact the Royalist army was hurriedly pulling back eighteen miles to Market Harborough.

At six in the morning Fairfax called a council of war. They agreed that the right course was to pursue the King and bring him to battle. In the middle of their discussions Cromwell rode in with 600 cavalry and dragoons. He was given a warm welcome and Fairfax at once put him in charge of the whole of the cavalry. The Army now set out after the Royalists, and by the evening was at Guilsborough, four miles south of Naseby, while a patrol under Ireton entered Naseby itself and captured a Royalist patrol carelessly feasting at a long table in the inn. The Royalists realised that they could no longer hope to avoid an action, and as day broke they took up position on a hill just south of Market Harborough.

Fairfax, meanwhile, riding his favourite chestnut mare, had in the small hours of Saturday, 14 June brought his Army up to the Naseby ridge. He was almost in the exact middle of England, on the watershed, with the streams on his left flowing westward and those on his right towards the North Sea. He and Cromwell rode forward to reconnoitre and a man who was nearby heard Cromwell say, 'Let us, I beseech you, draw back to yonder hill which will encourage the enemy to charge us.' Sprigge thus describes the scene:

the Enemies Army . . . we saw plainly advancing in order towards us: and the winde blowing somewhat Westwardly, by the Enemies advance so much on their right hand, it was evident, that he designed to get the winde of us: which occasioned the *General* to draw down into a large fallow field on the Northwest side of *Naseby*, flanked on the left hand with a hedge, which was a convenient place for us to fight the Enemy in . . . possessing the ledge of a Hill, running from East to West.

Fairfax took up this position, and then pulled his troops back a hundred yards behind the crest of the ridge to keep them out of sight, as Wellington was later to do at Waterloo. He made skilful dispositions. Slingsby noted in his diary that Rupert 'perceiv'd that General Fairfax intend'd not to quitt ye advantage of ye Hill . . . so advantageous was it, that they could easily observe in what body we drew up our men . . . when as they lay without our sight having ye Hill to cover them . . .' Fairfax and Skippon now put the Army in fighting order. Cromwell organised the cavalry, and at his request Fairfax made Ireton Commissary General of the Horse and gave him command of the left wing, while Cromwell himself took charge on the right, with five regiments of horse. Okey and his dragoons were sent to line the double Sulby hedges on the left to protect that flank and enfilade any attacking cavalry. Fairfax gave the word 'God our strength' while the Royalist word was 'Queen Mary'. The Royalists put beanstalks in their hats to identify themselves.

Now, only 41 days after he had started putting together the New Model, Fairfax faced a decisive battle and was saddled with ultimate responsibility. Opposed to him, in supreme command of the Royalist army, in full armour with his sword drawn, was his Sovereign, with the two Palatinate princes, Rupert and Maurice. One must wonder what thoughts ran through Fairfax's mind at this moment.

But there was to be no long wait as at Marston Moor. The two armies swept forward from their low ridges into the shallow valley and the struggle began. Rupert charged slightly uphill on Fairfax's left. His advancing lines were raked by Okey's dragoons, who emptied some saddles but did not check the advance. Rupert struck Ireton's left and swept it aside, charging on victoriously for another mile.

In the centre the Royalist foot gained ground and pushed the Parliamentary foot back over the crest of the ridge. Skippon was shot and badly wounded. The position was critical. Fairfax's left wing had collapsed and now his centre was giving way. At any moment the retreat could become a rout and the day might be lost. At such times Fairfax was at his best. He called in his reserves, threw himself into the thick of the fight, and brought the Royalist advance to a halt. The General was 'not in one place but everywhere as occasion required'. In this sort of crisis he was like a man inspired. Sprigge wrote of him that:

> When he hath come upon action, or been near an engagement, it hath been observed, another spirit hath come upon him, another soul hath lookt out at his eyes; I mean he hath been so raised, elevated, and transported, as that he hath been not only unlike himselfe at other times, but indeed more like an Angell, then a man.

He had lost his helmet and was riding about bare-headed. He put spirit into his untried foot soldiers and with him in their midst they rallied and stood their ground. One who was present wrote, 'Sir, had you seen him and how his spirit was raised, it would have made an impression on you never to be obliterated; God knows I speak the truth and do not hyperbolise.'

The newly promoted Ireton had lost half his horse but Rupert and his men had disappeared. With admirable presence of mind Ireton charged with the remnants into the right flank of the Royalist foot. Those tough men — mostly Welshmen — resisted him fiercely. Ireton himself had his horse killed under him, was run through the thigh with a pike, wounded in the face with a halberd and taken prisoner. But after him came Okey, who had remounted his dragoons and threw them into battle on this flank.

Away on the right Cromwell, reinforced by Rossiter and his troopers, who had ridden in from Lincolnshire just as the battle started, now had 3600 sabres behind him. He watched Marmaduke Langdale's troopers making their way towards him through the broken ground below. Waiting until they were halfway up the slope he then launched Whalley with three regiments of Ironsides down at them.

Langdale's men fought bravely but they were outnumbered nearly two to one and fighting uphill and were, as Slingsby says, 'out fronted & overpour'd'. They were driven back, pursued by Whalley. Cromwell still had two regiments in hand and with these he now sent in a series of waves of cavalry to attack the exposed left flank of the Royalist foot, who were thus being assaulted on three sides.

The tide of battle had turned and it had become critical for the Royalists. It was the moment when they needed to throw in their reserves, as Fairfax had done earlier. The King, watching the battle from the summit of Dust Hill, saw this and began to lead the reserve cavalry forward. But an officious Scot, the Earl of Carnwath, seized his bridle and pulled him aside, saying 'Will you go upon your death?' Charles was a brave man but at moments of crisis authority and determination seemed to desert him. It is difficult to imagine anyone grabbing Fairfax's bridle, or Cromwell's. They would probably have been cut down. Now someone called out 'March to the right,' and the whole body of the Royalist reserve cavalry (Slingsby wrote defensively, 'we but a few horse only, & those mightily discourag'd') rode back to Dust Hill. Even if the King had been killed at Naseby, it would have been a noble and courageous end. As it is, he sat on the hill with his advisers watching his infantry being destroyed. They were now surrounded, but fought, says Sprigge, 'with incredible courage and resolution'.

One regiment still held out. Fairfax came up to his lifeguard, commanded by Captain D'Oyley, who remonstrated with him for exposing himself to danger. Fairfax brushed this aside, saying, 'It is well enough, Charles,' and then asked D'Oyley whether he had charged the regiment of bluecoats opposite. D'Oyley said he had twice done so but could not break them. Fairfax told him to try once more, while he himself took a party of horse round to attack them in the rear, saying that they would meet in the middle. So indeed they did. D'Oyley met Fairfax who had just killed the regiment's ensign and himself taken its colours. A soldier later boasted that he had done this. When D'Oyley called him a liar, saying that any number of people had seen the General do it, Fairfax simply said, 'I have honour enough, let him take that honour to himself.'

And what of Rupert? He had swept on with uncontrollable momentum until he reached the Parliamentary baggage. The baggage master suddenly saw a commanding person ride up wearing a red *montero* whom he assumed to be Fairfax. Doffing his hat, he went forward to pay his respects. He was startled to be asked by the horseman, who was in fact Rupert, whether he would take quarter. The baggage master refused and his musketeers fired on Rupert and his men and drove them off. Now, an hour or so later, Rupert brought his cavalry back to the field. But it was too late.

Fairfax was taking no chances. He formed his Army up again in battle order — in itself no mean feat — in case the King and Rupert did decide on a desperate last attack. But the King and Rupert turned and rode sadly away. The Parliamentary cavalry pursued them for eighteen miles, to within two miles of Leicester.

Fairfax's victory had been complete and devastating: He took some 5000 prisoners, 500 of them officers, all the King's artillery, 200 horses, a vast amount of arms and ammunition, 200 carriages, 55 colours, all the Royalist baggage, and the King's personal correspondence, which was soon published with damaging effect. Perhaps another 1000 Royalists were killed, but Fairfax lost fewer than 200 men. The Parliamentarians found a large group of women following the Royalist army. To their shame, they killed a good many of them out of hand under the impression that they were Irish, though more probably they were Welsh, and slit the noses of others they asserted were harlots.

The King had fought his last battle and from now on, as Sir Philip Warwick put it, flitted about like a hunted partridge. Fairfax sent back a bare account of the victory, while Colonel Fiennes marched the prisoners to London where they were paraded through the town. Cromwell, as an MP, did not hesitate to comment on the performance of his chief in writing to the Speaker:

> Sir, this is none other but the hand of God . . . The General served you with all faithfulness and honour . . . as much for bravery, may be given to him, in this action, as to a man. Honest men served you faithfully in this action, Sir, they are trusty; I beseech you, in the name of God, not to discourage them . . .

In London a day of thanksgiving was observed and the Lord Mayor gave a celebration dinner attended by Rupert's brother, the Prince Elector, who no doubt had a eye on the succession. Parliament voted £700 for a gold, enamel and diamond locket to be made for Fairfax, with himself on his chestnut mare on one side and the House of Commons on the other. For Ludlow, the Member for Wiltshire and a prominent soldier on the Parliamentary side — 'This success was astonishing, being obtained by men of little experience in affairs of this nature, and upon that account despised by their enemies . . .'

Mr Hales, a former fellow of Eton, remarked that 'he saw now that Fairfax's Army would master both King and Parliament too; and rule as the Roman Emperors . . . in despight of the Senate . . .'

Ranke observed that Naseby gave the Parliamentary Army 'self-reliance and confidence in their leaders' and Clarendon 'that the capacity to rally after being beaten disclosed the better discipline which had been introduced by Fairfax and Cromwell'. It was the decisive battle of the Civil War.

Langport
and the Siege of Bristol

FAIRFAX wasted no time after Naseby. Next day he set out for Leicester and prepared to storm it, but it was promptly surrendered just three days after the battle. Then, as Robert Blake in Taunton was still being besieged by Goring and was in some danger, he turned south-west, joined now by Lambert from Yorkshire. Though it was the height of summer and extremely hot, he travelled at a formidable pace, 17 to 20 miles a day, by-passing the Royalist garrisons.

He entered Wiltshire and marched to Marlborough and Salisbury, happily resisting the urgings of the preacher Hugh Peters that he should demolish 'the monuments of heathenism at Stonehenge'. Near Salisbury he encountered for the first time the movement known as the 'clubmen'. These were armed local gatherings, often of some thousands of men, who wished above all to protect their lands and possessions from the marauding armies of both sides. Their motto was, 'If you offer to plunder our Cattel, be assur'd we'l bid you Battel'. In Wiltshire and Dorset they tended to be sympathetic to the Royalists, perhaps because their leaders mostly came from the local gentry, but in Somerset and Gloucestershire, where they had experienced the excesses of Goring's troops, they were better disposed to Fairfax and the New Model. Fairfax's firm discipline helped — he had a soldier executed for 'robbing a Gentleman'. And when he met the clubmen, he treated them with tact and skill. As Gardiner said, 'No man living was better qualified than Fairfax to deal with such a movement.' The leader of the Dorset clubmen, whom Fairfax met near Dorchester, spoke threateningly and demanded a cease-fire. But Fairfax refused to allow himself to be ruffled and explained that he could not call a halt to his march when letters captured with the King's correspondence at Naseby made it clear that an invasion of England by French and Irish troops was likely. He persuaded the clubmen to let him pass through unmolested.

His rapid march was tough going. His men had no tents. 'For the most part,' says one account, 'we took barns and hedges for our night's repose, after our hard and hot days' marches.' He was also short of supplies, reporting that 'It grieves me to see men not at all armed, badly horsed . . . horses spoiled for want of saddles, many men afoot who had their horses killed, and yet all so willing and ready to serve you to the uttermost.' Many men had deserted, but he pressed on to Blandford and Beaminster, picked up Weldon's brigade and Massey's western force on the way, and relieved Taunton on 8 July. Goring did not wait for him but advanced southeastwards towards Yeovil. Fairfax took a southerly route so that he could get supplies through the ports of Weymouth and Lyme.

The speed of his march gave the Royalists no time to recover from the shock of Naseby and concentrate their forces. The King still had some 4000 cavalry and had scratched together about 3000 foot. Clearly his best course was to join Goring. Indeed Fairfax told his father that the 'King had given Goring strict commands not to engage before himself, with the Welsh forces, were joined with him, and Greenwill with those out of the West, which, altogether, would have made a very great army, besides many thousands of club-men in Wiltshire and Dorsetshire, which was ready to declare themselves for the King, as soon as he had crossed the Severn.' But the King was still at Hereford and Fairfax was upon Goring before anything could be done.

Goring moved right across the line of Fairfax's advance from the south — perhaps to try to keep contact with the King — and took up a position along the river Yeo from Langport to Yeovil, destroying the bridges across the river. Fairfax and Cromwell rode out from Crewkerne to reconnoitre and Fairfax decided to force a crossing of the river at Yeovil, on Goring's extreme left. This he did without difficulty, taking Yeovil and Ilchester and forcing the Royalists back on Langport.

He now learnt that Goring had sent a large force of cavalry under his exceptionally incompetent brother-in-law, Porter, south-west towards Taunton. This mysterious move may have been a ploy to confuse Fairfax and get him to divide his forces. If so, it was partially successful. For Fairfax sent off Massey with 3600 men to pursue this body and himself moved the main army to Long Sutton, north of the Yeo and three miles from Langport. Hearing no news, he became anxious and sent off two further bodies, amounting to another 2000 men, to reinforce Massey.

But Massey had unexpectedly surprised Porter's cavalry at Isle Abbas while they were dismounted, some of them asleep, others swimming or strolling about and leaving their horses grazing in a meadow. They were driven off in confusion, many being taken prisoner, while the rest fled back to Langport, where they were met by a disgusted Goring, who then decided to fall back gradually on Bridgwater, while holding a strong position on a small brook in a dip, east of Langport and Huish Episcopi. He lined the hedges with musketeers, posted his cavalry on slightly higher ground behind, and left two guns to cover the ford, or 'pass' as it was called, by which any hostile cavalry would have to cross.

Fairfax began by tackling the two guns. His own were drawn up in a line 700 yards away and an artillery duel began. The result was not in doubt as the Parliamentarians had more guns, and in due course the two Royalist pieces were knocked out. Then he sent forward his own musketeers to engage the Royalists. There was a brisk exchange of fire but the Parliamentarians eventually pushed their way forward.

Then Fairfax decided that the time had come to force the crossing of the brook and to this end he ordered a cavalry charge through the ford on a front so narrow that only four horsemen, riding knee to knee, could make their way over. This was a risky course — it sounded like the charge that largely failed at Marston Moor — but could be decisive if carried out with real determination. The job was given to Major Bethell, who led three troops at the gallop straight through the ford and into the waiting Royalist cavalry. The charge was carried through with great dash — Fairfax and Cromwell described it as 'one of the bravest that ever their eyes beheld' — and was a success, but eventually the sheer numbers of the Royalist cavalry brought it to a halt and began to push Bethell's men back. Fairfax however sent in three more troops under Desborough, who charged the Royalist cavalry in flank, and sent his musketeers forward

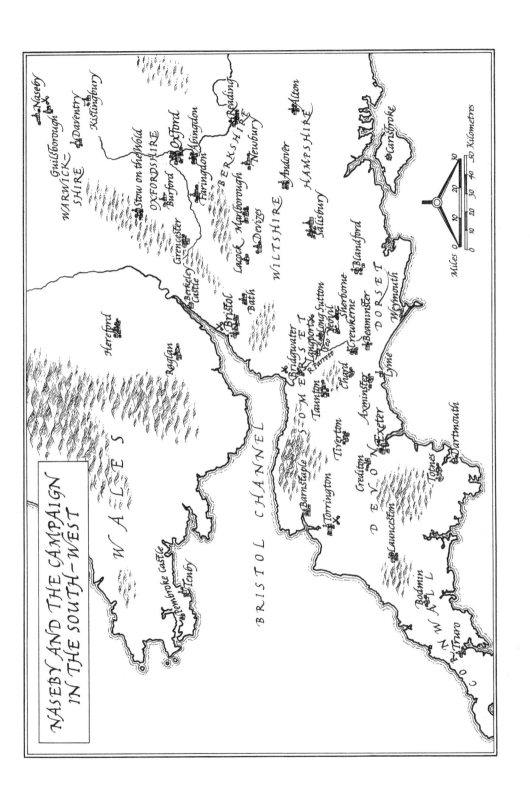

NASEBY AND THE CAMPAIGN IN THE SOUTH-WEST

to maintain a withering fire. The Royalists resisted bravely for a time but then broke and fled to Bridgwater, pursued by the Parliamentary horse, who found it hard to see them because of the great clouds of dust. The Royalists' spirit was broken and after Langport they were reluctant to face the New Model in the open field.

Fairfax himself looked on the battle of Langport as his greatest success. The numbers on both sides were more nearly equal than at Naseby. He was facing a very capable general in a prepared defensive position. But he had succeeded by a correct estimation of the staying power of the two armies. He had taken a risk but it had been fully justified by the result. He captured 2000 prisoners, 800 of whom took the Covenant and entered Parliament's service, the two guns, many arms and 32 colours, and told his father, 'we cannot esteem this mercy less, all things considered, than that of Naseby fight'.

In no time at all he was in front of the important port and fortress of Bridgwater, on the Parrett near the Bristol Channel, a place the King had been advised was impregnable. Riding forward over the river to inspect his advance posts, Fairfax had a narrow escape from being cut off by the incoming tide and drowned. He told his father on 16 July that he had to give his soldiers a few days rest and that he was short of match for his musketeers but that he intended to storm or blockade Bridgwater, as 'this town is of greater consequence, as we conceive, than any in the western parts; for if we have it, we shall garrison in a line which will reach from Severn's mouth to the South Sea, and so divide Devonshire and Cornwall, where their chief force is driven'. Six days later, he stormed the outer defences of Bridgwater and set two or three houses on fire as a warning. Next day Sir Hugh Wyndham surrendered. Fairfax took another 1600 prisoners and sent up the captured 'plate and rich hangings' to Parliament, which ordered them to be sold and the proceeds sent to Fairfax's soldiers 'for their encouragement'. In a postscript to a letter to his father Fairfax wrote: 'The King is expected this night in Bristow if the newes of taking Bridgewater stay him not, his greatest hopes now seems to be in the club men, and god's Providence is much seene in the timely taking of this towne. If the King had had time enough to have got his forces and these numerous club men together, we must have left it.'

Here in Somerset some of the clubmen were quite well disposed to Fairfax, who twice addressed meetings of 2000 of them near Bridgwater. They subsequently gave him some useful help. But others were interfering with his supplies and this had to be stopped. In another letter Fairfax wrote that 'the clubmen of Wiltshire, Dorsetshire, and Hampshire, are like to be of dangerous consequence, if not prevented. We have taken thirteen or fourteen of their chief leaders. Lieutenant-General Cromwell is gone out with some horse to hinder the clubmen's meeting . . . We must not neglect this business, for their violence is probable to lead them to some foolish attempt . . .' Cromwell and Desborough dealt firmly, but with the minimum bloodshed, with the recalcitrant clubmen, whom Cromwell described to Fairfax as 'poor silly creatures'.

Fairfax was anxious to pursue Goring into Cornwall, and his council of war recommended an immediate westward march, but he thought it unsafe to go there until the clubmen had been suppressed and Bath and Sherborne taken. So he turned back towards the east, telling Ferdinando, 'We find nothing more difficult than sieges, where things are not provided for that work. Necessity and reason now puts us upon that way; for no army, God be thanked, now for the present is like to keep the field against us.'

He sent forward a brigade to begin besieging Sherborne and detached Colonel Rich with horse and dragoons to try to seize Bath. There Okey's dragoons crept forward to the gate and gripped the barrels of the guards' muskets sticking out through the loopholes. The guards fled, the dragoons fired the gate and Bath surrendered before Rupert, who was only four miles off, could come to its rescue. Fairfax himself came in and made sure that the town would be securely held and then rode on with a small party of cavalry to Sherborne.

Sherborne was stoutly defended by Sir Lewis Dives, and there was fierce fighting round the walls. Fairfax battered them with siege artillery and employed miners from the Mendips to undermine them. When he went forward to see the work being done on the mine he had another narrow escape, this time from some of his own soldiers who were shooting deer. They managed to shoot one of their fellows and narrowly missed their General.

Money, sorely needed, came in and Fairfax gave his soldiers an extra shilling a day to encourage them. He sent a message to Dives to send out his wife and any other women if he wished. The guns made a wide breach but began to run short of cannon balls, so the soldiers collected used ones under the walls, and were given sixpence for each one they brought in. Dives was told he could have no terms but quarter and Fairfax ordered a storm, with the soldiers cutting and throwing in 6000 faggots to fill up the ditch. So the Parliamentarians fought their way in. They spared the lives of the garrison but took plenty of booty.

Fairfax's rear was now secure, but he still had his anxieties. He told his father, who had the advantage of being an MP: 'I am sorry money is so slowly sent to the army; indeed our soldiers have been put to hard service and strict obedience; but if they want pay, both these will be neglected, and nothing carries on our business with more advantage than keeping our soldiers from doing violences . . .' Nevertheless he decided that 'the next designe' must be to besiege the great city, port and fortress of Bristol, held for the King by Prince Rupert himself, who had captured it for the Royalists in July 1643. Plague had broken out there, but Fairfax declared that, 'As for the Sicknesses, let us trust God with the Army, who will be as ready to protect us, in the Siege, from Infection, as in the Field, from the Bullet.' So on 21 August the siege began and the city was blockaded for the next three weeks, Fairfax telling Ferdinando, 'We have shut Prince Rupert, with all his horse, up in Bristol; the plague is much there. I hope God will direct all things for the best . . .' Various sallies by the garrison were beaten back, but the dragoon leader Okey was captured by the defenders.

Fairfax, having established his headquarters in a small farmhouse, sent in a summons to Rupert to surrender. But it was no ordinary summons. Fairfax took the opportunity to set out his own views on what the conflict was all about and to remind Rupert of the support Protestants had given to his family in the Palatinate, saying that he would

a little expostulate with you about the surrender . . . which I confesse is a way not common, and which I should not have used, but in respect to such a person, and to such a place. I take into consideration your royal birth, and relation to the *Crown* of *England*, your honour, courage, the vertues of your person . . .

Sir, the *Crown* of *England* is and will be where it ought to be; we fight to maintain it there. But the *King*, misled by evill Counsellors, or through a seduced heart, hath left his Parliament, under God, the best assurance of his Crown and Family: the maintaining of this Schisme is the ground of this unhappy war . . . what sad effects it hath produced in the three Kingdomes, is visible to all men. To maintain the rights of the Crown and Kingdom joyntly, a principal part whereof is, that the King in supream acts is not to be advised by men of whom the Law takes no notice, but by his Parliament, the great Counsel of the Kingdom, in whom (as much as man is capable of) he hears all his people as it were at once advising him; and in which multitude of Councellours lyes his safety, and his peoples interest . . .

Sir, if God makes this clear to you, as he hath to us, I doubt not but he will give you a heart to deliver this place, notwithstanding all the other considerations of honour, courage, fidelity etc . . . It would be an occasion . . . joyful to us, for restoring of you to the endeared affection to the Parliament, and people of *England*, the truest friend to your Family it hath in this World . . . But if this be hid from your eyes . . . let all *England* judge whether the burning of its Towns, ruining its Cities, and destroying its people, be a good requital from a person of your Family, which hath had the prayers, tears, purses, and blood of its Parliament and people . . .

'The *Crown* of *England* is and will be where it ought to be; we fight to maintain it there.' This is something Cromwell would never have written. But a limited monarchy, advised and controlled by Parliament, was central to Fairfax's beliefs. At this stage what he wrote to Rupert was not far from being orthodox in a Parliamentarian. When in due time a more radical and revolutionary tide swept all before it, Fairfax was left high and dry. His views remained those set out in this letter.

Rupert 'received the paper, he looking in it, swore God damn him, it was a summons, and called for a cup of sack, and sat down and read it . . .' He replied in a high, imperious tone, but in substance made it clear that he was prepared to surrender the city, provided that

myself, all Noblemen, Commanders and Souldiers of Horse and Foot . . . shall have free liberty to march away . . . with their Arms, flying Colours, Drums beating, Trumpets sounding, Pistols cockt, Swords drawn, Matches lighted at both ends . . . and with all their bag and baggage, horses, arms and other furniture [and that] no Churches be defaced.

He also asked for permission to consult the King and, when this was refused, dragged out the negotiations until Fairfax concluded that he must attack. He now heard that, following Montrose's victory at Kilsyth, the Scots had abandoned the siege of Hereford. He himself had made thorough preparations for an assault. He rode round with his officers to view the works — 'no soldier was to shew any obedience to him as general, lest the enemy . . . make shot against him . . .' His preparations show how meticulous was his planning and staff work:

Colonel Welden with his Brigade . . . to storm in three places, *viz* 200 men in the middle, 200 on each side, as forlorn hopes to begin the storm; 20 Ladders to each place, two men to carry each Ladder, and to have 5s. a piece; two Serjeants that attended the service of the ladder, to have 20s. a man; each musquetire that followed the ladder, to carry a fagot . . . the Party . . . to possesse the guns, and turn them; A Gentleman of the Ordnance, Gunners and Matrosses [a gunner's assistant], to enter with the Parties; the Draw-bridge to be let down; . . . the bridge over *Froom* to be made good against horse with Pikes, or to break it down . . . Colonel *Rainsboroughs* brigade . . . to storm on this side the river *Froom*, beginning on the right hand of the Sally-port up to *Pryors-hill* Fort, and to storm the Fort itself, as the main busines: 200 of this brigade to go up in Boats with the sea-men to storm *Waterfort* . . . One regiment of horse, and a regiment of foot, to be moving up and down in the closes before the Royal fort, and to ply hard upon it, to alarm it . . .

It was all detailed and professional and, when it came to the point, effective. Weldon's brigade failed to carry the walls but Rainsborough's did, in what Fairfax described as 'a fierce and resolute storm'. Prior's Hill fort was captured, after a struggle lasting nearly three hours, and its garrison put to the sword. Sadly the brave Major Bethell was mortally wounded. To avoid further useless bloodshed and destruction Rupert surrendered on terms not fundamentally different from those he had earlier proposed. Fairfax escorted Rupert for two miles out of Bristol, while angry crowds shouted for Rupert's death. No less angry was the King, who wrote to Rupert:

Nepueu . . . what is to be done? after one, that is so neer me as you ar, both in Blood & Frendship, submits himselfe to so meane an Action . . . you asseured me, (that if no Muteny hapned) you would keepe Bristol for fower Monthes; did you keepe it fower Dayes? . . . my Conclusion is, to desyre you to seeke your subsista[n]ce . . . somewhere beyond Sease . . .

The King told Prince Maurice that the surrender had upset him more than anything 'since this damnable rebellion' and that Rupert must have had his 'judgement seduced by rotten harted villains'.

Fairfax asked Cromwell to send the Speaker an account of the storm, which he did, describing the whole course of the operations and the results, such as 140 cannon and 2–3000 muskets captured. Cromwell took occasion to tell the House: 'Presbyterians, Independents, all had here the same spirit of faith and prayer; the same pretence and answer; they agree here, know no names of difference: pity it is it should be otherwise anywhere.' When they published the account the House took care to leave out this passage, and doctored the text to suggest that the account came from Fairfax.

Triumph in the West

AFTER BRISTOL was taken Fairfax observed that the Royalists were much dejected. One of them, indeed, wrote despondently: 'Sir Thomas Fairfax is mightily triumphant daily and takes strongholds hourly.' He now decided to consolidate. He despatched Rainsborough to take Berkeley Castle, held by Sir Charles Lucas, and Cromwell to take Devizes and Lacock House, while he himself went to Bath to join Anne and rest for a few days. As usual, his health had been bad. These operations went well; in due course he went to Devizes and on to Lacock where he saw the Royalists march out. Cromwell went on to take Winchester and the great Catholic stronghold, Basing House.

Although it was autumn, Fairfax now resolved to push on into the south-west and destroy the Royalist forces there. He moved to Axminster but Goring was not yet an entirely spent force and during the night raided Fairfax's quarters with a strong body of cavalry, capturing sixty prisoners. But Fairfax pushed forward to Chard and Tiverton, which was quickly taken as a round shot broke the chain holding up the drawbridge. Once again the supply of money from Parliament ran out and the Army got no pay for a month. It was not at all easy for Fairfax to maintain discipline in these circumstances but he moved his Army to Crediton and dispersed it round Exeter. The winter rains made a Devonshire campaign impracticable and, as he wrote, 'the extreme coldness of the weather, and want of clothes, makes us act slower'. His army was troubled with sickness, as he was himself. Men were dying every day. He told Ferdinando,

> I am exceedingly troubled with rheumatism and a benumbing coldness in my head, legs and arms, especially on that side I had my hurts. It hath pleased the Lord to help me through much extremities. I trust He will lay

no more on me than He will enable me to bear. The mercies I have received
ought to stop all complaints in His service.

In London, Parliament had been devising impracticable peace
terms under which Ferdinando would have become Earl of Holder-
nesse and Tom Fairfax Baron of Naseby, with £5000 a year. When
the negotiations of Uxbridge broke down Parliament did settle
lands worth £5000 on their victorious general, while a Parliamentary delegation arrived to present him with the Naseby jewel. On
the other side Goring, weakened by illness and drink, gave up and
went to France, leaving an army that was hated by the local people
for its plundering and misconduct.

Fairfax had to detach Fleetwood and Whalley to watch the
King's cavalry at Oxford and had news from Ireland that 'Sir
Charles Scott and Sir Robert Stewart have slain a bishop and 1000
rebels.' But on 8 January, forwarding to an unresponsive Parliament a peace overture from the young Prince of Wales, who, with
his Council, was in overall charge of Royalist affairs in the south-
west, he set out once more, the Army's health improving once it
was on the move. Next day Cromwell captured 400 of the enemy
horses, while the Prince of Wales retreated to Launceston. Fairfax
wrote to Ferdinando:

Our business here (God be thanked) goes on very prosperously . . . There is
so great a fear, through the hand of God, upon them, as three of our men
did chase a hundred of them. We shall pursue (God willing) our advantage
as soon as this sharp season will permit. Without prejudicing the army too
much, I staid one day behind the army, to see my wife: a little better before
I left her . . .

A few days later the Prince gave Goring's former command —
for what it was worth — to Ralph Hopton. As Clarendon grimly
remarked: 'It was a heavy imposition, I confess, upon the lord
Hopton . . . to take charge of those horse whom only their friends
feared, and their enemies laughed at; being only terrible in plunder,
and resolute in running away.' Fairfax himself, disregarding the
intense cold and using pack horses to carry supplies, pushed on
without his artillery, through heavy snow, from Totnes to just
outside Dartmouth. Here he called a council of war and proposed
storming the town. His council argued that this would be rash,
that the town was strongly fortified, having 2000 troops to man the

defences, blockhouses in the streets and a hundred guns. 'Some of them spoke that it was impossible that any good could be done in that attempt.' But Fairfax held to his view that a determined assault would succeed without excessive losses, and his view prevailed. So the next night, at midnight, the attack was made, and after a short but stiff fight was entirely successful. 1500 prisoners were taken and the capture of Dartmouth did much for the Army's morale. But Fairfax treated the Cornishmen he found there well and news of his clemency spread fast. He told his father: 'I fear nothing, but the soldiers' want of money to pay their quarters. Good carriage towards them being the best way to gain them, desire the Parliament would be pleased to consider how to supply the army timely with money . . .'

Devonshire recruits were coming in in large numbers. And Fairfax had intelligence of serious divisions in the Royalist high command. He was able to go over to Tiverton for two or three days to pay a further visit to Anne, still gallantly following the drum. He left Sir Hardress Waller with a strong force to continue investing Exeter, and himself set out after Hopton on 10 February. Hopton had fewer infantry than Fairfax but he had more cavalry — some four and a half thousand. They were however undisciplined and morale was low. Captain Berry, sent out 'to amuse the enemy', routed a body of 200 Royalist horse and captured their commander.

Fairfax now came up with Hopton at Torrington, and when the dragoons went into action at midnight, the infantry advanced to help them and so brought on a general engagement. Despite the low morale of his troops, Hopton made a stout defence. Fairfax, who led in the cavalry himself, described it as 'as hot service as any hath been since our coming forth; the enemy showed more resolution than ever'. But he drove Hopton's men out of the town, capturing eight colours and about 400 prisoners. He himself had yet another narrow escape:

> their magazine, which lay in the church . . . took fire, and blew up all the church; timber, stones and sheets of lead, showering down . . . on all parts of the town. I believe there were 200 of the enemy prisoners, and some of our own men blown up, and buried in the ruins of the church. I must acknowledge God's great mercy to me, and some others that stood where great webs of lead fell thickest, yet, praised be God, no man hurt; only a horse of a gentleman of the Life Guard, that stood by me, killed.

Hopton did his utmost but the greater part of his troops were demoralised. Like Marston Moor, much of the battle took place in the early part of the night.

The hunt was nearly over. Fairfax drove forward to Launceston and then to Bodmin, his disciplined troops being now welcomed by the Cornishmen, though on his own side Rushworth noted that the 'General's greatest trouble is, how to order the army so, as not to be too harsh to the Cornish, who were so harsh to our men formerly.' The Prince of Wales retreated to Pendennis Castle and thence, on 2 March, sailed for the Scilly Isles. Hopton's forces were melting away, and now that the heir to the throne had gone there was no point in prolonging a useless resistance.

Fairfax for his part wanted to remove the danger that the large body of cavalry Hopton still had with him might join the King. He had learnt from intercepted letters that a large Irish force might soon be landing in England. So negotiations began at Tresilian Bridge, while Fairfax advanced to Truro. These led to the disbandment of Hopton's army, beginning with its French brigade, and on 13 March the commanders on both sides sat down to supper with Fairfax. The terms were generous. Hopton himself was 'to be allowed for his owne use all his horses, provided they exceed not the number of forty', lieutenants were allowed four horses and three cases of pistols and even 'Schollers and Clergymen . . . one horse at the least . . . at the Generall's discretion.' To 'English Gentlemen of considerable Estates' Fairfax offered 'my Passe and Recommendation to the Parliament for their moderate composition'.

Hopton himself Fairfax addressed as

> one, whom (for personal worth and many vertues, but especially for your care of, and moderation towards the country) we honour and esteem above any other of your party, whose Errour (supposing you more swayed with the Principles of Honour and Conscience then others) we most pity, and whose happinesse (so far as consistent with the publike welfare) we should delight in more then in your least suffering.

Fairfax was now able to say: 'Through God's goodness, we have almost put a period to the Western War.' Sprigge commented on the 'hard task the Army had in forcing up so great a body as 5000 of the Enemies Horse, into such a narrow neck of land, through a County so cragged, in such a season of the year, the ground all covered over with Snow, the wayes so slippery, and the Weather so bitter cold, by a hard frost of that continuance as had not been knowne for many years before', and compared it to Hannibal's passage of the Alps. Certainly the New Model had had an even harder time with the elements than with the Royalist army.

Fairfax returned to deal with Exeter and Sir John Berkeley agreed to negotiate. Terms were settled, the infant Princess Henrietta being allowed to go anywhere in England the King might appoint. The city was surrendered (one of its defenders being Lord Paulet, married to one of Anne's sisters). But Fairfax, though far from well, was already away seeing to the surrender of Barnstaple and in no time was off to besiege the place which had been the heart and soul of the Royalist cause, the city of Oxford.

His campaign in the south-west was over. It had been a complete success. Hugh Peters the preacher wrote an unctuous letter to him, saying, 'One of the greatest comforts I have had in this world, next to the grace of God in Christ, to my poor soul, hath been to be a member of your army . . . I have seen you upon earth, and doubt not to meet you triumphing in heaven . . .' Fairfax's Army had preserved its cohesion and discipline in appalling winter conditions and he had never allowed himself to be diverted from his essential objective, the destruction of the Royalist army of the West in the field. He had shown great flexibility in tactics — at Langport the skilful blending of musketeer attack and cavalry charge; at Torrington the gradual reinforcement of advance guards at night, bringing on a general engagement; at Dartmouth a rush against defenders rightly judged to be irresolute. He had consolidated his reputation as a military commander, and his troops had complete faith in his integrity and judgment. He had become the chief man on the victorious side. But he still began his letters to his father, 'May it please your Lordship' and could end one, 'So desiring your Lordship's blessing, I remain, Your most obedient son.'

Joshua Sprigge, chaplain and historian of the New Model, wrote of its Captain-General with personal knowledge. Fairfax had, he said, built up the Army gradually 'from seeds and small beginnings'. As a man of God Sprigge noted with approbation that Fairfax's 'way of steerage and conduct . . . was amongst men in reputation for Religion'. And he added, somewhat obscurely:

He wanted one thing, and yet had the more by such a want; and that was a
Privado or Favourite of passion, as if providence had intended him for *men*,
and therefore would keep him from *man*: Men were rather his *Friends* then
his *Favourites* . . . He never discovered passions abroad in counsels or actions,
what he had at home in himself, he (not others) knew . . .

This passage means, I think, only that he was a diffident and
reserved man, who had no intimates or cronies. I do not think that
by 'Favourite of passion' Sprigge meant to refer to any sexual
relationship. He was simply noticing the lack of any special con-
fidant on whom Fairfax depended. It was a seventeenth-century way
of expressing what Kipling meant when he wrote: 'If all men count
with you, but none too much.' He went on to say, justly, that Fairfax was 'not without love, clemency and meeknesse, by which he
kept his Army lesse stained in the Blood of his Enemy, but not lesse
Victorious'.

Of Fairfax's attitude to religious differences, he says that 'he
could beare the *different* opinions in their *unity* to the publick,
seeing the Work goe on as well as if all had been of one mind'. In
other words, he, like Cromwell, was, within limits, a tolerant man,
as few were at that time, and was indifferent whether his officers and
men were Presbyterians or Independents, provided that they did
their job well.

Finally Sprigge describes Fairfax as 'tall, yet not above just proportion, yet taller (as some say) when he is in the Field . . . as if
victory were in his spirit beforehand'. He noted that his 'body is not
without its infirmities, as of *Rheums* and *Distillations*', and that he
sometimes had 'an impediment in his speech'. Curiously, Ranke
records that Charles I also stammered throughout his life. Fairfax
and the King shared this infirmity. They had another thing in
common — both were superb riders. The King was able to 'govern
with safety horses that were hard to manage'. So was his great
opponent.

On the 1 May 1646, just twelve months after the New Model had
first set out from Windsor, Fairfax brought it for a second time
before Oxford, which had always been the Royalists' main centre.
Once more he moved swiftly. Whitelocke notes that 'many old
soldiers wondered at his speed'. The King himself was not there.

He had sent a message to Ireton offering to give himself up to Fairfax 'if only he might be assured to live and continue as King still'. This was sent on to Cromwell, who read it out in the House, but Parliament sent no reply. So, at the end of April, the King had surrendered his person to the Scots besieging Newark. But Rupert and Maurice and what Rushworth calls 'many of the prime Nobility and Gentry of England' were still in Oxford. Its defences were very strong, with around it outlying garrisons like Radcot and Borstal House, the rivers Isis and Cherwell, massive fortifications, and 5000 infantrymen to man them.

Fairfax, troubled again by the fearsome pains of the stone, invested the city, making his headquarters at Lady Whorwood's house at Holton, and being joined there by Anne. Banbury surrendered and Fairfax sent a summons to the Governor of Oxford, Sir Thomas Glemham, who had earlier been in charge of York, saying that he was anxious to preserve a place so famous for learning from the ruin that must be entailed by a storm. A long negotiation began. When this went badly, Fairfax increased the military pressure. When it went well he took a conciliatory line, sending in a 'brace of Bucks, two muttons, two veals, two lambs and six capons' as a present for the Duke of York. Rupert and a hundred horsemen rode out 'to take the Air' and were fired upon, Rupert being wounded in the shoulder. Radcot surrendered after a grenade exploded in the cellar, destroying its stocks of beer.

The siege took time. Rupert asked Fairfax for a pass to come out 'till the pleasure of the Parliament be known concerning him'. He at any rate knew that it was all over. Fairfax was embarrassed when orders came from the House of Lords to send two noble prisoners to Windsor, without any indication that the Commons concurred.

During the siege Fairfax had a foretaste of troubles to come, for one day General Watson, 'a most pernitious factious fellow', gave Cromwell, the Lieutenant General, a black list with 'the names of all those officers in the army that were Presbiterians'. Of Fairfax it was recorded that the

> General was ignorant of it, and knew not what it meant when one Major Fincher Quarter Master Generall of the Horse discovered it unto him and told him of what daungerous consequence would be if this liste came to the knowledg of those officers whose names were written in it. The generall made answer that for his parte he made noe differance of their opinions

but was confident that all his officers were faythfull to the Parliament, and that the Lieutenant Generall as he conceived would not doe any thing to the prejudice of any man that wisht well to the Parliament or Army. The Quarter Master Generall was noe way satisfied with this answer . . . Both houses took this soe haynously that their was an order sente to our generall that none should preach or teach in the Army but those that are lawfully called to it . . .

Fairfax wrote to the Speaker saying that he would like his friend Bulstrode Whitelocke, the lawyer and diarist, to join his staff. Whitelocke duly went down and records complacently that Fairfax 'used me with extraordinary respect and courtesy' and 'sent for me to his councils of war, and made use of my advice in most of his affairs of greatest consequence'. This gave Whitelocke a unique opportunity to observe Fairfax exercising his command, and to form the judgement that 'The general was a person of as meek and humble carriage as ever I saw in great employment and but of few words in discourse or council; yet when his judgement and reason were satisfied, he was unalterable, except it were by better, whereof (as was fit) he was the only judge.'

On 15 June, at Fairfax's headquarters, Ireton married Cromwell's daughter, Bridget. Ten days later Oxford was surrendered and the keys handed over to Fairfax. Under the agreed terms, signed by Fairfax in the Audit House at Christ Church, the Duke of York was brought to London, Princes Rupert and Maurice and their retinues were allowed to have passes to go abroad within six months, and the Great and Privy Seals were, oddly, locked up in a chest and left in the public library. A few days later the seals were broken up by a smith in the presence of both Houses of Parliament. Fairfax had sent the articles of surrender to the House of Commons but forgot to send separate copies to the Lords, who, when they did see them, expressed their pique by writing to him asking whether they were really authentic.

In Oxford, as earlier in York, Fairfax took special care to avoid destruction and looting. Aubrey noted in his *Brief Lives* that 'the first thing generall Fairfax did was to sett a good guard of soldiers to preserve the Bodleian Library . . . He was a lover of learning, and had he not taken this speciall care, that noble library had been wholly destroyed.'

Mopping up took a little time after Oxford had surrendered, but within a month Worcester and Wallingford were taken. Fairfax told his father, 'Finding myself at some leisure, I thought it the fittest time for Bath. I did not see my coming to London could be in any way serviceable . . . I shall endeavour to keep together . . . the army and shall wait on the Lord . . . My wife . . . hath been very ill in her head. I hope we shall both have some benefit of Bath.' Colonel Morgan had more trouble in securing the surrender of the great Catholic magnate, the 84-year-old Marquis of Worcester, in Raglan Castle. The marquis kept proposing new terms and was concerned that a debt of £20,000 owed to him by the King might be repudiated if he displeased him. Fairfax joined Morgan at Raglan and took over the siege, telling his father, 'I should be exceeding glad to receive often such light and help as I might have from your lordship in this troublesome condition I am in.' White-locke records that 'the marquis of Worcester wrote with much respect to sir Tho. Fairfax; that he honoured his family, and was more willing to agree to his proposals than if they came from any other. That he was intimately acquainted with sir Tho. Fairfax's grandfather . . . and concluded to agree to a treaty.' The castle was duly surrendered on 19 August, and the marquis and his home were treated far more leniently than the strongholds taken by Crom-well. This was the last of the Royalist castles to be taken, and Fairfax was able to join Anne at Bath and have a much needed rest.

The war was over, and Fairfax's reputation as a commander was firmly established. His style as a soldier had remained that of a cavalryman. Speed and dash were its characteristics. There was never anything ponderous or deliberate about his military opera-tions. He was the sort of general Churchill or Lincoln would have liked (and did not always get). As Sprigge wrote:

He was still for action in Field or Fortification, esteeming nothing un-feasible for God, and for man to doe in Gods strength, if they would be up and be doing; and thus his successe hath run through a line crosse to that of old Souldiery, of long Sieges and slow approaches; and he hath done all so soon, because he was ever doing.

Parliament and the Army

IN SEPTEMBER Fairfax left Bath and returned to his command. No doubt he now hoped to send his soldiers back to their homes and to take his wife up to London. He told Ferdinando: 'I hope we shall now settle the army so as there shall be fewer complaints. I hear very little of the foot; the horse hath been less payed, but no less restrained from injuries; I shall desire to prevent them all I can . . . I have sent Sharp to take an account of such things as are in the house in Queen Street. My wife doth intend to be there the next week . . .' But his hopes of relaxation were to be disappointed. There were still threats from overseas and next month the Independents in Parliament carried a motion to retain the Army in pay for six months.

There had been many complaints about the behaviour of Massey's horse and as early as 1 August Fairfax had written to the Speaker to report their 'robberies and insolencies'. He offered to undertake their disbandment, which he judged essential. This he now carried out quietly but firmly, with Ludlow, the member for the area, Ireton and two regiments, despite the threat of a mutiny. The brigade received only six weeks' pay out of what was owed to them. The order for disbandment came only from the Commons, and was countermanded by the Lords, who ordered Fairfax not to act without instructions from both Houses, but Fairfax ignored this and carried out the Commons' orders, which he thought were right. From London, Cromwell wrote to his daughter Bridget Ireton, ending, 'My service and dear affections to the General and Generaless. I hear she is very kind to thee; it adds to all other obligations.'

The same month Fairfax visited London for Essex's funeral. In November his Nantwich prisoner, Colonel Monk, took the Covenant and agreed to serve the Parliament in Ireland. In the north General Poyntz's troops mutinied, demanding money. Fairfax himself came up again for a triumphal reception. The City Militia met him outside London and on the 14th this young man of 34 had the unique honour of a visit to his house in Queen Street from deputations of both Houses of Parliament, first the Lords and then the Commons, led by the two Speakers. Speaker Lenthall, acting in accordance with a resolution that the whole House should 'give a visit to Sir Thomas Fairfax . . . and returne him the thanks of the Commons of England . . . upon his faithfull Services, wise Conduct and great Valour in the whole discharge of the great Trust committed unto him', made a fulsome speech, concluding that 'as the Title of *Caesar* was added to the succeeding *Roman* Emperors, so he'd propose that the Name of *Fairfax* be given to victorious Generals'. Fairfax made what was described as a 'very modest returne', saying that he 'accounted it his great happiness under God to be in the least kind instrumental for theirs and the Kingdom's good'. He had another congratulatory visit from the Lord Mayor and aldermen of London. The Recorder, in contrast to the Speaker, made an admirably brief speech.

In December the Lords ordered Fairfax to ensure that all his officers and men took the Covenant. Just before this he had, on Parliament's instructions, sent £200,000 to the Scots, in 36 carts escorted by 6 regiments and 500 dragoons. He went up to Northampton to settle the Army into winter quarters, and at Nottingham the sharp-eyed Lucy Hutchinson observed religious differences between him and Anne:

> The generall's lady was come allong with him, having follow'd his camp to the siege of Oxford, and layne at his quarters all the while he abode there. She was exceedingly kind to her husband's chaplaines, independent ministers, till the armie return'd to be nearer London, and then the presbyterian ministers quite chang'd the lady into such a bitter aversion against them, that they could not endure to come into the generall's presence while she was there, and the generall had an unquiett, unpleasant life with her, who drove away from him many of those friends in whose concentration he had found such sweetnesse. At Nottingham they had gotten a very able minister into the greate churche, but a bitter presbiterian; him and his brethren my Lady Fairfax caress'd with so much kindnesse, that they grew impudent to preach up their faction, openly, in the pulpitt, and to revile the others, and at length would not suffer any of the army chaplaines to preach in the towne . . .

This passage makes it clear that Fairfax himself preferred the ministrations of Independent chaplains, while Anne, always a Presbyterian, had now been persuaded to become an intolerant one. In the months ahead this must have been painful for Fairfax and made his life at home disagreeable, but it had no influence on his actions.

He still hoped for a quiet life and from Northampton wrote to Ferdinando saying: 'now it hath pleased God, in some good measure, to settle the general affairs of the kingdom, I should be glad to settle mine own . . . neither myself nor any with me can advise what is the best course . . . the public business having wholly taken up my thoughts, making me a stranger to my own business . . .'

The Scots, paid their money by Parliament, withdrew to Scotland and handed over the King, who set out from Newcastle on 3 February 1647, accompanied by Parliamentary commissioners. Ten days later Fairfax, described in a contemporary tract as being 'in a strait, how he should deport himselfe towards his Majesty', rode out from Nottingham to meet the King, dismounted and kissed his hand in silence, neither he nor the King saying a word. He escorted the King into the town. Next morning he did however have some talk with the King, who asked about affairs in Ireland, and 'was discreetly and wisely answered . . . by . . . the Generall'. The King afterwards said to one of his captors that 'the Generall was a person of Honour, Faithful to his trust, and one, that ever kept his word with him, that is, in keeping promises and Articles of War, and in using prisoners with such respect . . .' The King rode on to Holmby House, not far from Naseby, while Fairfax went to his headquarters at Saffron Walden. He visited Cambridge and was 'highly caressed', a Latin oration being made by a fellow of Trinity who had been a soldier in his regiment. He was given a 'rich Bible' and two banquets and made a Master of Arts. A few days later he wrote to the Speaker urging some reward for his fellow Yorkshireman Sir William Constable — 'hee hath bin vigilant in your service in this warre . . . I cannott but beleive him that hee hath laid forth out of purse more then hee hath hitherto received from the state'.

But a major conflict was at hand. The Presbyterians, under Holles and Stapleton, were now dominant in Parliament and were determined to get rid of most of the Army so that they would be free to come to terms with the King, and, in concert with the Scots, to impose compulsory Presbyterianism on England. To this end they planned to abolish the New Model Army as such, to do away with all the marching regiments of foot, retaining only the cavalry and 10,000 infantry as garrisons of 45 towns. Out of the old New Model a volunteer force of 12,500 men would be raised to serve in Ireland, where they would be out of harm's way. They hoped to force the retirement of Fairfax's most senior subordinates like Cromwell and Ireton. This done, they reckoned that the Scots, together with their own forces in London and the trained bands, would be adequate to ensure their control. It was a bold plan. But they committed the singular folly of trying to disband the New Model while giving the soldiers only a small proportion of what was owed to them, which was in all some £601,000. Pay had been very irregular since the summer of 1646, when some regiments had gone without pay for three months on end. Parliament owed Fairfax's own regiment thirteen months' pay and proposed to give them only two. Out of £36 8s due to every soldier, each would have been given only £5 12s. The cavalry was owed forty-three weeks' pay. Nor were the troops to be given any civil indemnity against being indicted for acts committed under orders during the war, for unpaid wartime bills or for stealing horses, a capital crime.

On 6 March the Lords forbade Fairfax to quarter his troops in the Eastern Association. The day before, the Presbyterian leaders in the Commons tried to deprive him of the command of the cavalry and dragoons, but their followers baulked at this. Nevertheless the motion was only lost by twelve votes. Fairfax himself wrote in conciliatory terms offering to cooperate in organising forces for Ireland. In a move against Cromwell the Commons also resolved that no one in the Army other than Fairfax should hold a rank above colonel and that no member of the House of Commons should hold any command in England. An exasperated Cromwell told Fairfax that there 'want not . . . men who have so much malice against the army as besots them'. Cromwell was so discouraged that he seriously considered going to the Continent to fight for the Protestant cause in Germany.

Parliamentary commissioners came down to Saffron Walden and met Fairfax and forty-three of his officers in the church. Their objective was to secure eleven New Model regiments for Ireland.

The officers asked who was to command the force, and what arrangements would be made for pay, arrears and indemnity. Meanwhile it was learnt that the soldiers were getting up a petition. The commissioners expressed alarm. Fairfax reassured them, saying that 'it should be his care to suppress whatsoever might give offense'.

But feeling among the soldiers was running high, which was not surprising, given their concerns about arrears of pay and the lack of an indemnity. Influential officers like Ireton, Whalley, Okey, Pride and the Hammonds, who had drawn up their own petition, persuaded the soldiers to tone down their language and address their petition to Fairfax rather than direct to Parliament. The petition was a moderate and reasonable document asking for indemnity for wartime acts, guaranteed payment of arrears, and pensions for widows and disabled soldiers. Nevertheless Parliament ordered Fairfax to stop its circulation. But the soldiers refused to allow their grievances to be suppressed.

Fairfax told his father that

> though it may seem strange the army doth make propositions to the Parliament about conditions of going into Ireland, yet it did seem to us more honest, modestly to desire such things as might enable them to carry on that service . . . The country here doth like very well of the army, and is very sorry that there should be any petition against them. [On a more personal note, he added:] I have my health but ill this spring . . . I had sent the Barbary to Denton before this, but that some grease is fallen into one of his legs, which, I hope, in a few days he will be recovered of . . .

Holles and the Presbyterians sought to put a stop to the Army's agitation. The Speaker was made to order Fairfax to send up the officers concerned in it to the bar of the House and Holles hastily 'scribbled on his knee' in the House a declaration that any persons proceeding with the petition would be regarded as 'enemies of the State'. This rash act of anger and haste made a confrontation inevitable.

Fairfax was now in serious difficulty, but he achieved the remarkable feat of persuading the soldiers to drop their petition, 'such', wrote Rushworth, 'is their Obedience, and Respect to their General'. He himself wrote much later that 'The Thinge seeminge just (but not liking the Way) I spoke with some Officers . . . and gott itt supressed for that Time . . .' He sent a tactful reply to the Speaker saying that his soldiers 'did generally express a very deep sense of their unhappiness in being misunderstood in their clear intentions', but had assured him that 'they would wholly acquiesce in whatsoever I should judge reasonable to offer, or you to grant, on their behalf . . . I trust the army will ever manifest their affections to the public by the constant perseverance in their accustomed obedience unto all your commands . . .' Parliament was however being the reverse of tactful. The Lords voted to summon Fairfax himself and one observer noted, 'I thinke the Lords are all madd.'

The Commons interviewed the discontented officers, who denied the charges made against them. Resentment grew among the troops at the way they, who had won the war for the Parliament, were now being treated. The politicians at Westminster had no idea of the fury their actions were creating.

On 15 April more Parliamentary commissioners, including Massey, a strong Presbyterian whose undisciplined brigade Fairfax had recently disbanded, and who had been chosen by Parliament to command the cavalry in Ireland, went down to see Fairfax. They first dined with him privately and tried to get him to sign a declaration denouncing those who criticised the Irish service. Fairfax refused to do this, crisply pointing out that the declaration, drafted by Holles and passed by both Houses, was an attempt 'to adjudge his Army guilty before any proof made that there were any that did retard the service'. He agreed only that if the commissioners could produce specific evidence against anyone in the Army he would look at it and punish anyone who was guilty. He told the commissioners that the Army 'was already in some heat upon occasion of a late declaration'. When they later saw the officers — some 200 of them — they were at once asked by John Lambert what Parliament was going to do about the conditions earlier requested. The officers received no satisfactory reply. They then raised the question of the command in Ireland. If they were to go, why, they asked, could they not serve under their existing generals. This was universally supported. 'All, All!' cried the officers, 'Fairfax and Cromwell and we all go!' At the meeting with the officers Fairfax nevertheless spoke about the importance of the Irish campaign and urged his officers to take part in it.

This was followed by the preparation of a message to Parliament asking for an answer to the points made about arrears, indemnity and pensions and arguing that if they kept their existing generals 'it

would conduce much to their encouragement and personal engagement'. The commissioners pressed Fairfax to order his officers
categorically to encourage men to enlist for Ireland. He replied, 'It
is my constant course to use the word "desire" to my officers and I
doubt not but it will find a ready obedience.' The commissioners
offered promotion to those officers prepared to go to Ireland. A
number agreed to do so but others refused, and one Ensign Nichols
was found to be circulating the soldiers' petition. Fairfax ordered
that each regiment should have the parliamentary resolutions on the
Irish service read to it and that new units should be formed composed of those willing to volunteer.

At this point, on 21 April, Fairfax, because, as was probable, he
was genuinely unwell, or because he wanted to allow time for tempers
to cool, or because he was sick of the whole business, went up to
London to see his doctors, undeterred by a letter from the Committee at Derby House urging him to stay with the Army. Typic-
ally, Denzil Holles maintained that he went only 'upon pretence of
taking physick'. He was to stay in London for the next thirty days.

In his absence the wrangle continued. The commissioners
brought Ensign Nichols to London and cast him into prison without
telling Fairfax. This was furiously resented by the Army as 'an
affront to his honor's power and dignity'. Out of more than 21,000
men in the Army the commissioners had been able to secure only
just over 2000 volunteers for Ireland. Skippon, though reluctant,
was persuaded to accept the command of the expedition. The
Presbyterians created a Committee of Safety and set about establishing a force of their own in London.

The discontented soldiers now decided to organise, and eight
regiments each selected two representatives to speak for their
interests. These became the celebrated 'agitators'. The Commons
for the first time showed signs of wishing to retreat, and voted to
add a fortnight's pay to the six weeks' already promised, with six
weeks' more for those willing to go to Ireland. It also asked its
military members to try to conciliate the Army.

Fairfax, though resting, did not forget his troops. On 26 April
he wrote to the Speaker on behalf of 'several gunners', who had
'most of them received maims in the service', asking that they might
be given gunners' places in the Tower of London. He stayed at his
Queen Street house throughout the first half of May under the care

of his doctors. Whether they did him any good it is hard to say. Seventeenth-century medicine was apt to be a weird affair. Baxter, for example, who believed that 'the excessive gluttonous eating of Apples and Pears . . . laid the foundation of that *Imbecility* and Flatulency of my Stomach', used as a remedy: 'Beer as hot as my Throat will endure, drunk all at once, to make me sweat.'

The Presbyterians in Parliament became more and more frustrated. A letter sent to the agitators on 18 May said that the Army (meaning all of it that had not volunteered for Ireland or was required for garrison duty) was to be disbanded by vote of the House of Commons and that members 'in the Commons House abuised the Generall as basely, they said "there was never Generall did like him, hee is now in Towne and courts Ladies, and itt is a shame for him that he should be now in Towne and his Armie in a distemper".' On the same day Rushworth wrote to Ferdinando saying:

> things are mighty uncertaine . . . The Generall is Comanded downe to ye Army, one saying in the House, hee had time enough to goe to Hide parke, but not to attend his duty, speaking it with much scorne . . . were it not for ye good of ye kingdom, were I as ye Generall, I would scorne to hold my Command an houre longer; but truly his patience is grate; and hee wishes hee had a fair oportunity to give over.

The Commons had voted that Fairfax should return to his headquarters if his health permitted. Thomas Widdrington, who saw him on the 13th, found that he was better and hoped 'he will continue so if the matters of the army have not too much influence upon his spirits'. He himself wrote gloomily to Ferdinando on the 18th saying, 'Nothing will be acceptable that comes from the army, but all things are hastened for a speedy disbandment . . . I still expect to have great difficulties put upon me.' An anxious Edward Bowles told Ferdinando that 'the proceedings of the Parliament and City against the army are very violent', and of Fairfax said, 'I pray God direct him to avoid the snares are laid for him.'

The Presbyterians decided on 25 May to disband most of the Army, beginning with Fairfax's own regiment, without giving the soldiers any assurance that they would receive their huge arrears of pay. This was provocative. Not only did it make it easy for the agitators to rally support for resistance, but it infuriated even moderate and reasonable men like Fairfax. He had now moved his headquarters to Bury St Edmunds. Angry though he was, he remained disciplined and obedient, and on 26 May he wrote to the chief officers of every regiment saying that their grievances had been forwarded to Parliament, and adding: 'I do . . . require soldiers to forbear any further actings by them selves without their officers in any irregular ways, and all officers are strictly to see to it . . . that there be no more such meetings or consultation of soldiers at Bury or elsewhere.' But his injunctions came too late and were ignored. Even the promise of eight weeks' pay was little solace to men who were owed fifty-six. He was now given a petition by the agitators of sixteen regiments saying that they were determined to act, and adding significantly that the 'promoters of our destruction' had not yet been called to account.

Fairfax summoned a council of war, which overruled his proposal that they should comply with the votes of Parliament, and decided on a general rendezvous at Newmarket. The committee which was to come down from the House to disband Fairfax's regiment on 1 June (voted £500 for their personal expenses — however behindhand the troops' pay might be, the politicians did not intend to be out of pocket themselves) was described as being like men sent 'among soe many beares to take away their whelps'.

Fairfax asked Skippon to come down to give him 'your Advice and company', but there seems to have been no response. His own regiment mutinied against their officers at Chelmsford and themselves marched off to the rendezvous. The Parliamentary commissioners, baffled, returned to Westminster.

Fairfax wrote to the Speaker on 30 May telling him of the officers' rejection of the votes of both Houses on disbandment, saying that he was 'much perplexed in my thoughts, that dissatisfactions betwixt the parliament and the army should rather increase than lessen', and concluding:

> I entreat you, that there may be ways of love and composure thought upon. I shall do my endeavours (though I am forced to yield to some things out of order) to keep the army from disorders, or worse inconveniences to the kingdom. I desire you to take some speedy resolution for the composing of things, whereby the kingdom may be happy in a timely deliverance from further distractions; for the effecting whereof I could be content to be a sacrifice, as the last service you can have from Your most faithful and humble servant,
>
> T. Fairfax.

These words of wisdom fell on deaf ears. Fairfax was now himself in a risky position between two increasingly militant factions. A fellow Yorkshireman, Colonel William White of Pontefract, wrote to him on the 28th saying:

> ... Your Excellencie I confesse hath a most difficult game to play ... God hath made your Excellencie his great Instrument of good unto this Kingdome in subduing the Enemies thereof. The Parliament honours and esteemes your Person and services most highly ... If any disturbance ... shall happen in the Army ... I beseech you forsee it in time, and write to the Parliament to give you leave so come upp to London to preserve them with your advice for the quieting thereof. I cannot see that your stay in the Army in any unquiet distemper ... can be for your safetie, nay I am sure it must be to your apparent danger ...

This advice Fairfax disregarded. He preferred to stay with his men, unruly and abused as they were, and if it came to a choice between the Presbyterians in Parliament and the agitators, when all was said and done he preferred the agitators.

Cornet Joyce

HOLLES and his colleagues had no intention of heeding Fairfax's appeal for conciliation. Instead they planned to try to secure the Army's artillery, stored at Oxford, and to seize the King, who was guarded at Holmby by a detachment under a Presbyterian officer, Colonel Graves. They began intriguing with the French and the Scots to arrange for the Scots to intervene on their side. On the other side the agitators, who were increasingly calling the tune in the Army, were themselves planning to secure the same artillery and to frustrate any Presbyterian plan to carry off the King. The man they chose to do this was Cornet Joyce, a hitherto unknown junior officer in Fairfax's regiment, who had been a tailor. They collected a body of several hundred troopers who rode with him. Fairfax, still a sick man — 'hee left his course of phissick too soone' — was struggling desperately to keep some measure of control, torn one way by his belief that the Army's grievances were well grounded and the other by his deep-rooted loyalty to Parliament, whose instrument in the field he had been.

Cromwell too had been in a dilemma. He had been acting as one of the Parliamentary commissioners. But he had undoubtedly been outraged by the Presbyterians' venomous attitude towards the Army and the decision to disband it. He may well have confirmed the agitators' instructions when Joyce saw him in Drury Lane on 31 May. What does seem likely is that Joyce had no orders from Fairfax, who, because of his known attachment to legality and correctitude, had been kept in ignorance of the agitators' design.

There is, however, evidence that Fairfax went some way towards favouring a line of resistance to the wholly unreasonable policy of the Presbyterian majority in Parliament. On 1 June one of his soldiers wrote: 'The greatest and newest newes is, our general hath declared his resolution to owne the Armie in this their just action, and hath sent for Lieut-Gen. Cromwell . . .' Cromwell had in fact decided to throw in his lot with Fairfax and the Army, and he joined Fairfax at Bury on 4 or 5 June.

Letters and papers of the time show that Fairfax, though cautious and conciliatory, did come down essentially on the side of his aggrieved Army. But in retirement, when he looked back on this period and came to write his own account in his *Short Memorials*, he told a different story. He was writing then in a climate of opinion which deplored the execution of Charles I and the militant puritanism of the Commonwealth. He had by then become much more conservative and sought to justify his earlier continuance in command of a mutinous army. He wrote:

> Here was ye vertical Poynt on which ye Armyes Honor and Reputation turned into Reproach and Scandall. Here the Power of ye Army (I once had) was usurped by those Forerunners of Confusion and Anarchy, the Agitators. My Commission as Generall bound me to act with Councell; but the arbitrary and unlimited Power of this new Councell would act without a Generall, and all that I could doe, could not prevaile against this Streame . . .

The contemporary record shows Fairfax in a different light, not simply as a powerless figurehead swept along by what he later chose to call 'factious Agitators' but as a commander to whom the Army continued to be devoted, striving first to bridge the gap between Army and Parliament and then to keep some control over a gathering revolution. His real role was more honourable and responsible than the one he later chose to depict.

He did say, reasonably, that 'ye Pay was withheld from ye Army, which heightened their Distempers'. He claimed that his 'private Sence and Reason' pointed to resignation of his command, but that he was persuaded by his friends to continue, which helped 'preserve ye Parliament . . . from . . . Concussions and Breakings'.

By this time the House had become alarmed. A newsletter from London dated 3 June said that 'the House was startled the day before when they understood from the Generall that the Army would not disband, and how it was moved to send for the Generall, and to raise 10,000 men to assist or compell a disbanding: but all that was laid aside . . .' The doors were locked. Holles and his supporters argued that the Army had mutinied and must be suppressed, but the

House shrank from the prospect of an armed conflict and preferred the path of appeasement. They decided to give soldiers (but not officers) their full arrears and to expunge Holles's earlier declaration from the records of the House. They also prepared an Ordinance of Indemnity. But it was all now too late.

Fairfax and Cromwell had made their decision and come down firmly on the side of the Army. But others decided differently, and at this time nearly a third of the New Model's officers retired, no doubt because their sympathies lay with Parliament and the Presbyterians. Those who departed included five cavalry colonels and three from the infantry. As a result the officer corps in the Army became from now on much more radical.

The Derby House Committee told Fairfax that 'Parliament expected Obedience to the Disbanding', but Fairfax, whose attitude continued to harden, 'desir'd to be excus'd'.

Now there came startling news. Cornet Joyce and his men had not merely secured the King against being removed by the Presbyterians but had themselves carried off the King (who seemed surprisingly cheerful and ready to go with them) and were bringing him to Cambridge. Fairfax at once informed the Speaker, despatched Whalley and a party of horse to restore the situation, and told the House what steps he was taking. He told Ireton that he did not like the business and asked 'who gave those orders'. Ireton admitted that he had given orders, but only for securing the King, not for taking him away. Cromwell, just arrived from London, said that if the King had not been removed, Parliament would have carried him off. He virtually admitted a share in responsibility for the agitators' design. Fairfax was reported to be 'amased' but to have been persuaded by Cromwell and Ireton that what they had done was essential. Joyce, told that Fairfax was displeased with him, said that his orders came from Cromwell. Fairfax himself later described what happened:

> I had Notice that Cornett Joyce (an arch Agitator,) . . . had seised on the King's Person . . . as soon as I heard itt, I imediately sent away twoe Regiments of Horse (comaunded by Colonel Whaley) . . . to sett all Things againe in itts due Order and Course . . . Col. Whaley acquainted the Kinge, he was sent by ye Generall to lett him know how much he was troubled att these great Insolencyes that had been committed soe neare his Person; and as he had not the least knowledge of itt before it was done, soe hee had

omitted noe Time in seeking to remove that Force which he had Orders from mee to see done; therefore desired His Majesty would be pleased to returne againe to Holmby . . . But the King refused to returne . . .

When the King had asked Joyce whether he had a commission from Fairfax, 'the Cornet desir'd the King not to ask such Questions', and when asked what commission he had, had pointed to the troopers, whereupon the King smiled and said it was as fair a commission as he had seen. Joyce's men had sent a message to the Parliamentary commissioners claiming that 'we, the soldiery now under his excellency sir Thomas Fairfax's command, have this day . . . manifested our true love to the parliament and kingdom, by endeavouring to prevent a second war . . .'

Whalley tried to carry out Fairfax's orders to treat the King with all respect but to settle him again at Holmby in the charge of the Parliamentary commissioners. The King, though, unaccountably, 'pleased to be a little merry', was adamant in his refusal, and so he was brought to Sir John Cutts's house at Childerley near Cambridge.

Next day, in the garden of that house, Fairfax, Cromwell, Ireton and other officers spent the whole day talking to the King. He refused to go back to Holmby, so Fairfax agreed to his being escorted to Newmarket. It was noted, incidentally, that Fairfax and Cromwell 'kneeled not' to the King.

Joyce was produced at the meeting and 'did avow hee told his Majestie hee had not the Generall's Commission'. The King said Joyce had asserted that he had the commission of the whole Army for what he did, 'and by consequence had the General's, he being the principal part'. Joyce denied again that he had had any instructions from Fairfax and told the King that he would be glad to appear before the Army, and if three out of four did not approve of what he had done, he would be content to be hanged. This was a curious conversation between a sovereign and a very junior officer.

Some remained sceptical. Sir Philip Warwick wrote: 'Fairfax and Cromwell wait on the King both together. He asks them, whether they commissioned Joyce to remove him: they deny it, *I'le not believe you*, says the King, *unless you hang him.*'

And Hobbes wrote in his *Behemoth*:

The General . . . by Letter to the Parliament, excuses himself, and Cromwell, and the Body of the army, as ignorant of the Fact; and that the King came-away willingly with those soldiers . . . assuring them withall, that the whole army intended nothing but Peace, and did not oppose Presbytery, nor affect Independency . . .

'Tis strange that Sir Thomas Fairfax could be so abused by Cromwell, as to believe this which he himself here writes . . . I cannot believe that Cornet Joyce could go out of the Army with a thousand Soldiers to fetch the King, and neither the General, nor the Lieutenant-General, nor the Body of the Army, take Notice of it . . .

The affair remains mysterious, but most historians believe, I think rightly, that Fairfax was sincere when he said he did not know.

When the talks in the Cambridge garden finally came to an end, Fairfax grimly recalled that 'as I took Leave of the Kinge, he said to mee Sir, I have as good an Interest in the Army as you'. The blinkered attitude this remark expressed staggered Fairfax. As he wrote, 'I plainly saw the broken Reed, he leaned on. These Agitators . . . had brought the Kinge into an Opinion the Army was for him . . .' The King was living in a fantasy world.

Fairfax made one more effort to restore discipline: 'I called for a Court of Warr to procede against Joyce for this high Offence and the Breach of the Articles of Warr; but the Officers (whether for fear of the distempered Soldiers, or rather as I feare a secret Allowance of what was done), made all my Endeavours in this ineffectual.' Joyce was not punished. Fairfax's authority on this occasion had been flouted. Joyce considered himself answerable primarily to the agitators, though, curiously, in a letter he sent from Holmby to Cromwell, he said, 'we are resolved to obey no orders but the General's'. The General had had to put up with a major affront to his authority. He even agreed next month to the payment of £100 for Joyce's expenses, though he resisted pressure to promote him.

Fairfax had at this time an extraordinary difficult choice. He could resign, on the grounds that his authority had been successfully defied in a major matter, or he could hang on, hoping to reassert control and prevent matters from getting altogether out of hand. He was a wholly honourable man, concerned above all with his responsibility for the future of his country in a dangerous situation. He chose to hang on. He was like a man who had won a race on a superb horse which had then bolted. He could slide off, or he could stay in the saddle and try to rein in the runaway horse. This is what he did. Undoubtedly he took this decision from a high sense of duty: few men have been less driven by personal ambition. He still believed that the essentials of the Army's case — now being pursued by the agitators — were right. It was also his army. He was proud of it and believed that it should have its due, and that its proper handling was a national imperative. And he believed that he, and perhaps only he, could act as a bridge between Parliament and the Army. He was also strongly opposed to the divisive, sectarian intolerance of the leading Presbyterians. It is misleading to say, as Clarendon does, that the Independent party 'comprehended all the superior officers of the army, (the general only excepted; who thought himself a presbyterian)'. Like Cromwell, Fairfax believed, before his time, in tolerance. So he remained at his post.

The March on London

AMIDST all this turmoil Fairfax still found time to write to the Speaker urging a proper allowance for a minister at Otley, 'the parish where myself was born'. While Joyce had been bringing the King to Cambridge Fairfax had held two rendezvous of the Army at Kentford Heath near Newmarket. At these, according to Rushworth, he 'exprest himself with great Judgement and Moderation', riding round to every regiment and urging restraint, saying that he was confident that their grievances would be redressed. He was received by the regiments 'with much Joy and Acclamations'. Hopes for a settlement rose. The Venetian Ambassador in France told the Doge and Senate: 'The army will be disbanded more quietly than was expected. Parliament has won over the superior officers and the rest will have to give way. General Fairfax will be the first to disband his regiment and the others can but follow the example of their chief.'

His optimism was misplaced. The agitators gave Fairfax two manifestos, a *Humble Representation of the dissatisfactions of the Army* and *A Solemn Engagement of the Army*. Both attacked the Presbyterian leaders, and the second called for the setting up of a Council of the Army to include both the senior officers and the agitators.

On 10 June Parliamentary commissioners went down to see the army at Triploe Heath, south of Cambridge. But all the regiments demanded that their offers should be referred to the newly established Council of the Army. The rendezvous at Triploe Heath was later seen by Fairfax as a turning point. In his *Short Memorial* he repudiated 'Papers and Declarations of the Army that came out in my Name' and asserted that 'from the Time they declared their Usurped Authority, at Triplow Heath, I never gave my free Consent to any Thinge they did; But . . . they set my Name . . . to all their Papers . . .' This, written after the Restoration, when he wanted to correct the record and was growing prematurely senile, is a lame and feeble justification. The truth was rather different.

From Triploe, the Army moved to Royston, and that night a letter signed (but certainly not written) by Fairfax, as well as by his chief officers, was sent to the City. This toughly worded letter contained a warning that if ruin befell London it would not be the Army's fault. But the Commons were now busy organising their own force to oppose the New Model. Massey rode through the City, calling for resistance to the 'madmen of the army'. And in Wales an insurrection broke out, the rebels declaring for the King and Fairfax. Fairfax wrote urging them to go home and to lay down their arms.

He wrote angrily to the Speaker from Royston on 11 June, in a letter that was unquestionably his own, saying:

> It is not many days since I wrote unto you about money for the army, to which, as yet, I have received no answer. It is very well known how long now the soldiers have been without pay: and how can it be expected that either I or my officers should have that influence upon them that is meet, considering the straits they are put into for want of pay?
>
> The private soldier is not ignorant that you have money by you: and certainly the knowledge of that, and the sense of their own wants, doth not a little heighten them in their discontents.
>
> I desire, therefore . . . that you would order the sending of a month's pay for the army . . . by Monday night.

Nothing was done. The Army moved down to St Albans. This alarmed Parliament and the City, which sent a conciliatory letter to Fairfax by the hand of four aldermen. And now, on 14 June, the anniversary of Naseby, 'the General and his Council of War finished the representation of the General and the army, concerning the bottom of their desires, in relation to the King, Parliament, and kingdom, which is very long, but set forth with much reason and arguments . . .' This account, written by Rushworth at St Albans on 15 June, twice refers specifically to Fairfax, and shows that he was indeed taking part in the drafting of the Army's declarations and not simply having his name affixed to them against his will as he later claimed.

The paper the Council prepared was called *The Declaration of the Army* and contained no longer merely material grievances, but political proposals. In a famous phrase it argued the right of Fairfax's Army to speak for England because it was not 'a mere mercenary army, hired to serve any arbitrary power of a State, but called forth . . . to the defence of their own and the people's just rights and liberties'. It put the question 'whether the Relief of Ireland was really intended, or rather, by breaking this Army, to raise such other Forces . . . as might serve to some desperate Designs'. The Army had reached the point of saying that it was as justifiable to resist an intolerable Parliament as an intolerable King. So the declaration called for the eviction of those corrupt members who had defamed them.

On the same day both Houses voted that the King should be taken to Richmond in Surrey and guarded by a regiment which did not belong to the New Model and was commanded by a Presbyterian. Fairfax simply stalled on this. But the City had no stomach for a fight with his Army and Parliament voted the month's pay for the New Model which he had earlier demanded.

The Army now issued 'a particular charge or impeachment, in the name of His Excellency Sir Thomas Fairfax, and the army under his command' against Denzil Holles and ten other MPs. Parliament, which was still striving to collect forces with which to resist Fairfax, ordered him to move forty miles away from London, but he ignored this and collected six more companies which had been detached for service in Ireland. The Army told Parliament that it insisted on the suspension of the eleven members.

Fairfax's secretary John Rushworth told Ferdinando on 22 June that nothing would be done about the eleven members unless the Army acted

> without delay before foreign forces or Scots come in . . . therefore, if in the next you hear the army is gone to court ladies in Hyde Park, think it not strange . . . I perceive the army will not part with the King without a peace settled. Great is the fear at London at the army's approach: but it is chiefly of those who have so provoked the army . . . which under God was their deliverance . . . the General is well, and hopes for good upon this business.

The Army now moved to Uxbridge. There Fairfax and his officers argued with six Parliamentary commissioners who sought to keep the Army at a distance from London. But the Army was moving steadily closer, though saying that it did 'no wise intend to awe the Parliament or be a Terror to them or the City'. The King was at Hatfield. On the 26th the eleven MPs thought it prudent to withdraw from the House. A bitter Presbyterian preacher said that 'If the wheels turn thus, I know not whether Jesus Christ or Sir Thomas Fairfax be the better driver.' Rushworth told Ferdinando on 27 June that 'all good men much confide in the General, and hope for a good conclusion', but that the 'General hath had sore conflicts in this business, and indeed he hath a hard game to play, in managing a matter so much out of method and rule.' Some of the letters written in these last days of June and signed by Rushworth on behalf of the General and the Council of War do not seem to be in his style. Nevertheless he was still very much in command of the Army. Only when Parliament had made substantial concessions and begun disbanding its own forces in London did he retire from Uxbridge to Wycombe. Still he made it clear that 'the army is unsatisfied, and do conceive themselves and the kingdom unsafe, until their last propositions . . . be fully answered'.

Some of the agitators had gone up to the northern forces, and the commander there, Sydenham Poyntz, a Presbyterian, told Fairfax that 'there are several gentlemen pretending dependence of your army, as also authority from yourself . . . who have appointed private rendezvous', and that Parliament had given him authority to arrest them. Fairfax replied that he had sent no emissaries, but that if any did go and speak honestly 'he and the forces under him would countenance and protect such good instruments'. At the same time he wrote to the northern agitators, welcoming their support for the 'proceedings of the Army in pursuance of our iust desires', and saying, 'I looke upon you as the same with the Army more imediatly under my command.'

The Venetian Ambassador told the Doge and Senate: 'What parliament fears most is the intention of Gen. Fairfax, as although he shows submission to the Houses and writes with protests of obedience and respect, his action belies it.' Fairfax and Cromwell were at this time still of one mind and remained so for some weeks to come.

Gardiner wrote that 'Fairfax, like Cromwell, whilst deeply sympathising with his soldiers in their grievances, had been anxious to cling as long as possible to Parliamentary supremacy as the surest means of averting military anarchy or military despotism,' and argued that 'it may fairly be concluded that they both hoped to find in the authority of the King that basis of a reasonable settlement which they had failed to obtain from Parliament'. Clarendon's remarks about 'the drowsy, dull presbyterian humour of Fairfax; who wished nothing that Cromwell did, and yet contributed to bring it all to pass' have little to do with what actually took place at that time.

The Presbyterians had wild thoughts of attacking Fairfax and rescuing the King. On 1 July Fairfax appointed nine officers — Cromwell, Ireton, Lambert and six others — to negotiate with Parliamentary commissioners about the Army's claims. Rushworth told Ferdinando five days later: 'The General is well, but much perplexed with business; the burden of the Kingdom lies upon him.'

Now that the eleven members had withdrawn, Fairfax agreed to move away to Reading. This, the Venetians noted, 'caused immense relief because it removes the cloud that seemed imminent over London'. They observed too that when 'the army was near the city many soldiers deserted and entered the city with a disposition to favour parliament', and that with these added to the demobilised forces (known as 'reformadoes') Parliament reckoned to have 10,000 soldiers ready to resist Fairfax if necessary. But on the 6th the Army presented to the House of Commons its accusations against the eleven members.

On 8 July the northern troops mutinied against Poyntz, and brought him down as a prisoner to Reading. Fairfax set him free, but Poyntz's authority was at an end. Fairfax was looked on as the key man at this stage and on the same day as the northern mutiny the French Ambassador, Bellièvre, called on him, and that eager opportunist the Prince Elector, Rupert's eldest brother, dined with him, 'showing great respect unto him', according to Rushworth. No doubt the Prince still had an eye on the throne. Fairfax, however, never lost sight of the problem of his troops' pay and on that date wrote to the Speaker pointing out that the Southampton garrison had had no pay since 25 March. On 16 July he wrote again asking that 'you would please to take some speedy course for the supply of soldiers with monys who are (as I am informed) 30 weeks in arrear'.

His thoughts now turned to the King. He first persuaded a reluctant Parliament to allow the King to see his three children, whom they held. He was warmly thanked by the young Duke of York. At the same time he told Parliament that the Army was not engaged in any underhand bargain with the King, but both he and Cromwell kept in touch with Bellièvre and told him that they were in favour of religious toleration, even to some extent for Roman Catholics.

They began discussions with the King through Sir John Berkeley, but these did not prosper, the King telling Berkeley that he distrusted the Army leaders because they did not ask him for any personal favours. He did not begin to understand men like Fairfax and Cromwell. Berkeley for his part formed the impression that 'the Army was governed partly by a Council of War, and partly by a Council of the Army, or Agitators, wherein the General had but a single voice; that *Fairfax*, the General, had little power in either; that *Cromwell* and his son *Ireton*, with their Friends and Partisans, governed the Council of War absolutely, but not that of the Army, which was the most powerful'. This may have been a reasonably accurate assessment. In the highly politicised, semi-revolutionary body the Army had now become, the straightforward Fairfax, with his stammer and lack of eloquence or any talent for intrigue, was not likely to exert decisive influence, but Parliament's failure to respond to his appeals for payment of the arrears hardened his attitude and disposed him to sympathise with those calling for strong measures.

On 16 July Fairfax spoke to the King about fears of a Scottish invasion. On the same day the Council of War was presented with a petition from the agitators making a number of demands and calling for a march on London. But Fairfax, Cromwell and Ireton were not yet fully persuaded that they had to take this extra step. In a letter to the Lord Mayor and aldermen of York Fairfax said, 'I hope you are no strangers to our papers and proceedings with the Parliament, and how the same necessitys that engaged us all at first hath continued us in pursuit of such things as concern the good and peace of this Kingdom, and that we are the same we ever were to the interest of the Parliament and Kingdom.'

Parliament was now losing its nerve. A number of Presbyterian members withdrew, and on 19 July, in a conciliatory move, both

Houses voted to put all forces in England and Wales under Fairfax's command. Two days later they ordered the disbandment of all deserters from his Army. The eleven members were given leave to go overseas. The Army was convinced that its views had at last prevailed.

On 17 July the Council of the Army met to consider Ireton's enlightened constitutional plan — the *Heads of the Proposals*. Under these the King and Queen were to be 'restored to . . . safety, honour and freedom;' Parliament was to set a date for its dissolution; future parliaments were to be biennial and their duration limited; a redistribution of seats would ensure a fairer representation of the population, and a Council of State would have substantial powers and control the militia for ten years. During that period Parliament was to make major military and civil appointments, after which the King was to appoint military commanders with the approval of Parliament and choose civil officials from a list of three put forward by Parliament; Royalists were to be treated leniently; bishops were to lose their coercive powers; the use of the Book of Common Prayer and the taking of the Covenant were not to be compulsory, though papists were to be 'disabled'; there was to be a general Act of Oblivion; taxation and tithes and the legal system were to be reformed; and the Army was to be paid its arrears.

Next day Fairfax appointed a committee of twelve officers and twelve agitators to revise it — though this effort was in vain, for the King, fatuously believing that he held the key cards and that the Army could not do without him, refused to compromise, at one stage suggesting, with amazing lack of perception, that Fairfax and Cromwell should be encouraged to 'fasten their affections to his Majesty's perfect restoration by proffers of advantages to themselves, and by fulfilling their utmost expectations in anything relating to their own interest'. On the 17th, too, Fairfax wrote to Ferdinando, saying:

Our treaty will, I hope, speedily have an end, being now almost ready to be sent to the House . . . this day we desired the Commissioners of Parliament to send a paper from us to the House, in which we desire they will declare against the bringing into this kingdom any foreign force whatsoever . . . Many turbulent spirits are yet in the city and army, but I hope their fury shall not prevail; and though some men's proceedings in this army have given some cause of jealousy, yet I trust, through God's assistance, we shall discern what is good, and not to be led along with the multitude to do evil. Colonel Lambart is coming down into the North to endeavour the settling of those forces . . . In three or four days we shall remove our quarters from hence — the plague has broken out in three houses in Reading . . . I shall not desire to have the Court so near as it is now; it brings a great number of cavaliers amongst us, which brings rather an ill name than danger upon us . . . My wife and Moll present their humble duty . . .

Things generally were looking better and Fairfax moved his headquarters to Bedford. On the way, at Aylesbury, he wrote to the Speaker saying that he had sent a hundred men to reinforce the King's guard at Windsor. He could not refrain from asking Lenthall 'to move the House for some pay for that Garrison, which, as I understand, is about a Twelvemonth in Arrear, and since March last hath not received one penny'.

Parliament's more conciliatory line had been a direct response to the Army's approach to London by way of Royston and St Albans and the tough wording of the *Declaration of the Army*. The Independents were joined by the moderate MPs in seeking compromise. But Fairfax's withdrawal to Bedford encouraged the militant Presbyterians — who in any case dominated the City of London — to try to secure absolute control of the House of Commons. With this end in view they decided to call out the mob, and frighten their opponents in the House into doing what they wanted.

Fairfax was suddenly appalled to learn of a 'petition and engagement' circulating in the City, which called for 'his Majesty's present coming to his Parliament . . . without the nearer approach of the Army'. He sent a furious letter to the Parliamentary commissioners, saying that 'our Fears of some desperate Designs hatch'd in and about the City, have not bin groundless'. Indeed they had not. Three days later a mob of apprentices forced their way into and terrorised Parliament and made them reverse their recent concessions to the Army.

There was now a real threat of a new sort of civil war. The City told Fairfax to stay away, the trained bands were called out and all men of military age called up. The City's forces were very large and the Presbyterians planned to fight. They made Massey their commander, with Poyntz to help him. Fairfax at last did as the agitators wanted and on 29 July began to move towards London. He might tolerate decisions being taken by agitators, but not by apprentices. Next day it was learned that the two Speakers, Lenthall and Manchester (though neither had much sympathy with the Independents) eight peers and fifty-seven Independent MPs had disappeared. They had decided to take refuge with Fairfax and the Army, which, as Clarendon wrote, 'appeared to every stander-by so stupendous a thing' and 'carried all the reputation and authority to the army'. The Presbyterians were left to themselves and at once recalled the eleven members.

Speaker Lenthall wrote to Fairfax: 'I am assured it will be strange to your Excellencie to heare of my being at Windsor . . . I pray God blesse your Excellencie and all the rest there, that you may be, under God, the Saviour of the Parliament and people's libertie . . .'

When Fairfax moved, he moved fast. On the 30th he was at Colnbrook. He secured both banks of the Thames, seizing Tilbury and one of the blockhouses at Gravesend, taking Deptford and threatening to cut off the trade by which London lived. He wrote to the Lord Mayor saying, 'We can't . . . but be deeply sensible of the unparallel'd violation acted upon the Parliament on Monday last by a Multitude from your City . . . I am assur'd from Eye and Ear-Witnesses, that divers of the Common Council greatly encourag'd it.' Although Poyntz killed some Independents who urged an accommodation, the City, as Clarendon wrote, 'grew every day more appalled, irresolute and confounded' and decided to submit.

Fairfax meanwhile had drawn up his forces on Hounslow Heath. He and the Members of Parliament who had taken refuge with him rode along the line of the troops and were received with acclamations, the soldiers throwing up their hats and crying 'Lords and Commons! A free Parliament!', which does not sound very spontaneous. The Prince Elector had found his way there too and was also well received. That night Fairfax was with the fugitive members at the Earl of Holland's house at Kensington.

Fairfax kept up the momentum. He sent four regiments over the river to Southwark, where opposition promptly collapsed, and at Hammersmith on the 4th he received word from the City of its submission, replying that he had no other design but a quiet and happy settlement. The Venetians noted that the 'city itself, seized with panic, lowered the sail of Fortune, with which it has dominated the whole island for several years, and by the consent of the crowd, surrendered at discretion to Fairfax'. On the 6th he brought the Army to Westminster in a triumphant but peaceful entry. Hammond's regiment of foot led the way, then Rich, then Cromwell's regiment of horse, then Fairfax on horseback with his lifeguard, then the Speakers and the members of Parliament in coaches. Every soldier had a piece of laurel in his hat. The Lord Mayor and aldermen welcomed Fairfax at Hyde Park and the Common Council met him at Charing Cross. The fugitive Speakers and members were returned to Westminster, after Fairfax had ridden into New Palace Yard. He was thanked by both Houses — Holles bitterly commenting, 'This General, (a setter-up and putter-down of Parliaments;) has a chair set for him in either House' — and appointed Constable of the Tower. Though pressed by the House 'to sit and be covered' he declined to sit down. Next day the Army marched through the City and over London Bridge 'with drums and trumpets, and colours flying'. Cromwell led the cavalry and Fairfax rode in a carriage with Anne and Cromwell's wife. The impression made by his disciplined force was profound. The Venetian report was that 'there were counted 9000 foot and 7000 horse, very fine troops, and so well disciplined that without injury to any one it resembled a gorgeous spectacle in the midst of absolute peace'. Fairfax, who made his headquarters at Chelsea, posted contingents in the Tower and at Westminster. When he himself entered the Tower, with his lifeguard and Pride's regiment of foot, a delegation from the City met him, suggested Colonel West as a suitable governor of the Tower and invited him to dinner. Fairfax replied that he had selected Colonel Tichburne for the job and asked to be excused from dining with the City, the Venetian report commenting, 'possibly because he did not feel entirely safe'. The City put in hand the preparation of a gold basin and ewer worth £1000, full of gold jacobuses, as a present for him. In the Tower he inspected the armoury and then went to the White Tower, where he looked at the records. Told that there was a copy of Magna Carta he asked to see it, 'This,' he said, taking off his hat, 'is that which we have fought for, and by God's help we must maintain.' He raised six new companies to garrison the Tower.

But the House of Commons was by no means cowed. The Presbyterians secured the rejection of a motion declaring null and void the proceedings during the absence of the two Speakers and

Thomas, first Lord Fairfax.
Fairfax's Grandfather

Ferdinando, second Lord
Fairfax. Fairfax's Father

His Excellencie
Thomas Fairfax &
Generall of the forces
raised by the
Parliament.

Fairfax in 1647

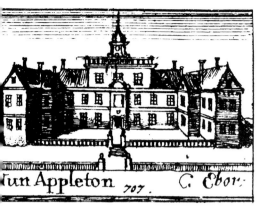

Nun Appleton in *c.* 1655–60

A lead bust of Fairfax

The armies drawn up before the battle of Naseby

ND FOOT OF HIS MAJESTIES, AND
all bodyes, at the Battayle at NASBYE;
of June 1645
The Lord Bard Tertia
Sir George Lisle Tertia
Sir Marmaduke Langdale and The Northe horse
The Generall
The right wing of horse commanded By Lieutennant generall Cromwell
The Generall Regt

Fairfax in 1650, by John Hoskins

Charles I by William Dobson

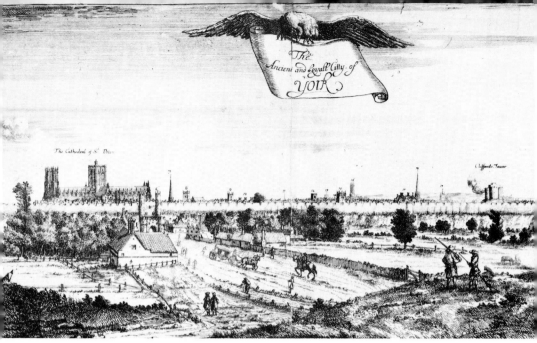

York in 1678

The Other Side – Lords John
and Bernard Stuart by Van Dyck

Cromwell in *c.* 1650,
by Samuel Cooper

Henry Ireton in 1649,
by Samuel Cooper

rejected another resolution approving the recent actions of the Army. The agitators at once asked Fairfax to purge Parliament. This at any rate persuaded the eleven members to flee, and Holles made his way to St Malo. Massey and Poyntz fled to Holland.

The Army Council supported the agitators in demanding a purge, as did Cromwell, but Fairfax, though no doubt as incensed by the behaviour of the Commons as any of his colleagues, hesitated to take a revolutionary, antidemocratic step. As he wrote later:

> it was resolved to remove all out of the House whom they conceived did obstruct . . . the publiq Settlement. Upon which Expedition of this March I was vehemently presst to; but here resolved to use a restrictive Power, when I had not a persuasive. Soe when the Lieftent Generall and others pressd me to signe Orders for marchinge, I still delayed the doinge it, as always dreadinge the Consequence of breakinge Parliaments . . . my delayinge but 3 or 4 Dayes, giving out Orders, diverted this Humor of the Army from beinge Statsmen to their more proper duty as Souldjers . . .

Cromwell, on his own, stationed a regiment of cavalry in Hyde Park as a demonstration. He then went to the House with the other military members and a guard of soldiers, who waited at the door. With the votes of these military members the House did finally declare the earlier proceedings null and void. Fairfax had prevented a formal purge, but had not been able to stop Cromwell using the threat of force to get his way in the House. This was the first time that there had been an important difference between the two men. Mrs Hutchinson wrote, 'While as yett Fairfax stood an empty name, he [Cromwell] was molding the army to his mind . . .'

On 17 August thousands of apprentices — now singing a different tune — presented an address to Fairfax saying that the memorial of his great services would 'be a Crown of Glory to his Excellency'. He wrote to the Speaker on behalf of disabled soldiers, making it 'my humble request unto the house, that these officers and soldiers, who are in this condition, may be taken into consideration, for some part of their arrears to be paid to them . . . This will be a great encouragement to such poor souls who have thus long languished in pain and misery.' On the 24th the King was moved to Hampton Court, and Army headquarters to Putney. Negotiations still continued with the King, and there survive draft articles of agreement between the King and Fairfax, providing among other things, for the restoration of bishops and for full liberty of conscience, but excepting Newcastle, Digby and others from pardon.

On the 30th Fairfax appointed a committee of twelve officers, including Cromwell, Ireton and Hardress Waller, to handle all matters 'of publique and common concernment to the Army or Kingdome'. Next day he appointed Colonel Hammond Governor of the Isle of Wight. Hammond was a New Model veteran who had fought at Bristol, Dartmouth and Torrington, but did not think that the Army ought to coerce Parliament and chose the governorship as a form of retirement. His scruples led the King's advisers to believe that he had become a supporter of the King's.

Fairfax now sent a tough letter to the Lord Mayor, demanding £50,000 towards the arrears and adding that 'Delay will be equal to a Denial.' The General Council of the Army authorised him to collect this amount himself if it was not forthcoming. The Commons decided to meet this by selling what was left of the bishops' lands, and those belonging to deans and chapters. Fairfax kept up the pressure and threatened to send Colonel Hewson's regiment into the City to collect the money.

Interminable debates continued in Parliament and in the Army, with the King in the middle, about a settlement. Cromwell spoke strongly in the House in defence of the monarchy. Gardiner accepts an Italian report that the King was told everything that passed in the Army Council by Anne Fairfax. ('La moglie di Farfax Generale appassionata per il Rè avvisa di quanta si passa nel Consiglio secreto.') But this sounds like insubstantial gossip. There is no other evidence that Anne was 'appassionata per il Rè' or that she was in contact with the King. Nor does there seem to be much evidence for the stories that Fairfax was held up on Hounslow Heath by the highwaywoman Mary Frith, or 'Moll Cutpurse', robbed of 250 jacobuses, and shot in the arm, and that Anne had her watch stolen at St Martin's, Ludgate Hill by another malefactor called John Cottington or 'Mull-Sack'.

The Levellers Crushed:
The King's Escape

O N 18 OCTOBER Fairfax was given a militant manifesto —
The Case of the Army Truly Stated — and replied judiciously
to the authors that he 'judged their intentions were honest'.
This was from the Levellers — a new force — men who believed
in equality and democracy and were against all constituted authority.

On 28 October there began the famous army debates in Putney
church. Fairfax was not present at the outset. According to Rushworth he was unwell and at Turnham Green. He was however
present after 5 November when arguments raged between the
Army 'grandees' and the radical Levellers and agitators. The
agitators attacked Cromwell and Ireton for attempting to come to
terms with the King, and they and Colonel Rainsborough urged
something close to a universal male adult franchise, which was not
to be seen in England until 1884. Ireton argued that the right to
have 'a share in the disposing of the affairs of the Kingdom' should
be restricted to those who had 'a permanent fixed interest in the
Kingdom . . . the persons in whom all land lies and those in corpora-
tions in whom all trading lies . . . because I would have an eye to
property'. Fairfax fully shared this point of view but did not himself intervene. He did no more than preside over the discussions.
Grand political schemes and constitution-making were not his line
of country. Yet, as H. N. Brailsford wrote in his book on the
Levellers: 'Doubtless Ireton was unpopular; even Cromwell had
his critics. But no one criticised Fairfax; this Olympian figure
played no part in party politics or church politics; he was the soldier
incarnate, round whose name blazed a legend of invincible
courage.'

Opinion in the country had grown weary of the Army radicals and had reacted strongly in favour of the King. A story circulated that Fairfax had been seen wearing the King's colours, and some soldiers were reported as saying, 'Lett my Collonell bee for the Devill an hee will, I will bee for the Kinge.' Fairfax wrote again to the Speaker on 8 November asking for something to be done about the Army's pay. He asked for six weeks' pay — or at least a month's, the arrears to be paid out of the sale of the bishops' and deans' lands. He told the Speaker that 'being very much troubled at the sad distractions of the kingdom for want of settlement', and at 'the distempers of the army for want of pay', he was calling the Army to a rendezvous. At the same time he sent the agitators back to their regiments. The Putney debates had shown a strong set of Army opinion towards Leveller views, as expressed in the *Agreement of the People*.

Four days after he had written this letter, Colonel Whalley came to report that the King had escaped from Hampton Court. But Fairfax had already heard the news the previous night and had at once written to a commander in the north (probably Lambert at York) urging him 'to use all possible care and diligence by setting guards uppon all passages . . . that if possible you may discover and stay his Majesty'. Next day Fairfax set out for Ware to hold his rendezvous. He was tired of the continual disaffection in the Army; with the escape of the King (who may really have thought that the Levellers intended to murder him, or may have been frightened away by Cromwell) he was prepared to be patient no longer. He sent both Houses a 'remonstrance' on behalf of himself and the Council of War, which was, however, addressed as much to the Army as to Parliament. He and the Council had, he said, 'been doing their Duty and best Endeavour for the Good of the Army'. But they had

found the greatest Interruption to their Proceedings by a few Men . . . who, without any Authority, or just Call thereunto . . . assuming the Name of *Agents for several Regiments*, have . . . taken upon them to act as a divided Party from the said Council and Army . . . have endeavoured, by various Falshoods and Scandals, raised and divulged in Print and otherwise, against the General . . . and Council of the Army, to possess the Army and Kingdom with Jealousies of them . . . have laboured to make Parties and Factions in the Army . . . to divide the Soldiers from the officers . . . and to withdraw

several Parts of the Army from their Duty and Obedience to the General's
Orders . . .

Fairfax had at last taken direct issue with the agitators. He said
he had urged Parliament 'more importunately than before' to
satisfy the Army's 'just Desires' (indeed he had, but had obtained
nothing but promises) and had now thought it necessary to assemble
the Army at three separate rendezvous. But even this the agitators
had 'laboured to pervert', sending 'Letters or Messages contradict-
ing the General's Orders.'

Fairfax now played his trump card, saying:

> That, without Redress of these Abuses and Disorders, his Excellency can-
> not, nor will, any longer undergo or undertake further to discharge his
> present Trust to the Parliament, the Army and Kingdom: And, tho' he is
> far above any such low Thought as to court, or woo, the Army to continue
> him their General; yet, to discharge himself to the utmost, and to bring the
> Business to a certain and clear issue, his Excellency doth now declare, That
> he is yet willing to adhere to, and to conduct, and live and die with, the
> Army, in the lawful Prosecution of these Things following . . .

He went on to present a consolidated list of the demands he had
so often made on the Army's behalf — for constant pay, security
for arrears, 'sufficient' indemnity against prosecution, provision for
maimed soldiers, widows and orphans of men killed in service, and
freedom from pressing and for apprentices who had served in the
war: He (or more probably his colleagues) added some political
demands — for a period for the Long Parliament, for Parliaments to
meet regularly for finite periods, to be properly representative, and
to redress the grievances of the people.

Finally the remonstrance said that, this done, the Army must
return to proper discipline and that all in it must sign a declaration
that they were 'satisfied in his Excellency the General's continued
Conjunction with the Army . . .'

Fairfax had sent his ultimatum. Either the Army returned to
being a disciplined force or he would go.

The crisis came at Corkbush Field near Ware on 15 November.
Fairfax brought together three regiments of foot and four of horse,
including his own regiments of foot and horse. The account by
William Clark, published immediately after the rendezvous, which
agrees on all points of substance with the modest but factual account

Fairfax sent to Manchester, acting Speaker of the Lords, is very specific and sounds authentic. It says that the

> Generall expressed himself very gallantly at the head of every Regiment, to live and die with them for those particulars which were contained in a Remonstrance read to every Regiment; And, notwithstanding the endeavours of Major Scott and others to animate the Soldiers to stand to the Paper called *The Agreement of the People*, they generally, by many acclamations, declared their Affections and Resolutions to adhere to the General.

Fairfax, whose account makes no mention of Cromwell, reported that all the regiments he had called together readily agreed with his conditions, but that two other regiments, Harrison's of horse and Lilburne's of foot, arrived uninvited, with copies of the Leveller *Agreement of the People* stuck in their hats, and 'very much inflamed towards Mutiny and Disobedience'.

Harrison's regiment came with a motto in large letters in their hats declaring *England's Freedom and Soldiers' Rights*, but Fairfax won them round and, according to Clark, 'they expressed their resolution to be obedient to his Excellency's commands'. His handling of these eight regiments showed Fairfax's enormous personal influence with his troops, even in an extreme situation like this. There was left only Lilburne's regiment, the most radical of all, which had driven away all its officers except one. Every effort was made to stir up their revolutionary spirit. As Clark wrote: 'upon the General's coming into the field, Colonel *Eyres*, Major *Scot*, and others, were observed to be insinuating divers seditious principles into the Soldiers, and incensing them against the General and General Officers: Upon which order was given for the commitment of Colonel *Eyre* . . . into the Marshal's hands, and Major *Scot* committed to the custody of Lieutenant *Chillenden*, and sent-up to the Parliament.'

Fairfax rode up to Lilburne's men with his officers and ordered them to pull the papers out of their hats. They refused, so his officers rode in and pulled some of them out, and the regiment then submitted. The ringleaders were arrested, three were tried and condemned to death, and one of them was shot at the head of the regiment as an example. The regiment was made to tear up the copies of the *Agreement of the People*. The soldiers claimed that they had been misled by their officers, and were told by Cromwell that they should have justice against them.

Edmund Ludlow claims that it was Cromwell who took the main part in suppressing the mutineers, and makes no mention of Fairfax. But his account is an attack on Cromwell who, he claims, was seeking 'to advance his own passion and power into the room of right and reason', and is therefore suspect. His version has been followed by many historians, but it seems more likely that the accounts given by Fairfax and Clark are nearer the truth, though Cromwell was certainly there.

When they heard of the suppression of the Leveller mutineers, both Houses agreed to send a letter of thanks to Fairfax and to try to meet the requests contained in his remonstrance. Cromwell gave Parliament an account of the rendezvous, telling them 'how by God's mercy, and the endeavours of his excellency and his officers, the army was in good condition'.

Underlying this clash was a profound difference between the moderates, led now once more by Fairfax, and the extremist Levellers, who were also republicans. Whalley's troop of horse denounced the agitators for having far exceeded their function. They had been chosen, the troop said, to act 'with the Consent and Advice of the General', to facilitate the just claims of the Army. Instead they had, contrary to their trust, 'cast-off all allegiance . . . to all present visible Authority in the Kingdom'. Okey's dragoons said that 'As we can't but with much Joy acknowledge your Excellency's extraordinary Care for preserving your Army in a Spirit of Unanimity, so we can't but admire the treacherous Proceedings of a Generation of upstart Agents . . .' ('Admire' then, in this context, meant 'deplore'.)

On the wider question, as one early nineteenth-century writer observed, the line taken by Fairfax and the moderates might have produced an acceptable reform

> If the Parliament . . . had not been interrupted and opposed by the violent and republican part of the Army . . . But, between the king's obstinacy on the one hand, in refusing the several moderate proposals that had been repeatedly made to him . . . and the violence of the republican party in the Army . . . the Nation continued in a state of turbulence and confusion for more than twelve years . . .

*

The King had now reached the Isle of Wight, where he took refuge with Colonel Hammond, who, after agonies of doubt, decided that his loyalty to Parliament came before his loyalty to the King, so that he became the King's reluctant gaoler. The Venetian view at this time was that 'the King hopes that Fairfax will ultimately take the royal side, though there is no sign of it yet'. The King did write a courteous letter to Fairfax, enclosing copies of his letters to the Parliament about his 'withdrawal to the Isle of Wight. He sent Berkeley to try to persuade Fairfax to support his demand for a 'personal treaty'. Fairfax would not meddle in such matters but said, looking severely at Berkeley 'after his manner', that his was the Parliament's Army, and that the question must be put to Parliament.

Negotiations now took place between the Army and Parliament which, with Fairfax's agreement, produced a plan for reorganising the Army, disbanding 'supernumeraries' and reducing the level of pay in time of peace.

Nervous at Royalist sentiment in the City, the House of Commons, which, because of his obstinacy and his attempted flight, had now turned against the King, asked Fairfax to send in 2000 troops to Whitehall and the Mews to protect them. He duly sent two regiments. But the Army radicals were still bitter at their defeat, though the General Council of the Army did all it could to conciliate them. Whitelocke records that 'Mr Saltmarsh, the minister, affirmed that he had somewhat revealed to him from heaven, wherewith he must acquaint the army; and presently went . . . to Windsor, where he spake to the general with his hat on, and told him, he had doted on him, but now must honour him no more because he had imprisoned the saints.' Having delivered this blast, Saltmarsh returned to Essex and promptly died. Had he lived he would perhaps have approved of the drastic ordinance passed by Parliament the next February, ordering all theatres to be destroyed and actors publicly flogged.

At the end of the year Hammond wrote to Parliament and to Fairfax, begging them to remove his Royal prisoner or discharge him from the task of guarding him. Fairfax sent three officers to the Isle of Wight to stiffen Hammond's resolution, while Parliament broke off all negotiations with the King by the vote of 'no addresses'.

They also dissolved the Committee of Both Kingdoms, replacing it by the purely English Committee of Derby House. Popular sentiment, however, was now strongly Royalist. There were, too, riots against the injunction that Christmas should no longer be observed. On the ninth day of the new year, 1648, the General Council of the Army held its last meeting, at Windsor Castle, with the agitators present, and no more differences between 'grandees' and Levellers. It voted unanimously to support Parliament in settling the kingdom 'without the King, and against him . . .' Afterwards Fairfax asked all the Council to dine with him in the castle. The King for his part had reached a secret agreement with the Scottish commissioners, who were planning to intervene on his side in conjunction with risings in England.

Even at so grave a time Fairfax did not fail to pursue a small individual injustice, writing to the Speaker about a Mr Jones who had done good service in 'reducing the town of Cardiff', in which he had spent £200 of his own money — 'Indeed, sir, the man is very poor, and much to be pitied . . . I conceive it just, at the least, that he should be speedily reimbursed his debt . . .'

On the 29th of January Fairfax came up to Queen Street, escorted by his lifeguards, and he and many of his officers were entertained in the City by the Lord Mayor. In the Army disaffection was not wholly at an end. Fairfax's own lifeguards made a mutinous demonstration on 23 February, and several men were judged by a court martial presided over by Fairfax and Cromwell. One Clerke was condemned to death, but, when the lifeguards humbly begged for mercy for him, Fairfax pardoned him. Soon after this, however, Fairfax disbanded the lifeguards. John Lilburne asserted that this was because the lifeguards were 'discerning men' and therefore politically unreliable. Whitelocke records at this time that 'the General, being tired with the multiplicity of business . . . appointed Cromwell, Ireton, Fleetwood and divers other officers, and such field-officers as were in town, or any five of them, to meet every day in Whitehall, to receive petitions, and consider of business relating to the army'.

On 13 March Ferdinando died at York. Tom Fairfax succeeded to the title and became not only the third Lord Fairfax, but keeper of Pontefract Castle, *custos rotulorum* (head of the commission of the peace) of Yorkshire and chief ranger in his father's place. He was now one of the principal men of Yorkshire. He inherited Denton, Nun Appleton, Bishophill and the Yorkshire estates, besides his father's plate, books, household staff, stallions, brood mares and foals.

In April there was a serious riot in the City. Some 3000 apprentices overcame the trained bands and bore down on Whitehall, shouting, 'Now for King Charles.' Fairfax and Cromwell were nearly surprised, but Fairfax got to the Mews, Cromwell attacked the rioters with a party of horse and Fairfax went to Ludgate and Smithfield to take charge, giving orders that everyone was to stay indoors. He then returned to Whitehall and went to bed, but despite a violent thunderstorm, news came that the rioters were out again and had secured Ludgate and Newgate and a piece of artillery — a drake. Colonel Barkstead's regiment of foot was sent out against them with some supporting cavalry and charged and broke them up in Leadenhall.

On 11 April the Scottish Parliament declared that the treaty between the two countries was at an end and demanded that the English Parliament should disband Fairfax's 'army of sectaries'.

Maidstone
and 'Colchester's Tears'

THE SPRING of 1648 was marked by a whole series of petitions, framed by the gentry in the counties near London, which called for a personal treaty with the King and the disbandment of the Army. In March a Colonel Poyer stood out against Parliament in Pembroke Castle, then took Tenby and declared for the King and the Book of Common Prayer. By the end of April all South Wales was in a state of revolt. This, with the menace of a Scottish invasion, the capture by the Royalists Sir Marmaduke Langdale and Sir Philip Musgrave of Berwick and Carlisle, and the strong Royalist feeling in the City, meant that the Army was faced with threats in the north, the west, London and the Home Counties. But, as always in a crisis, Fairfax was undismayed and acted swiftly.

On 1 May he wrote to the Speaker saying that, with the advice of his council of war, he had decided to send Cromwell with 'a considerable part of the army' to South Wales, to confide the protection of Parliament to Skippon and to withdraw the two regiments at Whitehall and the Mews. Parliament was reluctant to see the two regiments — their sole protection — go and Fairfax had to send the Speaker a reminder on the 7th. His council of war had been an extraordinary affair, marked by long prayer sessions and orgies of self-reproach — 'Loathing ourselves for our iniquities . . . none was able hardly to speak a word . . . for bitter weeping' — finally concluding that it was their duty to go out and fight their enemies, but also, 'if ever the Lord brought us back again in peace, to call Charles Stuart, that man of blood, to an account for the blood he had shed . . .' All this emotional breast-beating was hardly

Fairfax's style. He was much more concerned with the practical details of concentrating forces to deal with the rebellions which were breaking out.

Cromwell departed for Wales, though the principal rebel force was defeated before he arrived and he had to settle down to besiege Chepstow, Tenby and Pembroke. The main threat now appeared to be in the north. The House of Commons, Whitelocke recorded, voted on 9 May 'that the general be desired to advance in person into the north with such forces as he shall think fit, to reduce those places that are possessed by the enemy'.

But the situation near London was deteriorating rapidly. Royalist petitioners from Surrey threatened Parliament and invaded Westminster Hall on the 16th. They were broken up by troops, eight or ten being killed and a hundred or so wounded. On the 18th Fairfax sent Harrison and his regiment north to stop Marmaduke Langdale's advance into Lancashire. The Royalist leaders in Kent decided not to move until Fairfax had gone north and the Scots had come over the border, but popular enthusiasm was too much for them and on 21 and 22 May the whole county rose for the King. Four days later they had secured Dartford and Deptford. Given London's longstanding quarrel with the Army, it seemed entirely possible that the whole south-east might very quickly be won over by the resurgent Royalists. This might well have happened if the Army had had a sluggish or hesitant commander.

Cromwell was far away besieging Pembroke, and everything depended on Fairfax. But he was just the man for such a crisis. For some time past he had been building up the forces in London, bringing back elements of Ireton's regiment which had been dispersed at Chichester and Winchester. Now he swiftly sent over the bulk of the troops from the Mews and Whitehall to seize Southwark, and on the following day, 27 May, he assembled his limited but very professional force, 'our small bodie' as he called it, on Hounslow Heath. He had to abandon the plan to go north so that he could deal with the more immediate danger. A correspondent in York wrote gloomily that 'Affaires heere looke nott with soe plesant a countenaunce as by this time, if my Lord Generall had been heere, they would have done.' But Fairfax had no choice.

The Royalists gave up Deptford and fell back on Dartford. Six

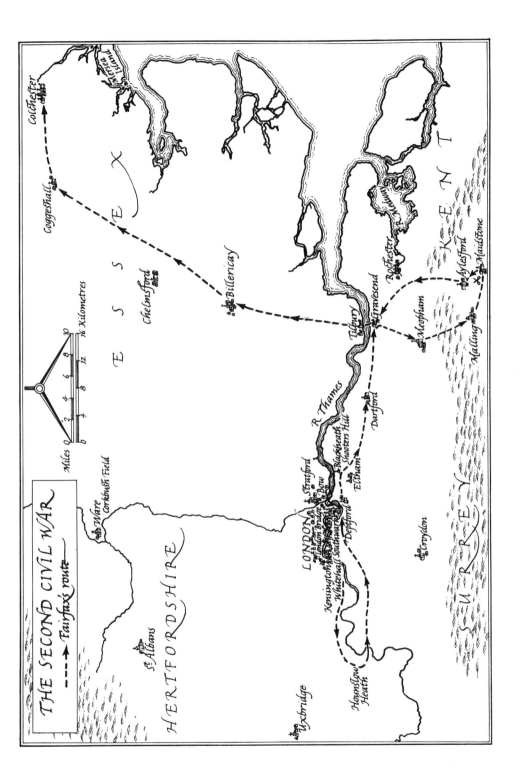

THE SECOND CIVIL WAR

- - - - Fairfax's route

Miles

Kilometres

HERTFORDSHIRE

St. Albans

Uxbridge

Ware
Corkbush Field

LONDON
Kensington
Whitehall Southwark
London Bridge
Bow
Stratford
Deptford

Hounslow Heath

E S S E X

Chelmsford

Billericay

Coggeshall

Colchester

Mersea Island

R. Thames

Blackheath
Shooters Hill
Eltham
Dartford

Gravesend
Tilbury

Croydon

S U R R E Y

K E N T

Neopham

Rochester
R. Medway

Malling

Aylesford
Maidstone

ships in the Downs, however, declared for the King and their crews were able to seize the castles of Deal, Sandown and Walmer. Sir Anthony Weldon wrote from Swanscombe to the Derby House Committee: 'Never was the faire face of such a faithfull County turn'd of a suddaine to soe much deformity and uglinesse.' An anonymous correspondent wrote to warn Fairfax that Sir Harry Vane had voted in the House 'with the malignant partie' and begged Fairfax to trust him no longer. But he had gladly put political squabbles behind him. Now he was in the field, doing work he thoroughly understood. With Major Husbands and several hundred horse leading the way, he prepared to advance into Kent. Once more he knew that failure on his part could destroy the cause for which he had fought so long.

On the 29th Colonel Barkstead reported to him that the enemy 'give out themselves to bee ten thousand butt the countrymen lessen every day; very many officers and souldiers that have formerly serv'd the Kinge come in hourely to them. The discourse among them is that if the county will nott stand to them they will immediately possesse themselves of all the castles and stronge holds, and therby secure landing for the Irish, French, or Danes . . .'

Fairfax rode through Blackheath with his own regiment and Whalley's, the foot following behind, and took some prisoners. He led his force up Shooter's Hill, where a trumpeter from the enemy asked to treat. Fairfax said that he could not negotiate while they continued in arms against the authority of Parliament. Husbands's cavalry pursued them to Dartford and Fairfax spent the night at Eltham to rest his infantry, who had done a lot of marching in the wet. It was clear to the enemy that he meant business, and Rushworth noted that 'most of the cunning cavaliers, who see their danger, have deserted them'. Less cunning cavaliers hung on, hoping that Cromwell would come to grief,

> Or that Tom Fairfax and his Rout
> Should be so bang'd by Kent
> He forcéd by his pockey Gout
> From life and Parliament.

Fairfax once again enforced strict discipline, and issued a firm declaration against plundering, which his troops would do 'at their peril'.

The Royalists outnumbered his troops by half as much again, but they divided their forces, one group going to Maidstone, another to blockade Dover and a third to Rochester. Fairfax sent a small party to relieve Dover and stationed another at Croydon to cover his rear. Then on 31 May he moved down the right bank of the Thames to Gravesend. Lucy Hutchinson wrote, 'A greate company of these Kentish men were gotten together about Gravesend, with fifteene knights, and many commanders of the king's armie to head them, who, although they were more in number then Fairfax his men, yet durst not bide his coming.' He sent a detachment to reconnoitre the enemy's position at Rochester and then struck south by what he described as 'very long marches' across the North Downs to Meopham. Then he turned east to Malling. From there it was only a short distance east to Maidstone. Here the enemy forces came out to confront him at Penenden Heath. They were commanded by the Earl of Norwich, 'the old Lord Goring' as Fairfax called him, father of his old adversary George Goring. The position was strongly held by some 7000 men, with another thousand at Aylesford and 3000 in Maidstone itself.

The battle that followed, like that at Torrington, began with a clash by the advance troops — in this case a body of dragoons — at seven in the evening, which grew into a general engagement. The fighting was severe, according to Fairfax's own account 'four or five hours' hot service', and as Whitelocke records, 'every street in the town was got by inches', but Fairfax's disciplined forces fought their way forward under cannon fire from barricade to barricade and by midnight had secured Maidstone. Fairfax was suffering severely from gout, but, says Whitelocke, 'with his foot wrapped up he mounted on horseback, led on his men in the greatest danger, and was one of the first in all this action'. He himself singled out Colonel Hewson and his regiment for their valour and resolution. Fairfax took 1300 prisoners afterwards among the woods and hopfields. Norwich's main force took no part in the fighting and he withdrew to Rochester, many of his men deserting. From there, with 3000 men, he moved towards London and by 3 June was at Blackheath. Fairfax did not appear to be seriously concerned and only sent Whalley in pursuit. His confidence was justified. Hobbes later wrote: 'the Londoners, I think, might easily and suddenly have mastered, first, the Parliament, and, next Fairfax's 8000 . . .

but the City was never good at venturing; nor were they . . . principled to have a King *over* them, but *under* them.'

The City kept its gates shut against Norwich, who, harried by Whalley's horse, crossed the Thames and rode to Chelmsford. Most of his troops fled but 500 went over in boats or swam their horses over the river and rallied in Stratford and Bow. Skippon was prepared to resist any move on London and Whalley rode over London Bridge and sent his cavalry to take up positions in Mile End.

On 6 June Rich relieved Dover Castle and two days later Ireton took Canterbury. Leaving Rich to lay siege to the castles of Deal, Walmer and Sandown, Fairfax decided that he could safely leave Kent, where his terms were accepted by the beaten Royalists and five of the warships agreed to submit in return for an indemnity. Mopping up there continued until September.

Whalley however sent back word from near Chelmsford in Essex that the Royalists were so much stronger in foot that he could not risk an engagement and that they were 'like a snow ball, increasing'. Norwich at first found little support there and some of the Royalist leaders decided to give up, but they were suddenly galvanised into action by Sir Charles Lucas, a brave but disagreeable cavalryman who had been captured by the Parliamentarians at Marston Moor and again at Stow on the Wold in 1646, subsequently, it seems, being released on parole, undertaking that he would not again bear arms against Parliament. He arrested those who had wanted to submit and was soon joined by Norwich and by Lord Capel with a body of horse.

On Sunday 11 June, Fairfax, still racked by gout, crossed the Thames at Gravesend and advanced to Billericay. He rode on ahead of his men to Coggeshall, where he met Whalley. The Royalists had shut themselves up in Colchester, Lucas's home town, which, Clarendon observes, 'was not glad of their company'. Fairfax was close behind them and reached the city on 13 June. He tried to carry it with a swift rush. Barkstead's regiment launched a direct assault, but after an initial success they were repulsed and driven out. So Fairfax had to undertake a siege, as Cromwell was doing away in the west at Pembroke.

The siege was a long, wearisome business, carried on in continuous, soaking rain, which in due course produced floods. Fairfax did not have the men or equipment to storm the city, so he had to settle down to starve it out, blocking it up with ten forts connected by makeshift walls. There was however fierce fighting when the Royalists made sorties in force. The defenders set the suburbs on fire, while Fairfax seized Mersea Island in the Colne and repulsed one effort to bring relief from the sea.

The Royalist leaders concealed his offers of generous terms from their men, compelling Fairfax to have arrows shot over the walls, with papers wrapped round them containing his offers. Those in the city gradually came down from eating bread to living on horseflesh. dogs, cats, and eventually rats. After three weeks came the news that Cromwell had taken Pembroke after a six weeks' siege. On 8 July, after Parliament had rejected the Scottish demand that Fairfax's Army should be disbanded, Hamilton's Scottish army crossed the border and moved down into Cumberland. The besiegers in the 'leaguer' before Colchester heard that in a minor action the Duke of Buckingham had escaped but that his brother had been killed. The Prince of Wales was at sea off Yarmouth and thus a potential threat to Fairfax: if he could bring off a landing he might rally a substantial force. In London the City merchants were thoroughly Royalist and hoping for a Scottish victory. A broadsheet told them that Fairfax had perished at Colchester. On 14 August Denzil Holles resumed his seat in the House.

The siege of Colchester became more and more bitter, as the rain came relentlessly down. The Royalists hung on, hoping for relief from the Scots. Fairfax became increasingly impatient. The dashing adventures of the war in Yorkshire and the New Model's *annus mirabilis* seemed years away. The Royalist leaders were desperate men, and on the Parliamentary side there was fury that the Royalists had again plunged the country into war. The fighting took on a new, savage aspect, one writer rejoicing that twenty dead Royalists were gentlemen — 'their good apparel and white skins speak no less'. The Parliamentarians accused the defenders of using poisoned bullets 'boyled in Copprice' and 'chew'd Bullets rolled in Sand'. One of Fairfax's colonels, Rainsborough, turned back several hundred unfortunate women who sought to leave the town, who were for a time abandoned in no man's land.

Eventually it had to end. Between 17 and 25 August Cromwell, helped by Lambert, destroyed the Scottish army at Preston. Three days later, after a siege of ten weeks, Colchester surrendered to

Fairfax, by which time many of the houses had been burnt and the population was in a sorry state. All the defenders under the rank of captain were allowed quarter; but though their lives were spared many of them were shipped off to work as labourers in the West Indies. The more senior officers submitted to 'mercy' which meant that their lives were in the hands of the victors.

There now took place an episode which has left a stain on Fairfax's memory. A council of war decided that three of the Royalist leaders — Lucas, who was held principally responsible for the whole business, Sir George Lisle, who was blamed for the burning of the suburbs, and Sir Bernard Gascoigne — should be shot. Norwich and Capel, as peers, or as Fairfax quaintly put it, persons 'considerable for Estates and Familys', were sent to London for Parliament to deal with, and Gascoigne was reprieved when it was discovered that he was really an Italian. But Lucas and Lisle, not landowners of mark, but as Fairfax put it, 'mere Souldjers of Fortune', died bravely facing a firing squad. Clarendon claims that

> As soon as this bloody sacrifice was ended, Fairfax, with the chief officers, went to the town-house to visit the prisoners; and the general (who was an ill orator on the most plausible occasion) applied with his civility to the earl of Norwich, and the lord Capel; and seeming in some degree to excuse the having done that, which he said 'the military justice required,' he told them, 'that all the lives of the rest were safe . . .'

Clarendon says that the deed was 'generally imputed to Ireton, who swayed the general, and was upon all occasions of an unmerciful and bloody nature'. Fairfax himself reported to Parliament, 'For some satisfaction to military Justice . . . I have, with Advice of the chief Officers . . . caus'd 2 of 'em, who were rendred at Mercy, to be shot to death.'

Lucas and Lisle were buried later under a stone which recorded that they had been 'by the command of Sir Thomas Fairfax, in cold blood barbarously murdered', and Charles II would not agree to Fairfax's later request that this be taken down. By those with Royalist sympathies, the executions were, and are, regarded as shameful. They took place at a time when tempers had been greatly inflamed. There had been others — for example of Windebank, killed by the King's orders after surrendering Bletchington House, and of Major Wandstead and fourteen others, hanged by the Royalists after submitting to mercy in Wiltshire. Under the rules of warfare as then understood, Fairfax had the right to refuse quarter to someone who had submitted to mercy. Above all Lucas had broken his parole. Fairfax had in June rejected an offer from Lucas of an exchange of prisoners, telling the defenders of Colchester 'that Sir Charles Lucas had forfeited his parole, his honour and faith, being his prisoner upon parole, and therefore not capable of . . . trust in martial affairs'. Lucas replied to this, arguing that despite 'being a prisoner still unto your lordship', he had compounded, that is, settled the fines, for his estate, and therefore 'the law of nature' justified his taking once again to the sword when a price had been put on his head by the Derby House Committee.

Fairfax is unlikely to have been convinced by this special pleading, and may have held that Lucas's breaking of his parole had deprived him of any claim to clemency. So too, perhaps, with Lisle, who had surrendered earlier at Faringdon. Nevertheless it seems likely that on this occasion Fairfax allowed his better judgement to be overridden by his council of war, and in particular by Ireton, now and subsequently the intellectual leader of the hard-liners in the Army leadership. Clarendon indeed maintains that he 'was left by Cromwell to watch the general as well as the army'. James Heath, in his contemporary *Flagellum*, asserts that Ireton persuaded Fairfax to order the executions in order to discredit him, as he was the only man who stood in the way of Cromwell's supremacy. This seems far-fetched. In his *Short Memorials* Fairfax claimed that 'upon Mercy, it is to be understood that some are to suffer, the rest to goe free'. The many who were sent off to the West Indies would have thought this an odd way of being 'freed'. His agreement to the executions was given when he and others were exasperated at having to fight the civil war all over again. But it was not a decision of which he can have been proud. Parliament was equally vindictive, and Lord Capel, after a trial at which Fairfax appeared at the request of Capel's friends to explain what he understood by submitting to mercy, was duly executed, though Norwich was spared. Capel claimed that Fairfax had promised after the shooting of Lucas and Lisle that 'no other of their lives should be in danger', but Fairfax did not confirm that he had given so positive an undertaking.

The second civil war was over. It had been a tense, bitter business. As Fairfax wrote, there was 'work enough that Summer', He held a review of his troops on 29 August and then went off to look at Roman remains at Maldon and to pay visits, at which he was received with honours and flattery, to Harwich, Ipswich, Solebay, Yarmouth and Norwich. He visited 'Sir John Wentworth's in *Lovingland*, and was entertain'd with the greatest varietys, for Ponds, Waterworks, Groves and Coy-Ducks, which are to be seen in England.' Then he returned to Bury, and on 22 September moved his headquarters to St Albans. A week before that Parliament had begun negotiations with the King at Newport in the Isle of Wight, an effort by the Presbyterians (who a fortnight later passed an ordinance making Presbyterianism compulsory throughout England) to reach an agreement with the King and so set the Army aside. Though warned that two cavaliers planned to stab him, Fairfax was, temporarily, back in the old routine of administering the Army, whose pay was eighteen weeks adrift, and he had once more to take up with the Speaker what he described as the unendurable problem of an unpaid army living off the land.

But his prestige was immense. It was during the siege of Colchester that Milton addressed a sonnet to him (not one of his best), beginning:

> Fairfax, whose name in arms through Europe rings
>> Filling each mouth with envy or with praise,
>> And all her jealous monarchs with amaze
> And rumours loud, that daunt remotest kings;
> Thy firm unshaken virtue ever brings
>> Victory home, though new rebellions raise
>> Their Hydra heads . . .

He went on to say: 'O yet a nobler task awaits thy hand' but was vague about precisely what that nobler task might be.

The shadow of the King lay across the future. Edmund Ludlow, the republican, records that 'by the advice of some friends' he went down to Colchester during the siege to see Fairfax and tell him of a design to betray the people's cause, and that the King would not hold himself bound by promises made under duress. Hence, he argued, the proposed Newport treaty between King and Parliament was a snare. According to Ludlow, Fairfax 'acknowledged what I said to be true, and declared himself resolved to use the power he had, to maintain the cause of the publicke, upon a clear and evident call looking upon himself to be obliged to pursue the work he was about'. Ludlow continues, 'Perceiving by such a general answer that he was irresolute, I went to Commissary-General Ireton, who had a great influence upon him . . .' Fairfax no doubt saw the problem clearly enough, but he was reluctant to commit himself to what could only be a revolutionary solution.

The Killing of the King

'It is said that the regicides killed Charles I only to
make Charles II king. It is not so. They killed the old
monarchy; and the restored monarch was by no means
its heir . . .'

> Frederic Harrison's *Oliver Cromwell*
> quoted by Gardiner in his *Great Civil War II*

'Why, Doctor! he gar'd Kings ken that they had a *lith*
in their neck.' (He taught kings they had a *joint* in their
neck.)

> Boswell's father to Dr Johnson on being asked
> what good Cromwell had done to his country.
> Letter from Sir Walter Scott quoted in *The
> Croker Papers II.*

FAIRFAX, though reluctant to become a full-blooded revolutionary, seems now to have come to the very reasonable
conclusion that the King himself was thoroughly untrustworthy. He may well have thought that he should be deposed. But
he had further trouble with Ireton, of whom Bishop Burnet wrote
that he 'had the principles and the temper of a Cassius in him; he
stuck at nothing that might have turned England to a commonwealth'. Ireton pressed Fairfax to put a stop to the proposed Newport treaty by purging the House. When Fairfax would not agree —
not only did he think this action excessive, but he may have resented
Ireton's having persuaded him to allow the executions at Colchester — Ireton sought to resign his commission, but this too
Fairfax would not accept, and Ireton retired temporarily to Windsor.
Cromwell was still in Scotland.

Ireton was not, however, to be repressed, and he now drafted a
Remonstrance of the Army, an impatient and angry document which

argued that it was dangerous to go on negotiating with the King, who would never hold himself bound by whatever he agreed to do; that the King, who had tried to set up an absolute monarchy and was responsible for the war and its bloodshed, ought to be tried quickly and, he hinted, executed; that the Prince of Wales and Duke of York should be declared incapable of governing unless they submitted to Parliament; and that future kings should depend 'upon the election of . . . the people'. Ireton had all the relentless logic, incisive analytical power and persuasive arguments that Fairfax lacked, but his clear intellect did not necessarily lead to sounder conclusions than did Fairfax's inarticulate instincts.

On 7 November Fairfax summoned a Council of Officers (excluding the agitators who had taken part in the Putney debates) to consider Ireton's remonstrance. They met in the Abbey Church of St Albans. Ireton, supported by Harrison, did his utmost to get them to agree that the Army should act on the lines he proposed. He organised petitions to Fairfax from three regiments supporting his views. But Fairfax, even at this late stage, declined to rule out a political compromise. Many of the colonels shared his anxiety that the Army should avoid revolutionary actions and hoped that 'the hearts of King and kingdom might be knit together in a threefold cord of love'. And Fairfax himself made a declaration, in which he said that

> . . . no worldly thing is so deare unto him, as the compleat settling of the liberties and peace of the Kingdome, and that he will proceed . . . without any overture tending to overthrow the government of the Kingdome, and that he will cleerly commit his stock or share of interest in this Kingdome, into the common bottome of Parliaments. And when his Majesty shall give his concurrence to what is . . . proposed by the Parliament . . . his Excellency will . . . maintain and defend his Majesty and his Parliament in that just long desired Agreement. And whereas it hath been suggested, or suspected, that the proceedings of the Army have been to overthrow Presbyterie, or hinder the settlement thereof, and to have the Independent Government up, he doth clearly disclaim and dissavour any such designe.

Fairfax persuaded the Council to agree to accept whatever treaty might result from the negotiation between Parliament and the King. He and the moderates may have made a private approach to the King, and the King may have written to Fairfax setting out his terms. But the evidence for this is cloudy.

Thwarted in the Council, Ireton and the militants now met with Lilburne and the Levellers at the Nag's Head tavern in London. These talks resulted in Leveller objectives being included in the *Remonstrance*. What happened next is obscure. It may be that, as the price for getting the agreement of the Council to accept a treaty, Fairfax had to agree that the Army itself should put its essential demands to the King. In the event, on 16 November, the Council of Officers sent their propositions to the King, which were in effect those contained in the *Heads of the Proposals* drafted by Ireton in July of the previous year.

Once these points were accepted, Fairfax and his officers undertook to restore the King, Queen and royal family in 'safety, honour and freedom'. What the King was being offered by the Army was indeed not very different from the solution Fairfax had sought all along. It was wholly consistent with the terms of his letter to Rupert at Bristol. But it was too much for Charles to swallow, brought up as he was to believe in his prerogative and the divine right of kings. This was not perhaps surprising, since, as Gardiner observed, 'Charles was . . . required to anticipate, in all essential points, the system which prevails in the reign of Victoria.' On 17 November, inevitably but fatally, the King set aside the Army's proposals. His last chance had gone.

He had also destroyed the case of Fairfax and the Army moderates, who were further undermined by the evident determination of the Presbyterian majority in Parliament to settle with the King on his terms. So, at their meeting on the 18th, the Council of Officers, feeling that there was now no alternative, accepted Ireton's uncompromising *Remonstrance* with only two dissenting voices, neither of them that of Fairfax. Like many others, he had been defeated by the unreasonableness of the King. The *Remonstrance* was sent to Parliament on the 20th under a covering letter which bore Fairfax's signature.

All this time it had been Ireton who had led the militants. Cromwell, away in the north, seemed not at all anxious to try to remove the King. But the King's rejections of the Army's proposals, while torpedoing Fairfax's moderate approach, also helped to make up Cromwell's mind. On the 20th he wrote to Fairfax, saying, 'I find . . . in . . . the regiments . . . a very great zeal to have impartial justice done upon Offenders; and I must confess I do . . . from my heart, concur with them . . .' A great man was preparing, perhaps reluctantly, to take the way of force, but, as Gardiner fairly observes, Cromwell 'had no appreciation of the instinctive horror with which the English people regarded an army which counted its impulses as the revelation of the will of God . . . it was beyond his power to lay broad the foundations of the peace for which he sighed.' Fairfax had, on this, a better appreciation of the instincts of ordinary English people, but after the King's rejection of the Army's proposals, the solution he himself wanted was unattainable. So the initiative passed to other hands.

The immediate need was to prevent the escape of the King from the Isle of Wight. He was trying to get away but Hammond declined to put him under stronger restrictions and held himself to be responsible only to Parliament, not to Fairfax. Fairfax recalled Hammond and sent the rough, determined Colonel Ewer to take his place. And he authorised the King's detention until Parliament had acted on the *Remonstrance*, one stated objective of which was the trial of the King. The reluctant Hammond was arrested and brought to Windsor and later sent to Reading on parole. Fairfax and the Council of Officers sent down positive instructions that the King should be removed to Hurst Castle, a blockhouse on the Solent. Fairfax was lending his name to instructions which were bringing the King to trial, but, despite his exasperation with the King, he must have been anxious. On 28 November he wrote to Cromwell asking him to come to headquarters, 'whereby I hope our councells and endeavours . . . wil bee giuen to the very great business now in agitation . . .'

If the King was to be tried and executed, as Ireton and the radical officers wished, Parliament had to be overawed, or dissolved, or purged. As Fairfax himself put it much later, 'agitatinge Councel had first Thoughts how to remove all out of ye Parliament who were like to oppose them in that Work'.

On 30 November a *Declaration* was published in Fairfax's name. This protested against Parliament's failure to debate the *Remonstrance*, said that the Army would preserve as much of the Parliament 'as can be safe' but wished to establish a 'more orderly and equal judicature of men in a just Representative', and called on Parliament to exclude corrupt members, failing which 'so many of them as God hath kept upright' should withdraw, as a preliminary to a dissolution and fresh elections. The *Declaration* said that, to achieve these objectives, 'we are now drawing up with the Army to London . . .' Even at this late stage the Army was seeking to force a dissolution, not to purge the House. Fairfax also wrote to the Lord Mayor warning him that he was coming to London and demanding £40,000 out of the arrears of the City's assessments. But he sent a reassuring letter to Bulstrode Whitelocke.

The House told the Speaker to ask Fairfax to keep away, but on 2 December he once more led the Army into London by way of Hounslow Heath and made his headquarters at Whitehall. Lord Grey of Groby held his stirrup while he dismounted and a group of MPs attended him to his lodging. As always, he insisted on rigorous discipline. Parliament meanwhile was debating the King's replies to the Commissioners at Newport, finally voting on the 5th that the agreement reached provided a basis for further negotiation, a resolution that directly defied the Army. An effort to reach a settlement, by sending a committee of moderate MPs to talk things over with the Army, failed. Prynne claimed that Fairfax was ready to listen but was overruled by his officers. Clarendon says they were kept waiting three hours and then told by Fairfax, 'sullenly and superciliously', that they must comply with the Army's *Remonstrance*.

The radical officers and the republican MPs (one of whom was Ludlow) now met and in the ensuing discussion Ireton was persuaded by the MPs to agree to a purge, rather than the dissolution he wanted. A sub-committee of six drew up the detailed plans. On the morning of 6 December Colonel Pride, with Lord Grey of Groby beside him, stood with his troops in the lobby and turned back all the members listed as unsatisfactory, that is those who had favoured the Newport treaty with the King. Of these some forty-one were held on this day, while outside the Army turned away the City trained bands. Fairfax's old colleague Skippon persuaded them to return quietly to the city. In the afternoon the preacher Hugh Peters, wearing a sword, came to make a list of the prisoners for Fairfax, returning later with orders for two of them to be released. The New Model troopers were glad to see the Members of Parliament put down. Clement Walker, one of the purged members, heard one of them say, 'These are the men who have cozened the state of our money and kept back our pay.'

It is not certain how far, if at all, Fairfax was told what was going on. According to Ludlow, 'Commissary-General Ireton went to Sir Thomas Fairfax, and acquainted him with the necessity of this extraordinary way of proceeding, having taken care to have the army drawn up the next morning by seven of the clock.' Fairfax certainly gave no orders for the purge, but he seems to have made no attempt to prevent it or afterwards to undo it. He did claim much later, 'I had not the least Intimation of itt till it was done,' describing the purge as 'the horrible Attempt . . . made by Colonel Pride upon ye Parliament' and adding, 'why it was soe secretly carryed, that I should gett noe Notice of it, was because I alwais preuented those designes when I knew them. But by this purging of the House . . . the Parliament was brought into such a consumptive and languishing Condition, as itt could never again recouer that healthful Constitution . . .'

The Rump, as Parliament had now become, at once asked Fairfax to liberate their colleagues. The reply was a demand that they should resume proceedings against Denzil Holles and his fellows and exclude from the House all who had not taken a strong enough line about the Scottish invasion. In the evening Cromwell, having taken his time about responding to Fairfax's summons, finally rode in from the north, having been conveniently absent while the revolution was taking place.

There was one point on which Fairfax did wholeheartedly agree with his military colleagues. This was the question of the Army's pay and arrears. On the 8th he took a very tough line with the City, sending in troops to seize the treasuries at Haberdasher's Hall, Goldsmith's Hall and Weavers' Hall, whence £27,000 was taken away. On this question Fairfax felt strongly, and had no objection to taking stringent measures.

Pride's purge marked the point at which the Army's action became frankly revolutionary. It had turned against the elected Parliament whose army it was. It also marked the point at which Fairfax lost control of the New Model. He had come to share the view that Charles I was impossible and was prepared to go quite a long way in putting pressure on Parliament, but he probably shrank from the unquestionably illegal use of force, and when it came to the point he was either kept in ignorance or, more probably, simply told by Ireton about the purge when it was too late to stop it. Since the decision by the Council of Officers to approve the *Remonstrance* and the launching of the Army on an illegal course, Ireton, not Fairfax, had been taking the major decisions.

At that point, or this, Fairfax ought perhaps to have resigned a command he could no longer exercise effectively. But he did not. He felt it his duty to carry on because a successor — Ireton or another — would have been able to do what he wanted with no restraint at all.

Moreover Fairfax instinctively felt that what he stood for — a moderate reform, a controlled monarchy, a free Parliament, and the countryside run by the gentry — was what most people in England really wanted. In this he was right. His problem was that for the present on both sides extreme views prevailed. The King seemed to have learnt nothing and to hope that by playing off one group against another he could eventually restore the autocracy he had enjoyed with Laud and Strafford. The Presbyterians in Parliament acted with notable folly, first by failing to give their Army adequate pay or security, and secondly by making it clear that they were prepared to restore the King more or less unconditionally, so only that he agreed to the establishment of compulsory Presbyterianism. On the other side, a fanatical minority of republicans, Levellers and religious zealots — Fifth Monarchists or whatever — sought to impose their vision of a brave new world by force of arms. Fairfax must have seen clearly enough that both sides were wrong, and that the regimes they hoped to create could not last. But for the time being the militants prevailed and he and those who thought like him could only look on in increasing dismay. It was a time when, as Yeats put it:

> The best lack all conviction, while the worst
> Are full of passionate intensity.

On 14 December, Fairfax presided over a meeting of the General Council at Whitehall which considered the question 'Whether the Civill Magistrate had a power given him from God?' John Lilburne, the Leveller leader, protested to Fairfax about the failure of this Council to adopt his views *in toto*, and demanded the reorganisation of the Council on popular, democratic lines, to become a sort of seventeenth-century soviet. Fairfax of course would have nothing to do with such ideas. On the same day, the House of Commons felt bold enough to ask on what grounds MPs were prevented by the Army from coming to the House. This was ignored. Next day the Council of Officers decided to bring the King under guard to Windsor, and Fairfax issued the necessary orders.

On 19 December four of the small group who still attended the House of Lords — Pembroke, Salisbury, North and Denbigh — came to see Fairfax, probably to discuss the very last overture to the King, which Denbigh was to make, with the approval of Fairfax and Cromwell. The Leveller and republican extremists were pressing for the King's execution, but up to this point Cromwell seems still to have been hoping to avoid it, and Fairfax was totally opposed to it. But the King would not see Denbigh, so yet another last chance had gone. On the 20th Fairfax and the Council of Officers had sixteen of the imprisoned MPs released. Meanwhile the Council, under Fairfax's chairmanship, was discussing with Lilburne and some of the Levellers, and with some Independent ministers, fundamental political and religious questions which needed to be addressed if a new constitution was to be worked out.

The King's refusal to entertain Denbigh's approach had, yet again, cut the ground from under the moderates in the Army and such as were left in the House. Influential and new voices were nevertheless raised against proceeding to extremes — they included Vane, Manchester, and Fairfax's old chaplain and historian, Joshua Sprigge — but the decisive factor was that Cromwell now concluded that the King was impossible and that the trial must go forward. Fairfax remained profoundly unhappy but his following in the Council of Officers had evaporated and his own hesitations and uncertainties sapped his influence. Appeals to him to intervene, for example from Edward Stephens, an excluded MP who begged him to prevent the murder of the King — 'the power is now yours . . . rouse yourself, my lord . . .' — were in vain. If he had favoured acting against the King, he, rather than Cromwell, could probably have led the Army movement. But he had not thought it right to use armed troops to evict members of Parliament; still less would he have thought it right to execute an anointed king. Again if he had vigorously and actively opposed Pride's purge and the trial of the King, he might conceivably have prevented both, at the cost of splitting the Army and perhaps fighting a third civil war. But this, too, was not in his nature. He believed in the supremacy of Parliament and in the monarchy, though a limited one, but he undoubtedly thought that both this Parliament and this King had behaved deplorably, and probably believed that some action should be taken against both. The pull of these two opposite forces resulted in paralysis. Burnet wrote: 'Fairfax was much distracted in his mind, and changed purposes often every day.' Cromwell shared many of his doubts but finally joined the extremists, though only for the duration of this particular crisis. Fairfax remained inert, immobilized by doubt.

The proceedings against the King now took their course. At the end of the year Parliament passed an ordinance setting up a special court to try him. Contarini, a Venetian Ambassador, reported that 'the military control everything', and, inaccurately, that 'Fairfax has great pretensions'.

On 6 January 1649 the Queen wrote to Fairfax from the Louvre — addressing him as 'Right trusty and right well-beloved' — asking for a safe conduct to visit the King. Fairfax never saw her letter, which was found unopened among waste papers in Parliament after the Restoration.

On the afternoon of 8 January, fifty-two of the Commissioners for the King's trial met for the first time in the Painted Chamber. The other eighty-three stayed away. Fairfax was one of those who did turn up — unlike Harry Vane, he had not refused to be appointed as a Commissioner — but it is recorded that he would not sit at the table but 'went away immediately'. He would not sign the order about the next sitting, and never appeared again at subsequent meetings. But he made no statement of his views and remained silent.

On 15 January he received a strong appeal and protest from forty-seven Presbyterian ministers, while another sent a passionate remonstrance to Anne. In the meantime the talks about the future pattern of government continued, with Fairfax in the chair. One of the militants reproached him for the 'spirit of fear upon your Excellency' and urged him to carry through the Army's great work.

When the trial itself opened in Westminster Hall on 20 January, the roll of the Commissioners was called over, and when Fairfax's name was reached, a masked lady in the gallery called out, 'He has more wit than to be here.' The lady was Anne Fairfax. The trial was intensely unpopular among the ordinary people of England, and Cromwell, having decided to go through with it, may have been anxious about the effect of Fairfax's opposition if it became widely known. One report says that 'Sunday was se'nnight Cromwell put a guard upon Fairfax, accusing him of an intention to deliver the King.' This would have been the day after Anne's outburst. But it seems unlikely that Cromwell resorted — or needed to resort — to such crude measures, though it is probable that he, Ireton and others were in constant discussion with Fairfax — a Royalist report described him as being 'baited with fresh dogs all Tuesday night to bring him into the Hall on the morrow'. But he would have nothing to do with their plans, which now included describing the King as 'a tyrant, traytor, murtherer and a publick and implacable enemy to the commonwealth of England'.

On the 27th the trial of the King continued, his skilful and dignified stand confounding his accusers. But the president of the court, Bradshaw, maintained that his Majesty was required to answer a charge of treason and other high crimes brought against him in the name of the people of England. A contemporary account adds, 'Here a Malignant Lady interrupted the court, (saying, not half the People,) but she was soon silenced.' The 'malignant lady' was, once again, a masked Anne Fairfax. Rushworth adds that she was silenced with threats, and ' 'tis affirm'd, the Lady Fairfax said with a loud Voice, 'Tis a Lye, not the tenth part of the People are concern'd in it; but all's done by the Machinations of that Traitor Cromwel.' Her courageous outburst not surprisingly infuriated the zealots in the Army, and a relative, Elizabeth Fairfax, was threatened with death by soldiers at Doncaster who at first thought she was Anne. After the Restoration, when Colonel Axtel, who commanded the guards in Westminster Hall, was tried, one of the charges against him was that he had ordered his musketeers to shoot the heckling lady, though they had refused to fire. It was also asserted that he had shouted, 'Down with the whores.' His unsuccessful defence — like that of some of the defendants at the Nuremberg trials — was that he was under military discipline and 'I was there by a command of the General.'

On Sunday the 28th the Dutch ambassadors, who had come over

to urge clemency for the King on behalf of the United Provinces, saw Fairfax, Cromwell and the principal officers at Fairfax's house and made representations to him (in French). According to the Venetians, one of the ambassadors, Adriaen Pauw, reported subsequently to the States General in these terms:

> They had encountered some difficulty over Farfax, who was surrounded in his chamber by a great number of officers . . . and when the ambassadors intimated that they wished to speak to him alone, he withdrew with them into another room, into which General Cromuel entered soon afterwards with a number of officers, without asking permission . . . These two, Farfax and Cromuel, did not venture to open the letters of credence except in the presence of a number of officers . . . and neither of them goes out without a guard of at least 300 horse. The Ambassador Pau praised Farfax for his great civility and Cromuel for his ability and eloquence.

But the Ambassadors could get no satisfaction.

The next day Fairfax is reported to have tried, unsuccessfully, to persuade the Council of Officers to put off the execution. His cousin Brian asserts that the night before the King was executed some of his friends proposed to Fairfax that they should rescue the King the following day, 'telling him that twenty thousand men were ready to join with him'. Brian says that his uncle 'said he was ready to venture his own life, but not the lives of others against the army now united against them'. But it was clearly in any case now too late to save the King though, according to Herbert, the King's attendant, on the 30th Fairfax was 'all that morning . . . using all his power and interest to have the execution deferred . . . and fully resolved with his own regiment to prevent the execution or have it deferred till he could make a party in the army to second his design'.

The Prince of Wales sent a direct appeal to Fairfax and the Council of War. It was put aside. The Dutch ambassadors saw Fairfax again at noon at his secretary's house. They reported that 'The general was at length touched by our animated and pressing entreaties, and declared that he would go directly to Westminster and recommend to parliament to grant the answer and the reprieve we requested, and that he would take a few officers of note with him to support the application.' When they came out they found the streets full of troops. A few hours later Fairfax was at the Banqueting Hall and saw Cromwell and Harrison. He was with one or other of them for the next two hours, and no record remains of what took place then.

All efforts were in vain. In the early afternoon of 30 January, after the Rump had rushed through a bill making it illegal for anyone to proclaim a new king, Charles I was beheaded in Whitehall. There can be no doubt that this was, for Fairfax, a traumatic shock. He may have believed and hoped right up to the end that Cromwell and Ireton would not carry matters to extremes, but were planning either to depose the King or to force him to abdicate or agree to a limited monarchy. He believed, too, that he had been misled, and perhaps Cromwell or Harrison had lied to him about their intentions. After the execution Herbert met Fairfax in the Long Gallery, and was amazed to be asked 'how the King did?' When he replied that the King was dead, Fairfax, he records, 'seem'd much surpriz'd'. The second Duke of Buckingham, who became his son-in-law, left a paper in his desk, which was found after his death, which said that Fairfax laid down his commission 'upon them deceiving him in the murder of King Charles the First'. Fairfax did not lay down his commission until some time later; but the memory of how he had been treated, festering in his mind, was probably a main cause of his resignation when it did come. His cousin Brian wrote that he 'utterly abhorred and lamented the death of the King to his dying day: and never mentioned it but with tears in his eyes'. And his chaplain said in Fairfax's funeral sermon, 'As for that horrible act of theirs in murthering of their sovereign he ever detested it, and used all the means that possibly he could for the preventing of it.' The breach between him and the regicides was now unbridgeable. But he was still to continue as Lord General for another eighteen months.

The End of the Road

'Farewell the plumed troop, and the big wars,
That make ambition virtue! O, farewell!
Farewell the neighing steed, and the shrill trump.'

Othello, Act III

A WEEK AFTER the King's execution, while acts were passed on successive days abolishing the monarchy and the House of Lords, Fairfax became a member of the now supreme House of Commons (from which his Scottish peerage did not debar him) as member for Cirencester, being one of the 'recruiter' members elected to fill the gaps in the Long Parliament. After another week he was made a member of the Council of State, set up by the House of Commons to be the executive of the new republic. Those selected for it included a number of moderates. Ireton and Harrison were excluded.

There could now be no oath of allegiance, but in its place those chosen were asked to sign an 'engagement', drafted by Ireton, approving what had been done in December and January and specifically the proceedings of the King's trial. Fairfax and some others, like Skippon, refused to sign this. Fairfax was prepared to serve the new regime but not to endorse what had been done, above all the killing of the King. But it was vital for the new regime to secure his support, so he was allowed to sign a special undertaking, omitting any expression of approval for what had been done but committing him to defend the actions of Parliament in settling affairs 'in the way of a republic, without King or House of Peers'. He accepted the new republic but not the way in which it had been brought into being, and was unmoved by occasional talk of 'King Fairfax'.

Collaboration between the Army leaders and the Levellers had broken down even before the King's execution. The Levellers were outraged that the House of Commons now seemed to be socially conservative and that they faced 'a new tyranny' by the Army leaders. Petitions from the dissatisfied started to come in. One from Norwich addressed Fairfax as 'Lord General of the forces raised for the defence of the Gospel of Jesus Christ and the enlargement of the liberty of the well-affected English.' Another, sent to him on 1 March by eight troopers, and probably written by Overton the Leveller, eloquently affirmed the rights of English soldiers, claimed that officers were nothing without 'the soldier that endureth the heat and burden of the day' and attacked the Council of State as 'composed of the most pernicious interests of our rotten state'. They were arrested and court-martialled and five of them were disgraced and cashiered. On 28 March Lilburne, Overton and other Leveller leaders were arrested. A monster petition for their release, signed, it was said, by 80,000 people, was sent to Parliament. Leveller broadsheets continued to circulate.

On 1 April a group calling themselves 'True Levellers' or 'Diggers', led by a New Model veteran, William Everard, began digging and planting 'parsenipps, and carretts, and beanes' on the common and felling trees at St George's Hill, near Walton-on-Thames, to assert a claim that the earth and its fruits belonged to all and not just to landowners. Alarmed, the Council of State asked Fairfax to disperse 'such ridiculous people'. Fairfax selected a Captain Gladman to do this job, who, sensibly, did not make heavy weather of it, but persuaded the leaders, Winstanley and Everard, to come and talk to Fairfax. This they did on 20 April, firmly keeping their hats on 'because he was but their fellow-creature'. According to Whitelocke, 'Everard said, he was of the race of the Jews; that all the liberties of the people were lost by the coming in of William the Conqueror' and that he had been bidden to dig in a recent vision. The Diggers appealed to Fairfax 'by vertue of yours and our victory over the King, whereby the enslaved people of England have recovered themselves from under the Norman Conquest'. He gave them a courteous hearing and the movement persisted for some time, but the local people, organised by the landowners, destroyed the Diggers' cottages and crops.

More serious were Leveller-inspired mutinies in the Army,

which, as in 1647, occurred when it became known that an army was to be sent to Ireland. They wished to have the agitators restored, to have tithes and the excise abolished, 'prince Charles brought in' and 'that the laws be Englished'.

The first revolt, led by Robert Lockyer, took place in Whalley's regiment in Bishopsgate in late April and was suppressed by Fairfax and Cromwell in person. Six men were condemned to death but all were pardoned except Lockyer, who was shot in St Paul's churchyard despite menacing letters to Fairfax from Lilburne and Overton. Lockyer's funeral became an immense Leveller demonstration, with thousands of supporters wearing the sea-green and black Leveller ribbons.

Next to mutiny, at Salisbury in May, was Scroope's regiment, one of those chosen by lot to go to Ireland. He and about eighty officers, finding that their men would not obey them, rode off to join Fairfax. The mutineers elected new officers and, joined by four troops of Ireton's regiment, marched north through Marlborough to Wantage. Fairfax sent a Major White and then Scroope himself to promise them pardon if they submitted but they went on to Blagrove, near Abingdon, and were joined there by two troops of Harrison's regiment, bringing their numbers to some 1200. Their leaders sent a defiant letter to Fairfax.

Fairfax decided that they must be crushed quickly, before they grew any stronger. He and Cromwell assembled a small force — his own regiment of horse, part of Reynolds's regiment, some Buckinghamshire horse and some of Okey's dragoons, in all about 4000 men. They reviewed this force in Hyde Park, where Cromwell addressed it. Then Fairfax moved with his old speed from London to Alton, Andover, Newbury and Abingdon. The mutinous troops crossed the Thames near Faringdon and reached Burford in the Cotswolds on 14 May. There they rested, but Fairfax was hot on their heels, moving at forty or fifty miles a day, and at midnight he was upon them, sending a small party — 'a forlorn under Captain Okey' to attack them while they slept, capturing three or four hundred, including Colonel Eyres, who had been troublesome at Corkbush Field in November 1647, and the arms and horses of as many more. A cornet and two corporals were shot. They died bravely, and Fairfax spared the rest. Whalley's regiment, now in Essex, decided 'to adhere to the Lord General, and instead of sea green and black, wear blew ribbands in their hats', blue being Fairfax's colour. It is striking that, despite his differences with Cromwell over the execution of the King three months before, Fairfax was now working with Cromwell without any friction in suppressing the Levellers, whose subversive ideas they both abominated.

The mutineers dealt with, Fairfax and Cromwell paid a visit to Oxford, where they stayed with Dr Palmer in All Souls, were received with all honours, waited on, and entertained by the Vice-Chancellor, the Heads of Colleges and the Proctors, given a feast at which they had 'good cheer and bad speeches', and made doctors of civil law. Fairfax established a lectureship and nominated three lecturers. He went on to the Isle of Wight, Southampton, Portsmouth and Guildford, being received everywhere 'with the great guns and feasting', and at Guildford talking to several regiments about the need for discipline and the dangers of mutiny.

On his return to London he found a letter from Colonel George Monk reporting on the military situation in Ireland, couched in positively servile terms — 'I am soe deeply obliged to your Lordship for your noble favours, and the good opinion that you have bin pleased to conceive of mee, that I am transported with joy that I have the happines to bee intituled one of your Lordships servants, whereby I may have occasion to manifest my affection.' No wonder Monk ended up as a Duke.

Fairfax and Cromwell were now hated by both Royalists and Levellers, but their authority was secure and on 8 June they were given a splendid banquet at Grocer's Hall in the City, when Fairfax was presented with a gold basin and ewer.

The rest of the year 1649 and the first five months of 1650 were, for Fairfax, uneventful. It was Cromwell who commanded the force which finally went to Ireland in the late summer, though when they approved his appointment the House also voted to make Fairfax general of all the forces in England and Ireland, Whitelocke commenting that this was done 'to take off any reflection on the general, or dislike of him'. While Cromwell was storming Drogheda and, in his own words, knocking Catholic priests on the head, Fairfax settled down to the routine job of administering the Army, as Lord General and a member of the Council of State, issuing from time to time ordinances forbidding soldiers to put horses into mowing grounds, petitioning Parliament with his Council that liberty 'should not extend to the toleration of popery, prelacy, the Book of Common Prayer, public scorn and contempt of God and his word', and forbidding soldiers 'to have hounds or greyhounds, or to kill deer or conies in any chases, parks, or warrens'.

In August the Venetians heard a rumour that the Scots had invaded England but concluded that 'the news is unlikely, since it has not called away Gen. Fairfax from the pleasures of his villa and the chase, which he is enjoying at Chinelenton'. Chinelenton was an Italian stab at Kensington. On 12 September 1649 he wrote from Kensington to a Colonel Cox saying, 'I perceive by Information given by some persons in the West that Captaine Bowen hath demeaned himself in verie uncivill Language against my self the Lieutenant Generall and ye Army in soe much that I hold him altogether unfit to continue in his Command . . .' so the Captain was to be dismissed. There was some talk of Fairfax at this time being replaced as Lord General by Cromwell, talk to which Cromwell himself gave no encouragement.

On 1 June, 1650 Fairfax, with 'many thousands of the well affected', met Cromwell at Hounslow Heath on his return from Ireland, and two days later Cromwell called on him at Queen Street, where, according to the paper *Mercurius Politicus*, 'there passed many remarkable expressions of mutuall love and courtesie, sufficient to check the false tongues and wishes of the enemies of the nation'.

The immediate 'enemies of the nation' were the Scots, who appeared to be planning to intervene again. Parliament decided that an army must be sent north, and on 12 June appointed Fairfax to command it, with Cromwell as his Lieutenant-General. Fairfax agreed to go, perhaps on the assumption that he was to go merely to the north of England to defend the country against the expected invasion. Two days later it was decided that a new commission should be drawn up for him in the name of the Commonwealth.

But on 20 June the Council of State (of which Fairfax was of course a member) decided that England must move first and invade Scotland — in other words stage a pre-emptive strike. As Whitelocke records, they 'thought it . . . not prudent to be behindhand with their enemy' and 'were satisfied that the convenant was by the Scots broken and dissolved before . . .' They directed that this decision should not be communicated to Parliament for six days, no doubt because they foresaw difficulties. Perhaps Fairfax had argued against this course in the Council. At any rate, after forty-eight hours he told the Council that he could not agree to take part in an invasion of Scotland. Defending England was one thing; taking the initiative in invading a sister country was another. His decision was embarrassing to the republican regime, still very new and anxious to avoid any public rifts. Cromwell suggested that Fairfax should remain Lord General, but not go on the expedition itself, as had been the case with Ireland. But the Council were reluctant to leave a disaffected Fairfax in London, where there might be a Presbyterian revolt.

Bulstrode Whitelocke has left a very detailed record of what happened next. He ascribes Fairfax's reluctance to the influence of 'the presbyterian ministers and his own lady, who was a great patroness of them', and says that the Council, 'somewhat troubled at his excellency's scruples', appointed a committee of five — Cromwell, Lambert, Harrison, St John and Whitelocke himself — to try to persuade him to change his mind, and to satisfy his doubts.

Fairfax welcomed the committee, 'where I find so many of my particular friends', and stressed his continuing 'duty and affection to the parliament'. But, he said:

> I think it doubtful whether we have a just cause to make an invasion upon Scotland. With them we are joined in the national league and covenant; and now for us, contrary thereunto, and without sufficient cause given us by them, to enter into their country with an army, and to make war upon them, is that which I cannot see the justice of, nor how we shall be able to justify the lawfulness of it before God and man.

Cromwell and his colleagues argued that Hamilton had previously invaded England and that there was 'too much cause of suspicion' that the Scots were planning another invasion. Fairfax saw the force of this but said that that was no reason for England to begin the war — 'what warrant have we to fall upon them unless we can be assured of their purpose to fall upon us?' — and pointed out that a later Scottish parliament had disowned Hamilton. When Harrison said that there was evidence which made it probable that their intentions were hostile, Fairfax replied: 'Human probabilities are not sufficient grounds to make war upon a neighbour nation,' adding 'I am to answer only for my own conscience.'

He conceded that what the committee had said had a good deal in it, but, as he differed from them and wished to be no hindrance to the Parliament, he would willingly lay down his commission. Cromwell replied:

> I am very sorry your lordship should have thoughts of laying down your commission, by which God hath blessed you in the performance of so many eminent services for the parliament. I pray, my lord, consider all your faithful servants, us who are officers, who have served under you, and desire to serve under no other general. It would be a great discouragement to all of us, and a great discouragement to the affairs of the parliament, for our noble general to entertain any thoughts of laying down his commission . . .

Lambert added that if Fairfax did resign, he was 'very fearful of the mischiefs which might ensue' and Harrison that it would 'sadden the hearts of many of God's people'. Lambert's point was a strong one, for Fairfax's departure would be a major setback to the regime's efforts to establish a puritan consensus and its own respectability. The discussion continued, 'allmost all the night' according to Lucy Hutchinson, but Fairfax was adamant. When the committee reported back on the 'lord general's total averseness to march with the army into Scotland' a fresh effort was made to get him to relent, but he would not budge. According to Lucy Hutchinson, her husband

> and other parliament men, hearing of his intentions the night before, and knowing that he would thus levell the way to Cromwell's ambitious designes, went to him and labour'd to dissuade him; which they had effected, but that the presbyterian ministers wrought with him to doe it. He exprest that he believed God lay'd him aside, as not being worthy of more, nor of that glory which was already given him.

Fairfax was prepared to make things as easy as possible for his old comrades, and though his letter to the Speaker did hint at the real problem by saying that 'it was fitt for mee seriously to consider how I might with good conscience take that trust', it made the grounds of his resignation 'debilities both in body and minde, occasioned by former actions and businesses'.

A committee of the House was then sent to thank him for his services and to assure him of the House's continued confidence in him. Rushworth returned Fairfax's commission to Parliament, which voted him £5000 a year, repealed the ordinance appointing him commander of all their forces and voted to make Cromwell 'Captain-General and Commander-in-Chief' in his place. Every effort was made to reassure the public. Gardiner quotes one preacher as saying, 'What though your old Lord General be not with you, he is not against you . . . You have his heart still in the camp, though his spouse has persuaded his weary body to take rest in her bosom.' The Council gave him a pass to go abroad, but it is not known whether he availed himself of it.

The break had been coming for a long time. Fairfax did not at this stage have any real sympathy for the Royalists, though they eagerly read reports which suggested that he might, and the new King in exile was prepared to make him Earl of Essex and give him an estate worth over £10,000 a year and 'what place he pleased in England' if he would come over to the Royalist side. He still undoubtedly believed, as he had all along, in a limited monarchy, and would do nothing to prevent that coming about at some stage in the future. But it was not in his nature to betray his friends. He had, however, been increasingly unhappy about the course they were taking. Pride's purge had been a bad moment and above all he had been alienated by the killing of the King. He was a man who reacted slowly, who could be persuaded — for the moment — by the articulate and strong-minded, but who was more and more uneasy about the legal and moral basis of the revolutionary regime. As T. S. Eliot observed:

> The persons who opposed Charles I and the persons who supported the Commonwealth were not all of the flock of Zeal-of-the-land Busy or the United Grand Junction Ebenezer Temperance Association. Many of them were gentlemen of the time who merely believed, with considerable show of reason, that government by a Parliament of gentlemen was better than government by a Stuart.

Fairfax had shown signs already of his dissent in his refusal to serve as one of the judges at the King's trial and in his refusal to sign the engagement. Now, talking it over with Anne, perhaps with Rushworth and some of the Presbyterian ministers, he had suddenly reached the point where his whole nature said no.

Those in the Army who shared his point of view felt let down. Lucy Hutchinson, reflecting her husband's views, asserts bitterly that the throwing up of his commission 'could not have bene done more spitefully and ruinously to the whole parliamentary interest', that 'this greate man was then as unmoovable by his friends as pertinacious in obeying his wife, whereby he then died to all his former glory'. The editor of her memoirs of her husband, the Rev. Julius Hutchinson, in a footnote on Fairfax's resignation, maintained (in 1808) that it was a disaster,

> For it was only with the co-operation of a man, who to his martial talents, which certainly exceeded all of his time, added that moderation and integrity, that the great politicians of those days could have planned and finished such schemes of representation, legislation, and administration, as would have rendered the nation great and happy, either as a commonwealth or mixed government. They had in some respects such opportunities as can never again arise; and if the presbyterians have nothing else to answer for, the perverting of the judgement of this excellent man was a fault never to be forgiven . . .

So, like Cincinnatus, Fairfax retired to Nun Appleton, the Yorkshire house he loved best.

Marvell and Buckingham

IT WAS EIGHT YEARS since Fairfax had defended the bridge at Tadcaster and raided Sherburn-in-Elmet with Captain Hotham. He had risen from being nothing more than the young heir to a Yorkshire country gentleman to become the victor of Naseby and Langport and Lord General of all the forces of the Parliament. Now his active career was over and he was himself only a private country gentleman. Yet he was only 38.

He at once dropped out of the public eye and from now on references to him are rare. He was not included in the new Council elected in February 1651. He was a magnanimous man and observed Cromwell's victorious campaign in Scotland, which he might himself have commanded if he had wished, with no bitterness or jealousy. When, in September, news came of the brilliant victory won at Dunbar by Cromwell and by his own fellow-Yorkshireman, Lambert, Fairfax was with Ludlow at Hampton Court. Ludlow wrote that he 'seemed much to rejoice at it'. And later, when Cromwell fell ill in Scotland (suffering, like Fairfax, from the stone and the ague) Fairfax sent up his own doctors, Dr Wright and Dr Bates, in his own coach to look after him. When the Scots did come down into England it was reported that 'Sir Thomas Fairfax, through infirmity of body, desires to be excused from stirring in the work,' but he met Cromwell at Ferrybridge and drove three miles with him in his coach, so he was clearly still on good terms with him.

He built a new house in York, in Skeldergate, which was described as having a 'fine situation, by far the best in the town, with a noble ascent to it . . . and gardens extending to the ramparts of the city walls'. And now at last he was able to spend more time at Nun Appleton, where the brick house his grandfather had planned had just been finished. Here he settled down with the devoted, courageous and tough-minded Anne, and was able to see more of his only daughter Mary — little Moll — who as a child had been carried on the great ride to Hull but who was now a girl of 12. He needed a tutor for her, especially to give her a grounding in languages.

The man he chose was the 29-year-old Andrew Marvell, son of an Anglican clergyman, who had travelled on the Continent, acquired some knowledge of foreign languages, written some poems displaying Royalist sympathies and, just recently, 'An Horation Ode upon Cromwell's Return from Ireland', a brilliant but even-handed topical poem. Marvell came to Nun Appleton towards the end of 1650 or early in 1651, and somewhere about this time he was converted from being an opponent to becoming a supporter of the Puritan cause. Perhaps talking to Fairfax may have played a part in this. Aubrey describes him as 'a great master of the Latin tongue', as 'roundish faced, cherry-cheek't, hazell eie . . . in his conversation very modest, and of very few words'.

Marvell stayed at Nun Appleton for two years and was clearly very happy there, loving the place — especially the garden running down to the water meadows, or 'ings' as they were called, and the river, the Yorkshire countryside, the ordered life of a manor house, the company of the general and the delightful and talented small girl he had to look after and instruct. He wrote several notable poems at Nun Appleton, including probably his four poems about mowers, inspired by the hayfields below the garden wall, and elegant epigrams in Latin and English addressed to Fairfax and the local hills which 'quake as equals under Fairfaxian sway'. 'Upon the Hill and Grove at Bill-borow' was dedicated to Fairfax and invited steeper mountains to

> Learn here those humble steps to tread,
> Which to securer glory lead.

It was probably Moll who, disguised as 'Celia', 'Now learns the tongues of France and Italy,' but remained essentially York-shire:

> no other grace
> But her own smiles commend that lovely face;
> Her native beauty's not Italianated,

> Nor her chaste mind into the French translated:
> Her thoughts are English, though her sparkling wit
> With other language doth them fitly fit.

He celebrated the house and its ordered life, the Fairfax family, the garden and his own happiness in two poems, 'Upon Appleton House' and 'The Garden.' Again he stressed its quintessential Englishness:

> Within this sober frame expect
> Work of no foreign architect . . .
> . . . all things are composèd here
> Like Nature, orderly and near:

Curiously Marvell remarked on Nun Appleton's modest size:

> And surely when the after age
> Shall hither come in pilgrimage,
> These sacred places to adore,
> By Vere and Fairfax trod before,
> Men will dispute how their extent
> Within such dwarfish confines went:

reflecting that

> Humility alone designs
> Those short but admirable lines

though Nun Appleton was hardly then or now what most people would call 'dwarfish'.

He noted the Fairfaxes' hospitality, inviting in

> Daily new furniture of friends

and reflected that the house, like all houses, was a temporary resting place

> And for an inn to entertain
> Its Lord a while, but not remain.

Fairfax was to hark back to this later when he himself wrote a poem about the reconstructed house — 'the new building at Apleton' — saying

> Thinke not O Man that dwell's herein
> This House a Stay, But as an Inne.

Above all Marvell celebrates Nun Appleton's situation, deep in the English countryside, with

> . . . fragrant gardens, shady woods,
> Deep meadows, and transparent floods.

where the stock-dove, nightingale, kingfishe, throstle, heron and landrail nested and

> I, easy philosopher,
> Among the birds and trees confer.

Here the general had laid out his flower beds in the form of a fort, with five bastions, where war was far away, and

> Tulips, in several colours barred,
> Were then the Switzers of our Guard.

But Marvell could not fail to think aloud:

> And yet there walks one on the sod
> Who, had it pleasèd him and God,
> Might once have made our gardens spring
> Fresh as his own and flourishing,
> But he preferred to the Cinque Ports
> These five imaginary forts . . .
> For he did, with his utmost skill,
> Ambition weed, but conscience till —

It was no more than a hint, but it was the same thought that Lucy Hutchinson had had when Fairfax had resigned.

There were stanzas full of extravagant conceits about the delightful Moll:

> Maria such, and so doth hush
> The world, and through the evening rush

> 'Tis she that to these gardens gave
> That wondrous beauty which they have

> This 'tis to have been from the first
> In a domestic heaven nursed,
> Under the discipline severe
> Of Fairfax, and the starry Vere.

Their lessons sound to have been agreeable:

> She counts her beauty to converse
> In all the languages as hers;

And in this enchanted world, Marvell was blissfully content:

> What wondrous life is this I lead!
> Ripe apples drop about my head . . .
> The nectarene, and curious peach,
> Into my hands themselves do reach;
> Stumbling on melons, as I pass,
> Ensnared with flowers, I fall on grass.
>
> Meanwhile the mind, from pleasures less,
> Withdraws into its happiness . . .
> Annihilating all that's made
> To a green thought in a green shade.

Marvell left Fairfax's employment late in 1652 or early in 1653. Fairfax may not himself have thought his life at Nun Appleton 'wondrous' but it was agreeable enough, even for a man with damaged health. He was a greatly respected figure with, living round him, a wide circle of relations and friends. His uncle Henry was the rector of Bolton Percy, with his two young sons Henry and Brian. Sisters, uncles and cousins lived close by. The formidable old Lady Vere was still alive and came to stay with them. He had his estate and garden, his oaks, cows, horses and three hundred deer in the park. He had his great hall, fifty yards long, hung with armorial shields, and his collection of coins and medals. He was, like the late Lord Wavell, a soldier who loved words, and spent long hours in his splendid library. In a volume preserved in the Bodleian Library are his own metrical version of the psalms and Biblical songs, entitled 'the Imployment of my Solitude', translations of Latin authors and painstaking verse (entitled 'The Recreation of my Solitude') which, sadly, altogether lack the magic touch of his young tutor. Horace Walpole commented characteristically on this, saying:

Of all Lord Fairfax's works, by far the most remarkable were some verses which he wrote on the horse on which Charles the second rode to his coronation, and which had been bred and presented to the king by his lordship. How must that merry monarch, not apt to keep his countenance on more serious occasions, have smiled at this awkward homage from the old victorious hero of republicanism and the covenant!

Fairfax was more at home in putting down in prose the fruits of his long experience in the breeding of horses. He described with expertise and authority the qualities he looked for in them, such as 'courage to bear themselves gracefully and not to faint upon light Causes'. He wrote of the need to improve the old English breed 'because naturally ours be more phlegmatic than those which are bred nearer the Sun', of the high qualities of the horses of Naples, of 'the Barbary Jennet and Turk', of the breed he himself liked best of all, the 'Courser', and of Dutch mares. He gave his considered views on how horses should be looked after — they could be pastured with cows, but not with deer, sheep or conies — how they should be fed and how breeding should be managed.

He had been voted large sums of money by Parliament. It appears that these were never paid to him, but in partial payment of his own arrears he was given some portions of the immense confiscated Buckingham lands. These were the estate of Helmsley, where he had been wounded outside the castle walls, which included the lands of Rievaulx Abbey, the magnificent York House in the Strand in London, and the estates of Burley in Rutland and Newhall in Essex. But these, according to Brian Fairfax, he 'never accounted his own'.

In October 1651 Parliament, 'in public gratitude of his high deserts', granted him the seignory of the Isle of Man, previously owned by the Stanleys. He appointed commissioners to look after it, and directed them to apply the funds of the sequestrated bishopric to the needs of the ordinary clergy, and to the establishing of four new grammar schools. All the ordinary rents, which most people in those times would have unblushingly pocketed, he had paid over to the former owner, no less than the 'lady of Lathom', the widowed Lady Derby.

He was of course out of sympathy with the republic, and the agents of Thurloe, head of Cromwell's intelligence service, brought their master regular reports of Fairfax's involvement in Royalist intrigues. But most of these were almost certainly false. In 1653, a year in which he was apparently offered but refused a place in Cromwell's new council, some members of Parliament may have hoped to involve him and Lambert in other plots against Cromwell, but they received no encouragement. There was too, little substance in the fears of some Independents in the army that Fairfax might be brought back to replace Cromwell and inaugurate a Presbyterian millenium. He and Lambert were included among the commissioners appointed in Yorkshire to judge the fitness of those appointed to benefices and remove those who were 'ignorant, scandalous' or 'insufficient'.

Next year Fairfax was elected one of the Yorkshire members in Cromwell's parliament but appears again not to have taken his seat. In 1655 a Cromwellian agent reported that Sir Henry Slingsby had given Anne a letter from the King, and Fairfax wrote to Cromwell apologising for having been in touch with the King and asking permission for a person of quality, in fact Rochester, to leave the Kingdom. That year Cromwell set up the rule of the Major-Generals, who, according to Clarendon, 'carried themselves like so many bassa's [pashas] with their bands of janizaries and were extremely odious to all parties'. The Major-General for the northern counties was John Lambert, but he governed through two deputies, the one at York being Colonel Robert Lilburne. In 1656 Fairfax and Anne were in London a good deal and were visited, 'by his Highnes' command', by Richard Cromwell and Fleetwood and some members of the Council. But they themselves did not go to see Cromwell and his wife. They had evidently drifted apart.

In 1657 Mary was 19 and was engaged to be married to Philip Stanhope, Lord Chesterfield. It appears that Fairfax and Anne had, uncharacteristically, paid more attention to their prospective son-in-law's rank than to his character, for Swift later described Chesterfield as 'the greatest knave in England'.

But in that year there suddenly appeared in England a grander catch altogether, the 30-year-old George Villiers, second duke of Buckingham. He and his brother, sons of James I's catamite, had been brought up with Charles I's children. They had been abroad during the first civil war but had fought for the Royalists in the second, when Francis had been killed. George had been with Charles II in Scotland and at the battle of Worcester before which, according to Clarendon, he annoyed the King by asking to be made commander-in-chief. After that he, like the King, had fled to the Continent, where he had been living off the sale of his father's splendid collection of pictures, including Titian's *Ecce Homo*, and had paid court to the widowed Princess Royal, mother of the future King William III. He had now come to England with a pass given to him by Cromwell, who seemed to want to win him over from Charles II's circle at the Hague. It is difficult to form an impression of what he was really like. Seventeenth-century portraits are frequently inadequate, and those of Buckingham give little idea of his personality. The Lely in the National Portrait Gallery shows a rather pudding-faced, aldermanic figure, but contemporaries agree that he was irresistibly attractive. Bishop Burnet describes him as a man 'of noble presence', Horace Walpole as 'this extraordinary man, with the figure and genius of Alcibiades'. Fairfax's cousin Brian called him 'the most graceful and beautiful person that any Court in Europe ever saw'. Evidently he was a sort of seventeenth-century Gary Cooper.

Not only were his physical attractions legendary, but he was clearly a man of many talents, perpetuated in Dryden's lines:

> A man so various that he seemed to be
> Not one, but all mankind's epitome:
> Stiff in opinions, always in the wrong;
> Was every thing by starts, and nothing long . . .

Buckingham was a brave man but he wasted his talents, dissipated his great fortune, and was eventually described as 'worn to a thread with whoring'. But in 1657 it was by no means apparent that he was an unsatisfactory character.

When he arrived in London, with extremely expensive tastes but no money, and his only asset his personal attractions, his first objective was, obviously, the repossession of some at least of his estates. According to Brian Fairfax, 'The Duke heard how kind and generous my lord Fairfax was to the countess of Derby' and 'had reason to hope my lord had the same inclinations as to this estate of his.' Fairfax had a noble, selfless notion that he held his part of the confiscated Buckingham estates in a sort of trust. To a man like Buckingham the solution was obvious — marry the sole heiress, the innocent Mary, and recover the estates.

There is no record of precisely how the thing was done. But done it was. Colonel Bampfylde, a Parliamentary agent, was soon telling Thurloe: 'It is believed that Buckingham is privately in England with [your] consent, and treating for a marriage with Lord Fairfax's daughter. This seems a little romantic . . .' The report went up to Cromwell, who, not surprisingly, refused to believe it. Edward Hyde, the future Earl of Clarendon, was equally incredulous, writing, 'Did not till this very minute believe that Fairfax would or could have given his daughter to my Lord of Buckingham.' But a member of the Council noted that, although Mary's banns had twice been published at St Martin's, Westminster, her engagement to Lord Chesterfield had been broken off, and commented, 'I think the sole design to be a Duchess made them forbid the banns.' Chesterfield went off to console himself with the 17-year-old Barbara Villiers, the future mistress of Charles II.

It is hard to believe that Fairfax and Anne — and old Lady Vere — had become dedicated social climbers in the evening of their days, and were prepared to consign their only child to such a husband, but the fact remains that they did it. It is impossible to say why. It is difficult not to share the bafflement of Clarendon and Cromwell, though Cromwell was in no position to cast a stone, for he had earlier thought of Buckingham as a husband for his own daughter Mary. Of course Buckingham was still young, and his life so far had been relatively blameless. And he was a dazzling figure, only just short of royalty itself. Fairfax seems to have been bowled over by Buckingham's personality. Mary, when she met him, fell hopelessly in love, and remained devoted to him through all that followed. And yet it must have been so obvious that Buckingham's designs were strictly material.

Mary was no longer the enchanted child of Marvell's poems seven years before. She had turned out a plain girl, described as 'laide, intelligente et cultivée'. It must have been clear enough that Buckingham did not want to marry her for her personal attractions. But still Fairfax, brought up in a stern Yorkshire school, agreed to it. It is sad, and inexplicable.

The wedding took place at Bolton Percy in September with Abraham Cowley the poet as best man, who celebrated the affair with a mildly fatuous sonnet. Cromwell, who not unnaturally regarded an alliance between Fairfax and Buckingham as potentially dangerous to him, did what he could to prevent it and even sent a squadron of cavalry north to arrest Buckingham and take him to Jersey, but his men were too late — Fairfax telling them that Buckingham and Mary were no longer at Nun Appleton. Nevertheless they forced Buckingham into hiding and he had to abandon his bride for a while. Not surprisingly, she, poor girl, was described as being 'transcendentally pensive'.

Buckingham duly had the Helmsley estates and York House restored to him and he and Mary went to live in London. When, in due course, he went on a clandestine visit to his sister, the Duchess of Richmond, he was arrested and thrown into the Tower. Fairfax was incensed and went up to London, this time to see the Protector. He saw him twice and Anne went to see Cromwell's wife. Cromwell, according to Thurloe, told Fairfax that he should have consulted 'with his old freinds, that had wente alonge with him in all the warrs', while Fairfax argued that Buckingham 'was a better man then the world tooke him to be'. Cromwell seemed inclined to set Buckingham free, but his council advised against it.

In February 1658 Fairfax came up to Parliament, but refused to take the oath. One of Edward Hyde's informants told him

> that the major part of the House had resolved to remove into the City, vote the old Parliament [in], make Fairfax general, and re-establish the Common-wealth; that the Duke [of Buckingham] who is the oracle of his father, mother-in-law, and wife (who is the best of the four) agreed to this. Cromwell has now humbled the Duke who does all he can to incense Fairfax to revenge, but he is more likely to be prevented than brought to act for he is a slow beast and inconstant.

In August Fairfax tackled Cromwell again about Buckingham, still confined to the Tower. Cromwell, who was by then a very sick man, remonstrated with him for marrying his daughter to an out-and-out Royalist. Fairfax defended Buckingham. The conversation inevitably became acrimonious. Fairfax, according to Brian, was 'put into a great passion, turning abruptly from him in the gallery at Whitehall, cocking his hat, and throwing his cloak under his arm, as he used to do when he was angry'. Ten days later Cromwell was dead.

When Richard Cromwell convened his first parliament in January 1659 Fairfax was elected a Yorkshire member. This time he did take his seat, and next month petitioned for Buckingham's release. He was well received and Sir Arthur Hazelrig said, 'I bless God that the noble Lord who sits by me, having received so many wounds, is here on my right hand.' Members, including Harry Vane and Anthony Ashley Cooper, supported Fairfax's plea, Mr

Onslow arguing that as Fairfax had 'been trusted with three nations, he may well be trusted with a single person'. Buckingham was released, but only after Fairfax had to give security amounting to £20,000 that Buckingham would 'peaceably demean himself for the future' and not join with the enemies of the Lord Protector. Buckingham returned with Fairfax to Nun Appleton. He and Mary spent the rest of the year there with the Fairfaxes. In the House Fairfax was extolled by Hazelrig and his friends, but he rarely spoke. When he did, he did not make much of a mark as an orator, one speech being described as only 'so, so'.

Fairfax and the Restoration

I N THE SPRING of 1659 the inadequate Richard Cromwell was thrust aside by the Army under Fleetwood, Lambert and Desborough. They recalled the Rump of the Long Parliament, which had been ejected six years before. Fairfax was made a member of the Council of State set up the following month, but he ignored the appointment and stayed in Yorkshire. In August a series of Royalist revolts, some under old Civil War veterans like Massey and Byron, were suppressed, the only serious threat coming from Sir George Booth in Cheshire and Lancashire. But his forces were crushed by republican troops under Lambert. Yorkshire stayed quiet. Charles II and his court at Brussels, hoping to take advantage of a rising to restore the monarchy with the help of foreign troops, had their hopes dashed. The victorious army demanded independence from Parliamentary control, and when the Rump tried to assert its authority in mid-October Lambert and his troops threw it out. Fleetwood and Lambert then set up a Committee of Safety to run the country.

Fairfax's old Yorkshire comrade-in-arms, John Lambert, became the central figure in the new regime, and there was even talk of marriage between his daughter and Charles II. But military rule, by a group of generals who seldom agreed, was intensely unpopular. The Rump and the Army were equally detested in the country and the military failed entirely to establish their authority. The commander in Scotland, the cautious but astute George Monk, whom Fairfax had long ago captured at Nantwich, now came out against his fellow generals and for the Rump, and proceeded to purge his forces of anabaptists and extreme republicans.

Fairfax concluded that what he had stood for ever since the beginning of the first Civil War could best be achieved by a free

Parliament — that is, the re-establishment of the full Long Parliament, including the secluded members who had been ejected by Colonel Pride twelve years before. He, and those who thought like him, undoubtedly recognised that an inevitable consequence of such a free Parliament would be the restoration of a (hopefully chastened) monarchy. Since restiveness under the Committee of Safety was becoming universal and Monk was in Scotland, Fairfax had a pivotal position in Yorkshire, midway between Scotland and London. York was the heart and soul of northern England, and his great personal prestige, above all in the Army, offered him a crucial role. He alone could propose an honourable alternative to doubting troops.

In late October one of Monk's most trusted officers, Major-General Morgan, was in York, suffering (like so many officers of that time) from gout, and being looked after by a surgeon called John Troutbeck. The two of them went to sound out Fairfax at Nun Appleton. They showed him Monk's declaration. According to Brian Fairfax, his cousin 'approved of it, but added withall that if Generall Monk had any other designe then to restore Parliaments to their antient freedome, and settle the Nation upon its antient Government Hee would Oppose him, but otherwise Hee would hartely Joyne with him.' Edward Bowles, described as 'Lord Fairfax's Chaplain, Counsellor, and Agitator,' who 'dealt with the General about weighty and dangerous Affairs,' told them that while Fairfax and his friends were inclined to act with Monk they objected to his limiting that support to the Rump and a Commonwealth. Nevertheless, as one Thomas Gower wrote from York, 'It was thought fitting . . . to give the city of London encouragement that they might see such a considerable province as this county join in the same design and endeavour to vindicate themselves from slavery: these and several considerations . . . prevailed above the caution of many who thought it almost a desperate attempt to appear against 60 troops of horse quartered among and close by us.'

Morgan went north to report to Monk, who then sent down his brother-in-law Clarges to York to discuss plans for a rising. Clarges saw Bowles, who in turn went to Nun Appleton to see Fairfax. Fairfax who, according to Clarendon, had received a letter from the King, delivered to him by Sir Horatio Townsend, talked it over with his brother-in-law Henry Arthington and with Buckingham (it was safest at this stage to confine consultations to those with close family links) and agreed to lead an armed rising in January. He then brought in Major Smithson, who had married his niece, and one of his old officers, Colonel Hugh Bethell, and contacted the Royalist Sir Philip Monckton in York, who believed he had owed his life to an intervention by Fairfax in 1648. He brought in others too. Gower wrote from York on 17 December, 'There hath been a great meeting of several gentlemen of quality at York, which some take ombrage at.'

In the meantime the republicans had not been idle. Lambert marched north and reached York on 7 November, joining forces with Colonel Robert Lilburne. He had under him about 12,000 men and it was only two-and-a-half months since he had crushed Booth's rising in the north, so Fairfax's prospects looked cloudy.

Lambert made his headquarters at Newcastle and by December his troops had cut off communications with Scotland. Fairfax sent one Captain Bacon to try to reach Monk by way of Durham and Newcastle but he was arrested. Fairfax's cousin Brian now arrived at Nun Appleton. Fairfax 'sayd here is my Cosen Brian, I will undertake that hee shall do this business'. Brian was promptly sent off with an urgent oral message to Monk 'to desire him to bee carefull in case Lamberts Army or any part of ye Rere of it should fall back into Yorkshire . . .' He was briefed by Bowles and disguised by Buckingham as a 'yong Contry clowne'. He then had an epic and dangerous mid-winter ride over the fells of Westmorland and Cumberland, by way of Kendal, Penrith and Hawick, bluffing his way past Lambert's men, narrowly escaping from a disreputable moss trooper, finally reaching Coldstream and giving his message on Christmas Day to Monk, who assured him that he would watch Lambert as a cat watched a mouse. Brian also surprised his uncle Charles Fairfax, who was serving with Monk, and met his servant Richard Smyth, who was later to work for Thomas Fairfax at Nun Appleton. He had an equally hazardous ride back, finding that the troop of Lambert's cavalry at Brampton had decamped when they heard that Fairfax was coming out against them, 'for as Mr Bowles used to say of my Lord ff: hee was like a great Bull, long a raysing, but being up, hee made a great noyse'.

Brian's brother Henry had been despatched on a similar errand to Overton at Hull, but had met with no success, for Overton was preoccupied with religious enthusiasm, and decided to remain neutral.

Just before Brian arrived in Coldstream, Fleetwood and his colleagues in London, fast losing control, had given up, and the Rump took over again on Boxing Day. Lambert now had nothing behind him. But he got wind of Fairfax's intentions. He sent Lilburne down with 'a Captain of horse called Turner, a Quaker', 500 picked cavalrymen and orders to seize Fairfax and secure York. Fairfax and Buckingham had to move hurriedly, but temporarily, from Nun Appleton to avoid arrest by the party of horse sent to pull them in. Fairfax got away to Selby, 'passing Armin and Castleton Ferry into Marshland', while in York it was believed that they had fled to Leeds.

Fairfax had planned his rising for the first of January, but in the light of the leaks he decided to act a few days earlier. Dr John Price recorded that 'he was too politick to be taken napping' and 'thus Intelligence came to us that the Lord Fairfax was up, in and about York: and that to him had joyned almost all Col. Lilburn's Regiment of Horse, who, neglecting their Colonel, followed the commands of their Major, Smithson . . .'

Brian records that when he left Nun Appleton, Fairfax was 'very ill both with the gout and Stone', so that he had to travel in his coach, but that he was determined to keep his promise to Monk. While his friends in the East Riding came together at Malton and others in the North Riding were gathering at Kirby Moorside and Helmsley, he himself, with a party of about a dozen, set out in deep snow. 'My Lord,' writes Brian, 'was so ill that he was forced to stay at the Papermill in the Parish of Oglethorp, an hower, where he voyded a Stone.'

Near Harewood they met twenty troopers of Lilburne's regiment, three or four of whom, 'pulling down their Montero Capps' rode alongside the coach. Fairfax got ready his pistols but the men rode off. His party travelled on to Arthington, picking up twenty supporters.

Things did not look good. Fairfax, ill in bed, sent for Brian and told him, 'Cosen, you are unacquainted with these things, wee have here some honest contry gentlemen that are willing to venter their Lives, but alas what can wee do if any part of Lamberts Army come upon us. If I had (sayth hee) such a Troop as I had the beginning of the Warr, I would not feare him, for I would venter to go with them all England over.'

He planned to go to his other house at Denton and try to defend himself there until the situation cleared. But at this dark moment a 'Gentleman knocked at the Gates'. It was an officer of the 'Irish Brigade', that is the brigade brought across from Ireland to help suppress Booth's rising, who said that 1200 men of the brigade were at Fairfax's service and would meet him on Marston Moor to receive his orders. This was an extraordinary tribute to Fairfax's personal prestige — 'so much', wrote Bishop Burnet, 'did he still maintain his great credit with the army'. It changed the whole aspect of affairs, although the brigade was, in fact, torn by conflicting loyalties. The distracted troopers had confidence in their old Captain General, and were prepared to put their future in his hands.

Next day Fairfax moved to Knaresborough, where he picked up his son-in-law Buckingham and four cavalry troops commanded by Bethell, Smithson and Cholmley. He travelled on to Marston Moor, where he had fought and been wounded sixteen years before. Here the Irish Brigade — nine or ten troops — was drawn up. Either they (according to Strangeways) or the officers with Fairfax (according to Brian Fairfax) objected to Buckingham being there, and he was compelled to withdraw.

The rendezvous now began to take on a political tinge, which must have been all too familiar to Fairfax, with his memories of Triploe Heath and Corkbush Field. The brigade, like the rest of the Army, were strongly opposed to the restoration of the monarchy, and a declaration supporting the Rump was read at the head of each troop. All present were asked to sign it. Fairfax and his friends refused, but in the subsequent discussion the differences were settled, or glossed over, and eventually the brigade expressed its support for Fairfax with loud shouts and set off with him for York, arriving outside the walls, where he had earlier taken part in the siege of 1644, on New Year's Day 1660. Fairfax sent in a trumpeter to summon Lilburne's forces to surrender. He naturally wanted to avoid an assault on his own city, most of whose inhabitants were wholly with him. Bowles and Monckton made contact inside the city and Monckton secured the Minster and rang the bells there, and elsewhere the cry was raised for Fairfax.

Lilburne now thought up an ingenious plan. He offered to let into York those who would subscribe a declaration for the Rump and against 'a King or any Single Person whatsover'. This was acceptable to the Irish Brigade, whose officers promptly signed it, but entirely unacceptable to Fairfax, who tore it up before their faces. Lilburne had skilfully managed to sow dissension in the ranks of his opponents.

The situation looked ugly. Brian records that his uncle 'immediately went to the head of his own troops . . . drawn out in the fields towards Popleton . . .' and continues disarmingly:

> I was now really afraid that we were going to charge one another, which was a new thing to me, and I did not like it. I never stirred from my Lord Fairfax, and I had an excellent horse that the Duke of Buckingham valued at £100 under me . . . But my heart had failed me had not my Lord Fairfax's looks encouraged me. He began to be another man, his motions so quick, his eyes so sparkling, giving the word of command like a General, that I took heart, and I think I could have charged with him.

But eventually Fairfax agreed that the Irish Brigade and some of Smithson's might enter the city, while he and his supporters stayed outside. Lambert's forces did approach, but had lost heart, and next morning Fairfax had a fresh reinforcement of 400 men. Lilburne now abandoned his efforts to keep Fairfax out of York. Lambert and the handful of men left to him rode south, where he gave himself up. In due course the Rump put him in the Tower.

Fairfax went off to spend the night with his widowed sister at Poppleton, whence he, Cholmley and Arthington wrote to the Speaker saying,

> We have this Day taken *York*, and now understanding that the Lord *Lambert* hath submitted, we conceive there will be no further use of us; and do therefore intend (after a Day's Refreshment of our Men) to send them home. And we desire you to be assured, that what hath been done, was only in Order to your Service . . . As for the Duke of *Buckingham* being with us, it was meerly accidental, and having been forced together with my Lord *Fairfax* to leave his own House, he came to us only for Safety as a private Man; and upon Exceptions against him withdrew himself . . .

Fairfax's job, essential though it had been, was done, and being without personal ambition, he had no desire to set up as a warlord or to take a hand in the political confusion in London. Provided that

Monk acted sensibly, he was content to leave the task to him. Many found this hard to understand. Gower wrote:

> My Lord Fairfax hath laid down his arms, and with them an opportunity, in some men's opinion, to make himself great, and the nation quiet by a free Parliament; it is most certain he might have done what he list; Lambert's army disbanded and melted, only by the fame of his rising; the Irish Brigade sent an officer to let him know that most of them had served under him, and now offered themselves to be ordered by him . . . most of Lambert's men had the same resolutions . . . we are assured London had their eye principally upon him; and though all this and more was fully represented, yet he chose rather to sit down contented with the thanks of the House, than to make use of these great opportunities. Some ascribe it to dulness, others that an order of Parliament hath more power upon him then all reason; some to farther design not yet ripe . . .

It was true that his intervention had contributed greatly to producing the disintegration of Lambert's army of 12,000, thus enabling Monk to make a bloodless march to London. Probably no other man could have won over Lambert's troops so quickly and so decisively.

Monk, telling the Speaker that Fairfax had been 'very forward to runne any hazards for the freedome of his Country and the priviledges of Parliament', now moved south and was in York from 12 to 17 January, appointing Fairfax's uncle Charles as its military governor. It was reported that the House had 'found Fairfax's letter satisfactory, in spite of charges by Lambert and Lilburn that he designed Charles Stuart's interest'. He dined privately with Monk, taking Bowles with him, and Monk dined with him at Nun Appleton. Bowles is said to have urged Monk to stay in York and declare for the King. No doubt Fairfax who, unlike Monk, said what he thought, argued for a free Parliament and the restoration of the monarchy. Brian Fairfax claimed much later that Monk offered to resign his command to Fairfax but that Fairfax refused, and Burnet has the same story, adding that Monk 'was so reserved to him, that Fairfax did not know how to depend on him'. Monk's version, in a letter of 21 January, that Fairfax had 'assured mee in a privat conference that hee would joyne with mee to the opposeing of Charles Stuart's family', sounds to be a fabrication. In fact Monk was keeping his options open and being careful not to commit himself. His public statements gave no comfort to the Royalists —

indeed he condemned the monarchy in a letter to the Devon gentry on 23 January, and next month broke down the City of London's chains and gates on the orders of the Rump.

Fairfax stayed in York when Monk marched south and ignored his own appointment to a new Council of State. He and his friends, and, increasingly, the gentry all over England, regarded the recall of the Rump as no solution, and a large meeting was held in York to consider what action to take. The worried Council of State in London sent orders to Colonels Smithson and Charles Fairfax to prevent any further meetings, if necessary by arresting the participants.

But Fairfax was not to be intimidated. Nor was he deterred by a letter from his uncle, the military governor, warning him that a further meeting might get him into trouble. He replied disingenuously that it would only be a very small meeting and would do nothing that was not just and honest. General Morgan, who arrived the day before, added his authority in claiming that a gathering would be 'of ill report and prove offensive' and might lead to the 'imbrueing these poor nations into blood again'. But these attempts at pressure miscarried. Fairfax and his friends, who included the most influential of the Yorkshire gentry, the High Sheriff, and the Lord Mayor of York, signed and published a declaration in forthright terms.

This pointed out that Yorkshire had no representation in the Rump to express their grievances, spoke of 'our common freedom as Englishmen, too much of late violated', and demanded the readmission of the members excluded in 1648 and the filling up of all vacancies. Otherwise they demanded that a new Parliament be elected with no other qualifications than those in force before 1648. If their demands were not met, they said, then they would be denied the fundamental right of Englishmen to give their consent to the laws of the land through elected representatives, and, that being so, they would pay no taxes.

Fairfax wrote two letters to Monk, one a covering letter to the declaration, the other a private letter, explaining that the meeting had not included any who had borne arms against Parliament, and that he had kept the numbers down to avoid stirring up trouble. But he pointed out that those who had signed were 'for quality, estate and callings the most interested in the country, with the concurrence of many thousand more'. The declaration, coming from Fairfax, who had himself a great name and had been so recently in touch with Monk, made more impression than any of the similar calls coming from other parts of the country, though Monk sent him only a temporising reply on 18 February. Lady Willoughby wrote to Edward Hyde on the 17th, saying that 'Fairfax and a great party with him are for the King.'

At this point Monk at last changed course and turned on the Rump, demanding (as Fairfax had urged) that the vacant seats in Parliament should be filled. So they were, and the new House elected a new Council of State, which included Fairfax, though he still preferred to stay at Nun Appleton.

On 16 March 1660 the Long Parliament at long last voted its own dissolution, and in the election which followed Fairfax was returned for Yorkshire as senior knight of the shire. Lambert escaped from the Tower next month, to be recaptured twelve days later. At the beginning of May Fairfax was chosen with, of all people, Denzil Holles, to be one of the House of Commons's twelve commissioners to take to the Hague their reply to a letter Charles II had sent to the House. In this the House described the killing of Charles I as 'the Act of some few ambitious and bloody Persons'. The commissioners urged the King's swift return to London to 'take the government of the Kingdom into his hands'. Fairfax spent a week in the Low Countries, had an interview with the King and was given the Royal pardon. But that was all he was given — or wanted. Monk soon had the Garter and a Dukedom and was made Master of the Horse and First Lord of the Treasury. Rewards were scattered far and wide. It was not a pretty business. The odious court toady Henry Jermyn 'received many rewards and offices' whereas next year the old cavalry leader Marmaduke Langdale 'begged to be excused attendance at the King's coronation on the ground that he was too poor'. Fairfax was another old soldier who had played a key part but who was given no mark of Royal thanks.

Fairfax was against the paying off of old scores. When the House discussed possible exceptions to an amnesty, Ludlow records that 'the Lord Fairfax on that subject plainly said that if any man must be excepted, he knew no man that deserved it more than himself, who being General of the army at that time, and having power sufficient to prevent the proceedings against the King, had not thought fit to make use of it to that end'. They were the words of an honest man, at a time when few had the courage to speak out, but clearly his conscience was troubling him.

The new King made no gesture to Fairfax, but Fairfax made a gesture to him, lending him the horse on which he rode to his coronation. Its dam was the mare Fairfax had ridden at Naseby.

Disillusion

The soul's dark cottage, battered and decayed,
Lets in new light through chinks that time hath made;
Stronger by weakness, wiser men become
As they draw near to their eternal home:

Edmund Waller

FORTUNATE is the man who, in his last years, enjoys fair health and vigour, can see his children happily married and his life's work bearing fruit, and can take pride in the standing of his own country. For Fairfax, sadly, none of this was true. When Charles II was crowned Fairfax was still under 50, but his health was bad and he was in constant physical pain. And what he heard about his only daughter and about the state of England must have given him a different sort of pain.

Mary was now a great personage, the first lady of the land after the Queen and the Duchess of York, but her life was not a happy one. Buckingham had married her to get his property back, and as time went on he paid less and less attention to her. He was sent to help escort the old Queen and the young Princess Henrietta on a visit to England and on the Princess's return to Paris he pursued her with such abandon that he became a nuisance and had to be sent home. In the summer of 1662, when another equally unfortunate wife, Catherine of Braganza, came to England, he took up with one of her suite, 'a Portuguese nymph'. Four years later he began a long affair with the notorious Lady Shrewsbury, was involved in numerous brawls and was three times sent to the Tower for rowdiness. Two years after that he killed Lord Shrewsbury in a duel. The story went that Lady Shrewsbury, dressed as a page, held Buckingham's horse while he fought with and killed her husband, and afterwards went to bed with him, stained with her husband's blood. This lady he installed at his house and lived with openly, ignoring Mary's protests.

The scandal was considerable. The new Queen, who had been treated in much the same way by the King, sympathised with Mary's fate. According to Hamilton,

> Comme la duchesse de Buckingham étoit une petite ragote, à peu près de sa figure, qui n'avoit jamais eu d'enfants, et que son époux abandonnoit pour une autre; cette espèce de parallèle entre leur fortunes intérressoit la reine pour elle; mais ce fut inutilement; personne n'y fit attention, et les moeurs du siécle allèrent leur train . . .

The Duke built a great house at Cliveden for Lady Shrewsbury, had their bastard son buried in Westminster Abbey, and gambled away his vast fortune. But just as the Queen seemed, through everything, to love the King, so Mary apparently continued to love her swaggering but worthless husband, and she had her more agreeable moments, as when she danced in a 'grand ballet' at court with the Queen, the Duchesses of Richmond and Monmouth and Louise de Kéroualle. Both Catherine and Mary seem to have been unfashionably petite, at a time when, to judge from Lely's portraits, the admired beauties of the day were sprawling and over-ripe. It is little wonder that Mary was described by the Vicomtesse de Long-ueville as 'much such another in person as the queen; a little round crumpled woman, very fond of finery'. Did Fairfax blame himself that his beloved little Moll should have come to this? He and Anne bore a heavy responsibility.

And what must his thoughts have been when, in a macabre and pointless gesture, the bodies of Cromwell and Ireton were dug up from under the floor of Westminster Abbey, dragged on hurdles to Tyburn and there first hung and then beheaded, their heads being stuck up to moulder on Westminster Hall, while the bodies of Sir William Constable, Pym, Admiral Blake and others were likewise exhumed and thrown into a pit? Or when his brave and brilliant commander of the dragoons, Colonel John Okey, and Colonel Barkstead, who had fought under him at Maidstone and failed to break into Colchester, were caught in Holland by the British Ambassador, Sir George Downing, brought back to England and hung, drawn and quartered as regicides? Downing, a former preacher in the New Model and chaplain to Okey's regiment, was described by

Burnet as a 'crafty fawning man', by Pepys as 'a perfidious rogue', and by Marvell as a man who 'like Judas betrayed his master'. He flourished after the Restoration and it is curious that it is after this dismal Vicar of Bray that we have chosen to name the London street where the Prime Minister lives and works.

Fairfax's friend and adviser Edward Bowles told Monk, 'As for me, I have buried the good old cause, and am now going to bury myself.' Fairfax himself lived through the humiliations of the reign of Charles II — a disreputable court, the Dutch fleet in the Medway, the shameful treaties of Dover, under which Charles II became the paid client of Louis XIV. It must all have been a misery to him, and no doubt he would have agreed with Macaulay's verdict that 'no part of our history, during the next three centuries, presents a spectacle of such general dreariness. The whole breed of our statesmen seems to have degenerated . . . their moral and intellectual littleness . . . in immediate contrast with the high and majestic qualities of the race which they succeeded.'

It was typical of the new regime that Buckingham, not Fairfax, was in 1661 made Lord Lieutenant of the West Riding. It fell to Buckingham to deal with two Yorkshire risings in 1662 and 1663, last despairing flings by supporters of the Good Old Cause, who apparently hoped that Fairfax might lead them. But they came to nothing and a hundred of the chief conspirators were arrested. Fairfax wrote to his son-in-law urging him to appoint officers 'whose discretion and moderation will more sweeten than exasperate the spirits of men' and advised him to take care to find out the real culprits and not to let others 'be destroyed and ruined by some men's private passions, under colour of doing public service'. We do not know whether Buckingham took any notice, but eighteen of the rebels were executed.

Some time during his last years Fairfax wrote his two *Short Memorials*, one a vivid account of his own part in 'the Northern Actions', the other — perhaps written later — a defence of his failure to prevent the purging of Parliament and the execution of the King. This last was a feeble effort, frequently inaccurate, the product of a tired, senile brain, and has done little for his reputation. Horace Walpole wrote of it tartly: 'One can easily believe his having been the tool of Cromwell, when one sees, by his own memoirs, how little idea he had of what he had been about.'

In those times, few people lived to a great age. Fairfax was only in his early fifties when Sir Thomas Widdrington, husband of his sister Frances, and his Uncle Henry died, and in 1665, the year of the Great Plague in London, Anne died at Nun Appleton. They had been married for twenty-eight years.. He himself was increasingly crippled by gout, and had to move around in a specially made chair with wooden wheels. Next year he made a will leaving Nun Appleton to Mary and Buckingham for their lives. He lived on for five more cheerless years.

The last of his letters to survive is a pathetic one, written in August 1670, to an unknown lady. It describes him as having been 'in the gout, and long time after lame in my hands' and thanks her for being 'pleased to let me know my daughter could not conveniently make a journey down this summer, which I did partly believe, though I should have been glad to see her'. That 'partly' makes one wince. He goes on:

> I shall beg once more you would be so charitable to deliver me from some trouble I am in, to let me know whither my daughter has gone, for I have not heard one word . . . it seems strange to me she should go to Calais, a garrison only of soldiers . . . neither can I think she would be so forgetful of me, without giving me some notice of her going out of the Kingdom, since it is no secret to others . . .

Fifteen months later he died at Nun Appleton and was buried with Anne in the medieval parish church at Bilbrough, 'in such manner', as he had directed, 'as may be convenient and decent rather than pompous'. Today only the chapel containing their fine tomb survives, for a later member of the Fairfax family had the small church demolished, allegedly because there was not room in it for all her staff. In its place her husband had erected, in 1873, a new, larger church which does not find favour with Pevsner.

The Duke and after him the Duchess held the Yorkshire properties for thirty years. Mary tried to sell Nun Appleton to settle her debts but could not do so as she had only a life interest. She died childless in 1704 and was buried in Henry VII's chapel in Westminster Abbey. The Yorkshire properties then went, as had the title, to the son of Henry Fairfax, who had been Rector of Bolton Percy.

The fifth Lord Fairfax, who took part in the revolution of 1688, married Catherine Culpeper of Leeds Castle in Kent, whose father had been given by the exiled Charles II all the vast tracts of land between the Potomac and the Rappahannock rivers in Virginia. After his death in 1710 she sold the Yorkshire estates. The new owner of Nun Appleton, Alderman Milner, demolished the two wings in 1712, divided the gallery into rooms and added a new south front with columns brought from Kirkham Abbey. The front elevation of the house is the only part that remains essentially as Fairfax left it. The park is still there, as are the vestiges of the nunnery and the meadows by the river, while not far away is the fine fifteenth-century church of Bolton Percy.

The sixth Lord Fairfax, a friend of Addison and Steele, sent his kinsman William to manage his estates in Virginia. William's daughter Anne married George Washington's elder brother. His sons were close friends of Washington when he was living at Mount Vernon. The sixth Lord then himself emigrated to America after he had been jilted by his fiancée. He gave his name to Fairfax County, Virginia, just outside Washington, between the Chesapeake Bay and the Blue Ridge Mountains, where today 'companies can locate in a quality suburban environment only minutes from the business and cultural advantages of the nation's capital'. Subsequent lords Fairfax lived in the United States. Two were killed in the American Civil War. Then the twelfth lord, Albert Kirby Fairfax, an American citizen, bought a house in London and eventually settled in England, making a collection of letters, tracts and pictures relating to the third Lord Fairfax and the Civil War. The Fairfax name has, therefore, lived on both in England and in the United States.

But Black Tom's own line came to an end when Mary died and he left no direct descendants. After more than three hundred years even his memory has faded. Yet he deserves to be remembered as one of the most interesting players in the drama of the English Civil War. He had notable qualities — dash, Yorkshire tenacity, and resilience. He was a splendid horseman and a sparkling though sometimes rash cavalry leader, courageous, moving very fast, taking risks and wasting no time. He never dawdled. In the north he won, or helped to win, some brilliant victories, on an increasingly large scale — at Sherburn-in-Elmet, Leeds, Wakefield, Nantwich and

Selby — a fine collection of battle honours. When he was defeated, as at Adwalton Moor or in his own part of the battle at Marston Moor, he was undismayed, and was swiftly in action again as if nothing had happened. He was at his best when things were at their worst. He played a major part, first in keeping Newcastle's large army pinned down in Yorkshire, and later in winning the north for Parliament. He was regarded with affection and respect by the men who fought under him.

He put together and commanded one of the finest armies England ever produced, the New Model. He led it to victory at the decisive battle of Naseby, at the battle of Langport, which he himself rated his greatest military success, and in the great winter campaign in the south-west.

Later, when he was caught up in a revolution, he was increasingly unhappy, for he remained a monarchist, had no use for the radical policies of Ireton or for those of the Levellers, and was shocked and dismayed by the killing of the King. But he believed all along in a monarchy controlled by Parliament, and was totally opposed to absolutism of the Louis XIV type, or to the doctrine of the divine right of kings. England did eventually evolve something like the system he would have liked to see. But when that happened Fairfax had been in his grave for two hundred years.

He was a modest man, absolutely honest, and lacking personal ambition. If he had wished to play a leading political role he could easily have done so by asserting himself after the close of the first civil war, or by taking charge of the northern movement for the restoration of Charles II, a role he was content to leave to Monk. He preferred to retreat to the gardens and water meadows at Nun Appleton, for at heart he remained a Yorkshire country gentleman, loving his horses, his books and his flowers.

He was no politician, but his reputation as a soldier is secure, and above all he comes down to us, after three centuries, as an attractive figure, a moderate, common-sense puritan and a gentle person, whom the rough forces of revolutionary change compelled to wield his sword all over England but who sought always to resist extremists and fanatics and to uphold the qualities of decency and good sense.

Book List

BOOKS ON FAIRFAX

(Fairfax MS Letters are to be found in the Bodleian, in the collection at Leeds Castle, Kent, and in that of Sonia, Lady Fairfax.) The principal published sources on Fairfax himself are Clements Markham's *A Life of the Great Lord Fairfax* (1870), a mine of detailed information, the four volumes of the *Fairfax Correspondence* (*Memoirs of the Reign of Charles the First* ed. George W. Johnson 1848 2 vols, and *Memorials of the Civil War* ed. Robert Bell 1849 2 vols) together with Fairfax's own *Short Memorials* of which the holograph is in the Bodleian Library (Fairfax MS 36) and the best published text in the *Antiquarian Repertory* (1808) Vol. III. There is another with notes by Sir Charles Firth in Arber's *Stuart Tracts 1603–1693: An English Garner* (1896).

M. A. Gibb's *The Lord General* (1938) includes the results of extensive research in the Thomason tracts in the British Library. For Fairfax's campaigns with the New Model army Joshua Sprigge's contemporary *England's Recovery* or *Anglia Rediviva* (1647) is of the first importance. Marvell's poems when he was tutor to Fairfax's daughter are in the *Complete Poems* (Penguin edition 1972). There is an article on 'The Fairfaxes of Denton and Nun Appleton' by Lockwood Huntley reprinted from the *Yorkshire Gazette* and published in 1906 and a chapter ('A Soldier') in G. C. Hesseltine's *Great Yorkshiremen* (1932). Other sundry pieces tend to draw almost entirely on Markham. An article on Fairfax and Culpeper portraits at Leeds Castle by David Cleggett appeared in *Virginia Cavalcade*, published by the Virginia State Library, Vol. XXXII, No. 3, Winter 1983, and one by Virginia Black on portraits of Fairfax ('The Search for "Black Tom" Fairfax') in *York Historian* Vol. 3 (1980) published by the Yorkshire Architectural and York Archeological Society.

CIVIL WAR PERIOD: GENERAL WORKS

For the period of the Civil War the rock on which every student has to build is Gardiner's *The History of the Great Civil War* (3 vols 1886–91) and the *History of the Commonwealth and Protectorate* (4 vols revised edition 1903). This seems to me narrative general history at its best (though Roland Usher's *A Critical Study of the Historical Method of Samuel Rawson Gardiner* (1915) needs to be looked at as a corrective. For texts, Gardiner's *Constitutional Documents of the Puritan Revolution 1625–1660* (1889) is valuable. The Thomason tracts in the British Library are of course invaluable. I found surprisingly useful — and readable — two earlier general histories, Guizot's *History of the English Revolution* (translated by William Hazlitt, 1854) and Ranke's

History of England principally in the Seventeenth Century (1875) — much quoted in Winston Churchill's *History of The English Speaking Peoples*. I found it a pleasure to have reason to read Clarendon's *History of the Rebellion*, since although too many documents are quoted at length it is a majestic work and contains many splendid passages. My own editions are those of 1704 and 1826. More recently there are Dame Veronica Wedgwood's volumes on *The King's Peace* (1955) and *The King's War* (1958) and her *Velvet Studies* (1946). There are of course many recent general works on the period, of which I have personally found valuable Barry Coward's *The Stuart Age* (1980) and J. P. Kenyon's *The Stuarts* (1958) and *Stuart England* (1978).

PRIMARY PUBLISHED SOURCES

These include *The Diary of Sir Henry Slingsby* (1836), *The Clarke Papers* (edited by Sir Charles Firth in 4 vols, 1891–1901), Henry Cary's *Memorials of the Great Civil War in England* (2 vols, 1842), *Reliquae Baxterianae* (1696), Carte's *A Collection of Original Letters and Papers . . . found among the Duke of Ormond's Papers* (1739) (which contains Colonel Edward Wogan's narrative of 'The Proceedings of the New-moulded army.'), Sir Philip Warwick's *Memoires of the reigne of King Charles I* (1701) John Vicars's three books — *Jehovah Jireh. God in the Mount* (1644), *God's Arke overtopping the . . . Waves* (1646) and *The Burning Bush Not Consumed* (1646), Francis Maseres's *Select Tracts relating to the Civil War in England* (1815) — which includes Denzil Holles's *Memoirs*, Major Huntingdon's *Sundry Reasons* and Hobbes's *Behemoth* — the *Autobiography* of Joseph Lister of Bradford (1842), the *Memoirs* of Sir Hugh Cholmley (1787), the *Lives of William Cavendish, Duke of Newcastle and of his wife* . . . by Margaret, Duchess of Newcastle (ed. C. H. Firth, 1886), the *Memoirs* of Edmund Ludlow, edited by Sir Charles Firth (1894), Thomas Malbon's *Memorials of the Civil War in Cheshire* (1889), *Bellum Civile. Hopton's Narrative of his Campaign in the West* (1902) and the *Memoirs of the Life of Colonel Hutchinson by his widow Lucy* (mine is the second, 1808, edition). Continuously useful are the various volumes of Bulstrode Whitelocke's *Memorials of the English Affairs* (1732 edition: first published 1682), Rushworth's *Historical Collections* (1680), the *Calendar of State Papers* Domestic Series & Addenda, 1625–1660 35 vols (1858–97) and the *Calendar of State Papers* (Venetian) 1628–60 (1911–35).

MILITARY WORKS

I found useful Alfred H. Burne's *The Battlefields of England* (1950) and *More Battlefields of England* (1952), *Sieges of the Great Civil War* by Peter Young and Wilfred Emberton (1978) and Peter Young's *The English Civil War: A military history of the Three Civil Wars* (1974), Sir Charles Firth's *Cromwell's Army* (1902), Sir John Fortescue's *Six British Soldiers* (1928), Lt Colonel T. S. Baldock's *Cromwell as a Soldier* (1899), Firth's and Davies's *Regimental History of Cromwell's Army* (1940) and Mark A. Kishlansky's *The Rise of the New Model Army* (1979).

SPECIALISED WORKS

I found particularly valuable J. T. Cliffe's *The Yorkshire Gentry from the Reformation to the Civil War* (1969). The same author has since written *The Puritan Gentry* (1984). R. R. Reid's *King's Council in the North* (1921) was of some use. D. Underdown's *Pride's Purge* (1971) is interesting and important.

BIOGRAPHIES

There are a great many of these. Of those on Cromwell I found helpful Christopher Hill's *God's Englishman* (1970) and his Historical Association pamphlet *Oliver Cromwell* (1958), Carlyle's *Oliver Cromwell's Letters and Speeches* (1845), W. C. Abbott's *The Writings and Speeches of Oliver Cromwell* (4 vols, 1937–47), Peter Young's *Oliver Cromwell* (1962), the biographies by John Morley (1900), Theodore Roosevelt (New York 1900), and John Buchan (1934) and Antonia Fraser's *Cromwell. Our Chief of Men* (1975).

Others I found useful were Maurice Ashley's *Cromwell's Generals* (1954), Geoffrey Trease's *Portrait of a Cavalier* (Newcastle) (1979), Ruth Spalding's *The Improbable Puritan* (an excellent life of Bulstrode Whitelocke) (1975), F. H. Sunderland's *Marmaduke, Lord Langdale* (1926), Carola Oman's *Henrietta Maria* (1936), H. G. Tibbutt's *Colonel John Okey* (Bedfordshire Historical Record Society 1955), Winifred, Lady Burghclere's *George Villiers, Second Duke of Buckingham* (1903), F. T. R. Edgar's *Sir Ralph Hopton* (1968), W. H. Dawson's *Cromwell's Understudy: The Life and Times of General John Lambert* (1938), R. W. Ramsey's *Henry Ireton* (1949), A. M. W. Stirling's *The Hothams* (1918).

Notes on Sources

ABBREVIATIONS

FC	*The Fairfax Correspondence:* I & II *Memoirs of the Reign of Charles the First,* 1848. III & IV *Memorials of the Civil War,* 1849.
M	Markham, Clements R. *A Life of the Great Lord Fairfax,* 1870.
SM	Fairfax's own *Short Memorials of Some Things to be Cleared Duringe my Command in ye Army.*
SMNA	Fairfax's *A Short Memorial of the Northern Actions, Duringe ye Warr there Fro ye Yeare 1642 till 1644.*
Clar.	Clarendon, Edward, Earl of. *History of the Rebellion.* Unless otherwise indicated, references are to the new edition 1826, in 8 volumes, though some passages quoted use the wording from the 1704 folio edition.
Sprigge	Sprigge, Joshua. *Anglia Rediviva, England's Recovery,* 1647.
DNB	*Dictionary of National Biography.*
Slingsby	*The Diary of Sir Henry Slingsby* (1836).
Gardiner *HGCW*	Gardiner. *History of the Great Civil War.*
Gardiner *HCP*	Gardiner. *History of the Commonwealth and Protectorate.*
CSP *Venetian*	*Calendar of State Papers* (Venetian) 1628–60 (1911–35)

SUB-TITLE

Fairfax's official designation when in command of the New Model Army, as given on the title page of Sprigge's *Anglia Rediviva,* was 'Captain-General of all the Parliament's Forces in England'. After succeeding his father, Fairfax was often referred to as 'the Lord General'. Usually he was simply called 'the General'.

PREFACE

Fairfax being forgotten: when in 1984 an appeal was launched for the restoration of his tomb at Bilbrough, the Department of the Environment's Historic Buildings Committee declined to help on the grounds that the matter was of 'insufficient historical importance'. There has also been an historical novel, *Born for Victory* by Juliet Dymoke (1960).

The quotation is from one Canon Raine and comes from the *Genealogy of the Fairfaxes* (privately printed).

The early history of the Fairfaxes is in Chap. 1 of *FC* I, M 2–9, an article on *The Fairfax Family* by C. C. Harrison from *Scribner's Monthly* reprinted in *Old Yorkshire*, New Series, Vol. 3, and another (in distinctly hectic prose) by Lockwood Huntley, *The Fairfaxes of Denton and Nun Appleton* (1906) in the Historic Families Series reprinted from the *Yorkshire Gazette*. For Thomas and Ferdinando, first and second Lords Fairfax, see the *DNB*.

The 'Order for the House at Denton, written by Thomas, Lord Fairfax of Denton' is in S. Croft's *Excerpta Antiqua*. For Tom Fairfax's young days see M. Charles's letter to the first Duke of Buckingham is in *FC* I 119. The letters quoted are from *FC*. The Admissions register at Gray's Inn records that Fairfax was admitted to that Inn on 26 March 1628. On the campaign in the Low Countries see Markham, *The Fighting Veres* and Ranke, *History of England* II 20–21.

I have relied heavily on J. T. Cliffe's *The Yorkshire Gentry*, an extremely thorough and valuable study. The division of the 679 families is his (Chap. XV). An article by J. W. Clay on 'The Gentry of Yorkshire at the Time of the Civil War' in the *Yorkshire Archeological Journal* 23 (1914–15) contains lists of the Royalist and Parliamentary gentry. The letter about the reluctance of men in the West Riding to contribute to the King's 'free gift' is in *FC* I 73. For the elder Thomas Fairfax's part in collecting the forced loan see R. R. Reid's *The King's Council in the North* 399. The 'historian of the Yorkshire gentry' is J. T. Cliffe. The letters about Tom Fairfax's marriage and subsequent illness are from *FC* I 296–313 as are those between Tom Fairfax and his grandfather (I 355–7). The quotation from Aubrey is from *Brief Lives*: 'The Olden Time'. Old Lord Fairfax's gloomy predictions about his grandson dissipating the family fortunes are in a memorandum by Charles Fairfax in *FC* I cvii (*Historical and Biographical Memoir of the Fairfax Family*). The Slingsby quotation is from *Slingsby* p. 11. That from Burnet is from the *History of His Own Times* p. 27. Old Lord Fairfax's will is printed in *FC*, as are Stockdale's letters about Strafford (I 104) and the Irish massacre (I 367). The quotation about the new Yorkshire families is from F. W. Brooks's Historical Association pamphlet *The Council of the North* (1953) The quotation from Professor J. P. Kenyon is from the preface to his *Stuart England* (Pelican Books 1978). The remark about Queen Elizabeth is from a letter of 24 Feb. 1627 quoted in *FC* I 90 and the remark about Charles I being conscientious but untrustworthy is by Gardiner *HGCW* I 227.

The Stockdale letter, the drawing up of the petition by Stockdale and the petition itself are in *FC* I 347–72. For the growing restiveness in Yorkshire see Cliffe *op. cit.* 314–31 The Slingsby quote is in *Slingsby* 76. For Heyworth Moor see Rushworth IV 632, *Sprigge* and *Slingsby* 77. The Fairfax quotation is from *SM*, Clarendon's from *Clar*.

III 186, Rushworth's from *FC* III 17. The remark about the 'drowsy and unactive genius' is from *Clar.* III 66, Sir Robert Poyntz's from Carte's *Original Letters* I 21.

Slingsby's quote is from *Slingsby* 80–81 and Fairfax's from *SM*.

For the passage on warfare in the seventeenth century I have relied mainly on Firth, *Cromwell's Army* 80–151, Col. T. S. Baldock's *Cromwell as a Soldier*, Markham's *The Fighting Veres*, Colonel W. G. Ross's *Oliver Cromwell and his 'Ironsides' as they are represented in the so-called Squire Papers* . . ., and Francis Markham's *Five Decade's of Epistles of Warre* (London 1622). I have also quoted the *Memoirs of Colonel Hutchinson* 259.

CHAPTER 3   THE RIDER OF THE WHITE HORSE
pp. 23–34

For the fighting in Yorkshire the principal source is *SMNA* which I have quoted freely. Other sources are *Slingsby*, *The Life of William Duke of Newcastle* by Margaret Duchess of Newcastle and contemporary tracts. Gardiner's account (HGCW) is clear and useful.

The Northern Intelligence quote is from *FC* I 419 as is Lenthall's letter to Lord Fairfax, I 30–31, and Ferdinando's report to the Committee, I 28. The Parliamentary declaration about Papists is in Rushworth's *Historical Collections* (Jan. 7, 1642).

The King's letter to Newcastle, of 15 Dec., is quoted in *Gardiner HGCW* I 83. For the Sherburn raid, see *SMNA*, *Slingsby* (87) and *A True Relation of the Fight at Sherburn* (1642) in Leeds Reference Library.

Bradford: see Siege of Bradford annexed to *The Original Memoirs of Sir Thomas Fairfax* (a printed version of *SM*), Fairfax's account in *SMNA*, *Brave News* . . . (British Library E.83(36)), *A Second Letter from the Lord Fairfax* (British Library E84(15)), *An Historical Narrative of the Life of Joseph Lister of Bradford in Yorkshire* ed. Thomas Wright, London 1842, *The Rider of the White Horse* (1642) (British Library E.88(24)). Fairfax's letter to his father is in *FC* I 33.

For the storming of Leeds see *SMNA*, *A true and plenary Relation* (1642), Leeds Reference Library (whence comes the quote about 'fresh-water Souldiers'), *A true Relation of the passages at Leeds* (British Library E.88(23)).

References to the Hothams are in *FC* I 36. Clarendon's comment is from *Clar.* III 441.

Seacroft Moor: see *SMNA*, the Duchess of Newcastle's *Life* of the Duke, Hodgson *Memoirs* 97. The Fairfax letter from Bradford (20.4.1643) is in the possession of Lady Fairfax. A version is in *FC* I 44–5. There is a good modern account of this and subsequent actions in Young and Holmes *The English Civil War: A Military History* Chaps 6 & 10.

Wakefield: the superior Royalist intelligence was in part based on intercepts. A letter from Belassis to Rupert of 17 May 1643 (at Leeds Castle) enclosed two intercepted letters of Tom Fairfax's. *SMNA*, Rushworth, V 269, the Duchess of Newcastle's *Life*, *Gardiner HGCW* I 163, John Vicars's *God in the Mount* 337; the Venetian Secretary's quote is from *State Papers Venetian* 26, (Gerulamo Agostini 12 June 1643). The letter from leaders of the Eastern Association is in *FC* I 46.

Adwalton Moor: *SMNA*, Duchess of Newcastle's *Life*, Lister's *Historical Narrative* 19, Hodgson's *Memoirs*, Warwick's *Memoires* 257–8, Slingsby 96, Rushworth. The Clarendon quote is in IV 137 note (addition from MS C).

CHAPTER 4   DISASTER AND RECOVERY   pp. 35–42

The best source for all this is *SMNA*. See also *Slingsby* 97–100, and Rushworth. The 'something' which 'came on the Lord's Day night' is in Lister's *Historical Narrative* 23–4. Lenthall's letter is in *FC* I 50.

The crossing from Hull: Cromwell's account is in W. C. Abbott, *The Writings and Speeches of Oliver Cromwell* I 261.

Winceby: see *A true Relation of the Late Fight Betweene the Right Honourable The Earle of Manchesters Forces, and the Marquesse of Newcastles Forces* (British Library E.71(5)) Manchester's account is in *Lords Journals* 16 October 1643. Firth *Cromwell's Army* 139 n. 2 says that neither Baldock (*Cromwell as a Soldier*) nor Hoenig 'does justice to the share of Fairfax and the second line'. *An Exact Relation of the Victory* . . . is quoted in *FC* I 62–5. The quote from Mrs Hutchinson is from her *Memoirs of Colonel Hutchinson* 167.

Nantwich: see *SMNA*, Rushworth, Carte *Original Letters* I 36–42 (Byron's account). *Memoirs of Colonel Hutchinson* 204, *Gardiner HGCW* I 346, Whitelocke *Memorials* I 237, *FC* III 67–75, and Young & Holmes *The English Civil War* 175–6. Fairfax's letter to Anne is in *FC* III. 74. The Clarendon quotation is from *Clar. IV* 425 note.

CHAPTER 5   THE LADY OF LATHOM AND MARSTON
MOOR   pp. 43–55

The letter to the Lancashire authorities is in *FC* III 76, as is the letter about the men following the plough (III 79, from Colonel Duckenfield). For the siege, see *A Journal of the Siege of Lathom House*, included in the 1906 edition of the *Memoirs of Colonel Hutchinson*, from which come some of the quotations about the castle.

The autograph draft of Fairfax's letter to the Countess of Derby was sold at Sotheby's on 21 July 1980 (Lot 41). A version is in *FC* III 85–6. The Countess's reply is quoted in the *Journal of the Siege* 495.

Lambert's letter is in *FC* III 94.

For Selby see Rushworth, Ranke *History of England* II 400, *Gardiner HGCW* I 396. Ferdinando's letter is quoted from *A Letter Sent from the Right Honourable The Lord Fairfax . . . concerning the great Victory . . . at Selby . . .* (19 April 1644) Slingsby's quotation is from *Slingsby* 106, Fairfax's from *SMNA*, Clarendon from *Clar. IV* 422.

Siege of York: see *Slingsby* 107 *et seq.*, Rushworth, *SMNA*, the Duchess of Newcastle's *Life*. For Rupert's approach see *FC* I 1, M, Young & Emberton *Sieges of the Great Civil War* 75–81. Clarendon's comment is in *Clar. IV* 509. Rupert's letter to the King, of 14 June 1644 is quoted in Young *Marston Moor* 86–7. This is a principal source for the battle. I have also found valuable P. R. Newman's *Marston Moor, 2 July 1644:*

The Sources and the Site (University of York, Borthwick Papers No. 53) and Alfred R. Burne's *The Battlefields of England* 213–29. See also Rushworth V 632, *Gardiner HGCW* I 436–48, Drake's *Eboracum* 168. The labourer's remark is in A. D. H. Leadman *Battles Fought in Yorkshire*. Fairfax's comment is from *SMNA*, which has a good deal about the battle. See also his 'A Modest Refutation of an Error Published in Print by Mr Fuller, in his Book of Worthyes . . .' in the Antiquarian Repertory (1808) Vol. III. The Slingsby quotation is from *Slingsby* 112. 'They stood at sword's point a pretty while . . .' is from Scoutmaster Lionel Watson's account — *A more Exact Relation of the Battell Neer York* (British Library, Thomason Tracts E.100(12)). Bowles's remark is from *Manifest Truths* E.343(1). *A Full Relation of the Late Victory . . .* by Captain Stewart is in E.54(19). The recent authority is P. R. Newman in his York University pamphlet *Marston Moor . . .* Sir James Lumsden's account is quoted in Young, *Marston Moor* 267–8. Denzil Holles's account is in his *Memoirs* in Maseres's *Select Tracts* I 199. Fairfax's appeal to spare the Whitecoats is from Vicar's *God's Arke overtopping the World's Waves* (1646) 284 as is the quotation about him having lost no honour this day (274). The quotation from Thomas Stockdale is from his letter to Rushworth quoted in Firth's *Marston Moor* 73–6. Ranke's remark is from his *History of England* II 410, Holles's from his *Memoirs* 199, Whitelocke's from *Memorials* I 276, Burne's from *The Battlefields of England* 226.

The official despatch by the victorious generals is in *Calendar of State Papers, Domestic 1644* p. 311. Cromwell's letter of 5 July 1644 to Colonel Valentine Walton is quoted in Carlyle's *Oliver Cromwell's Letters and Speeches* Part II Letter XXI, and in Abbott *The Writings and Speeches of Oliver Cromwell* I 287. For the aftermath see the *Memoirs* of Sir Hugh Cholmley 69–71.

CHAPTER 6   GENERAL OF THE NEW MODEL ARMY
pp. 56–66

The Trevor quotation is from Carte *Original Letters* I 78. The Sprigge quotation is from *Anglia Rediviva*, Fairfax's from *SM*. Cromwell's speech of 9 December 1644 is quoted in Carlyle's *Oliver Cromwell's Letters and Speeches* Part II and Abbott *op. cit.* I 314. Chaloner's letter is in *FC* III 155. Baldock's comment is in *op. cit.* p. 195, Baxter's from *Reliquae Baxterianae*, Sprigge's from *Anglia Rediviva* 7. Whitacre's diary (BL Add MSs 31, 116 f 188) is quoted in Kishlansky *Rise of the New Model Army* 38. Contarini's report is in *State Papers (Venetian)*.

On the debates in the House, see Kishlansky *op. cit.* 38–41, *Gardiner HGCW* II 64–75.

Fairfax's quotations are from *SM*. Widdrington's letter is in *FC* III 160. For his reception by the Speaker see Rushworth, Whitelocke *Memorials* I 392 and *FC* III 161. Chaloner's letter is in *FC* III 162–4.

'The most astonishing creation . . .' is from H. N. Brailsford *The Levellers and the English Revolution* (1961). On the forming of the New Model, see *Gardiner HGCW* II 61 and Chap. XXVIII, Coward *The Making of the English Revolution* 189, Rushworth, Kishlansky *op. cit.* 37, 42–51, 61–75, Firth *Cromwell's Army* and *Sprigge*

325–30, on all of which I have drawn. The volume of contracts in the Museum of London is reproduced in Gerald I Mungeam 'Contracts for the Supply of Equipment to the New Model Army in 1645': *Journal of the Arms and Armour Society* Vol. VI No. 3 Sept. 1968.

The secret code is in the possession of Lady Fairfax. The names of the staff are in *Sprigge*. For red coats see Vicar's *Jehovah Jireh* (1644) 204 and 215 and Firth *Cromwell's Army* 234. These contracts with Richard Downs for cloth are from Mungeam *op. cit.*

Whitelocke is quoted in Kishlansky *op. cit.* 49, his remark about pay is in Whitelocke *Memorials* I 421, the two ordinances he quotes are in *Memorials* I 431. Culpepper's letter is in *Gardiner HGCW* II 320 For officers preaching see Firth's *Cromwell's Army* 335. Holles's remarks are from his *Memoirs* 276–7. For the exclusion of Lilburne see *Gardiner HGCW* II 150. Warwick describes his talk with Fairfax in his *Memoires* 253. Firth's comment on Fairfax's powers is in his *Cromwell's Army* 55. Whitelocke's quotation is from *Memorials* II 20 and the King's from BL Thomason Tracts E.292(27) p. 3.

CHAPTER 7   NASEBY   pp. 67–75

Cromwell's letter is in Carlyle's *Oliver Cromwell's Letters and Speeches* Part II letter XXIV, and Abbott *op. cit.* I 336. For the numbers who set out in the New Model see Firth *Cromwell's Army* 36. For the control of the Committee of Both Kingdoms see *Gardiner HGCW* II 164–5. For Fairfax's disciplinary measures and his treatment of his own regiment see *Sprigge* 19. The capture of the carts of Canary wine is in Whitelocke *Memorials* I 436. The King's letter to the Queen is dated 8 June (BL Thomason Tracts E.292(27)). Cromwell's letter to Fairfax of 4 June is in Carlyle *op. cit.* Part II Letter XXVIII, and Abbott *op. cit.* I 352. Gardiner's comment is from *HGCW* II 170. Fairfax's letter of 4 June to Ferdinando was sold at Sotheby's on 21 July 1980 (Lot 40). A version is in *FC* III 228.

For the northern cavalry's refusal to move see *Slingsby* 149. The request for Cromwell is in *Sprigge* 28–9. The letter is quoted in *Cromwelliana* 18. The lifting of the Committee of Both Kingdoms' restrictions on Fairfax's authority on 9 June is in *Gardiner HGCW* II 200 quoting *Com. Letter Book*.

For the numbers at Naseby see *Gardiner HGCW* II 208 and the Note in *Gardiner HGCW* II 'On the Strength and Preliminary Movements of the Armies at Naseby' and the Additional Note by Lieutenant-Colonel Ross. For the battle see *Sprigge*, *Slingsby* 150–53, Gardiner *HGCW* II Chap. XXXI, Warwick *Memoires* 284–7, Baldock *Cromwell as a Soldier* 230–42, M Chap XX, Young and Holmes *English Civil War* 239–50, Burne *Battlefields of England* Chap XVII, BL Thomason Tracts E.288(22, 25, 28 and 38) and Carte *Original Letters* I 127–9 (Wogan's account). Cromwell's overheard remark is quoted in Fraser *Cromwell* 157. Sprigge's description is from *Sprigge* 34, Slingsby's from *Slingsby* 151, Sprigge's passage about Fairfax from *Sprigge* 42. Fairfax's lost helmet BL Thomason Tracts E.288(38), and the comment 'Sir, had you seen him . . .' from E.288(22). Slingsby on the defeat of Langdale's horse is *Slingsby* 152. Lord Carnwath's interference with the King is in *Gardiner HGCW* II

214. The story of Fairfax and Captain D'Oyley is in Whitelocke's *Memorials* I 449. Cromwell's letter from Harborough of 14 June is in Carlyle *op. cit.* Part II Letter XXIX. Ludlow's comment is from his *Memoirs* I 123, Hales's from Maseres's *Tracts II — The Mystery and Method of his Majesty's Happy Restoration* by John Price.

Ranke's comment is from *History of England* II 433, and he quotes Clarendon (IV 48 from the 1849 edition).

CHAPTER 8   LANGPORT AND THE SIEGE OF BRISTOL
pp. 76–85

The Clubmen's motto is in Rushworth. On the Clubmen see Whitelocke *Memorials* I 460, 477–510, Rushworth, Barry Coward *The Stuart Age* 188, *Gardiner HGCW* II 230–80.

The remark about barns and hedges is from *A brief narrative of the Expedition to Taunton,* quoted in Firth, *Cromwell's Army* 248. Fairfax's letter about the bad state of the army is in *Lord's Journals* VII 464.

For the battle of Langport see *Sprigge,* Burne *More Battlefields of England* Chap. XVIII, Whitelocke *Memorials* I 471–7, *Gardiner HGCW* II Chap. XXXII, Baldock *Cromwell as a Soldier* 248–53, Baxter *Reliquae Baxterianae* 54. Fairfax's letter to his father about the battle is in *FC* III 235.

Fairfax's letter to his father before Bridgwater is in *FC* III 239. The p.s. to his subsequent letter is in *FC* III 240, that about clubmen on p. 244. Cromwell's remark about them is from his letter to Fairfax of 4 August in Carlyle *op. cit.* Part II Letter XXX, and Abbott *op. cit.* I 369. Fairfax's letter about sieges is in *FC* III 246. For the taking of Bridgwater see *Sprigge.*

Fairfax's remarks about pay are in *FC* III 244–5. His declaration about the risks of the plague is in *Sprigge* 88, and his letter to Ferdinando in *FC* III 248. His summons to Rupert is in *Sprigge* 97. Rupert's reaction is in *Cromwelliana* 22 as is the note about no soldier being allowed to show Fairfax obedience while he rode round.

The detailed preparations for the storm of Bristol are in *Sprigge* 94.

The King's angry letter to Rupert was sold at Sotheby's on 21 July 1980 (Lot 30). His letter to Maurice is in *King Charles, Prince Rupert and the Civil War* ed. Sir Charles Petrie 16. Cromwell's account of Bristol is in Carlyle *op. cit.* Part II Letter XXXI, and Abbott *op. cit.* I 374 (see also note 172 on p. 378).

CHAPTER 9   TRIUMPH IN THE WEST   pp. 86–94

Fairfax's remark about the Royalists being dejected is in *FC* III 250. The remark about 'taking strongholds hourly' is in Gibb *The Lord General* 132 quoting Hist. MSS Comm. Report VII 452. Goring's raid is in Whitelocke *Memorials* I 528.

Fairfax's letter mentioning 'the extreme coldness' is in *FC* III 264 and that about his own ailments on p. 251. For the proposed honours see Whitelocke *Memorials* I 541, *Gardiner HGCW* II 374. Fairfax's letter about 'our business' going on prosperously is in *FC* III 274–5, Clarendon's quote from *Clar.* V 306. For the taking of Dartmouth see Whitelocke *Memorials* I 562–3, 567, *Gardiner HGCW* II 431, Baldock *Cromwell as a Soldier* 285. His own letter to the House of Lords is in *Sprigge* 170. His letter to Ferdinando is in *FC* III 284.

For Torrington see Rushworth, Whitelocke's *Memorials* I 573–6, *A more Full Relation of the Continued Success of His Excellency Sir Thomas Fairfax At, and since the Routing of the Enemies Forces at Torrington*, Baldock *op. cit.* 288, Carte *Original Letters* 110. Fairfax's letter of 18 February to Ferdinando is in *FC* III 285. Rushworth's in *FC* III 286. For the advance from Torrington see *A Letter sent to the Hon. William Lenthall . . . concerning Sir Tho. Fairfax's gallant Proceedings in Cornwall* 7 March 1645 (London Museum), *Gardiner HGCW* II 436–7, Ludlow *Memoirs* 131 and *The late victorious Proceedings of Sir Thomas Fairfax* 9 March 1645 (London Museum).

For Hopton's capitulation see Rushworth, *Sir Thomas Fairfax's Letter to the Hon. William Lenthall concerning the Agreement . . .* 23 March 1645 (London Museum), *A Summons from . . . Sir Thomas Fairfax to Sir Ralph Hopton* 11 March 1645 (London Museum), *Gardiner HGCW* II 438, Carte *Original Letters* 118–25. Fairfax's letter to Ferdinando is in *FC* III 288. See also *FC* III 316. For his comments see *Sprigge* 220 and 229. Hugh Peters's letter is in *FC* III 279–80. For a comment on Fairfax's generalship in his campaign see Baldock *op. cit.* 291.

The quotation from Sprigge is from *Anglia Rediviva* 321 — 'A Character of the Army. First, of the General Sir Thomas Fairfax'.

Whitelocke's remark about Fairfax's speed is from *Memorials* II 9. Fairfax's brace of bucks for the Duke of York comes from F. J. Varley *The Siege of Oxford* (1932) p. 143. For Fairfax's letter about Rupert's pass see Cary *Memorials of The Great Civil War* I 21, and for the House of Lords letter see ibid. 27. For Whitelocke's visit see his *Memorials* II 19–20. For the surrender of Oxford see Rushworth & *Gardiner HGCW* II 484–5. The Aubrey quotation is from *Brief Lives* (London, 1949 edition) 340.

Fairfax's letter to Ferdinando is in *FC* III 297. For Raglan see Whitelocke *Memorials* II 61 & 64, Rushworth, Fairfax's letter in *FC* III 316. The Sprigge quotation is from *Anglia Rediviva* 322: 'A Character of the Army'.

CHAPTER 10   PARLIAMENT AND THE ARMY
pp. 95–104

Fairfax's letter to Ferdinando is in *FC* III 317–18, that to the Speaker about Massey's Horse in Cary *Memorials* I 137–8. See also Ludlow *Memoirs* I 198–9, Kishlansky *Rise of the New Model Army* 117 and *Gardiner HGCW* II 530. Cromwell's letter to Bridget is in Abbott *op. cit.* I 416.

For his triumphal reception in London see *Sprigge* 312, Whitelocke *Memorials* II 84–7 and Rushworth VI 73–4. Lucy Hutchinson's observations are from *Memoirs of Col. Hutchinson* 270–71. Fairfax's letter from Northampton is in *FC* III 327. Holmby or Holdenby House, Northamptonshire, was an enormous palace built by Sir Christopher Hatton in the 1570s. It became a Royal residence in 1605 and was pulled down later in the seventeenth century. The visit to Cambridge is in Whitelocke's *Memorials*

II 120–21 and the letter about Constable in Firth and Davies *The Regimental History of Cromwell's Army* 399.

For the proposed disbanding of the army see Kishlansky *op. cit.* 154 *et seq.* and 184–5, *Gardiner HGCW* II 29–33 and H. N. Brailsford *The Levellers and the English Revolution* Chap. VIII. The figure for the total arrears owed to the army comes from 'The Arrears of Pay of the Parliamentary Army at the End of the First Civil War' by Ian Gentles in the *Bulletin of the Institute of Historical Research* XLVIII 1975. Cromwell's letter to Fairfax (of 11 March 1646) is in Carlyle *op. cit.* Part III Letter XLIII, and Abbott *op. cit.* I 430. Fairfax's letter to Ferdinando is in *FC* III 333–4.

Fairfax's account is in *SM*. His letter of 30 March to the Speaker is in Cary *Memorials* 187. The comment about the Lords being 'all madd' is in the *Clarke Papers* I 2. For the discussions with the Commissioners see Whitelocke *Memorials* II 127, Kishlansky *op. cit.* 192, *Clarke Papers* I 6–10, Rushworth VI 98–116 (from whom comes the quotation 'All, All . . .'), *Gardiner HGCW* II Chap. XLVIII. Holles's remarks from his *Memoirs* in Maseres's *Select Tracts* I 239. For Ensign Nicholl see Kishlansky *op. cit.* 214 and 331 and *Gardiner HGCW* II 58–9. Fairfax's letter about gunners is in Cary *Memorials* I 200–201. Baxter's medical notes are from *Reliquae Baxterianae* 2.

The letter to the agitators is in *Clarke Papers* I 85. Rushworth's letter of 18 May was sold at Sotheby's on 21 July 1980 (Lot 57). It is now in the Kent County Archives. A version is in *FC* III 343. Widdrington's letter is in *FC* III 340. His own of 18 May is in *FC* III 340. His own of 18 May is in *FC* III 344, and Bowles's in *FC* III 345. Fairfax's letter to the chief officers is in *Clarke Papers* I preface XV.

For the council of war at Bury see Brailsford *op. cit.* 195, Rushworth VI 125, *Clarke Papers* I preface. The letter to Skippon is in *Clarke Papers* I 106–7. That to the Speaker of 30 May is in Cary *Memorials* I 217. Colonel White's letter is in *Clarke Papers* I 103–4.

CHAPTER 11   CORNET JOYCE   pp. 105–110

For this affair see the *Clarke Papers* I (preface and 120–39), Fairfax's own account in *SM*, Whitelocke *Memorials* II 154–7, Rushworth VI 129–49, *Gardiner HGCW* II 84–94, Kishlansky *op. cit.* p. 339 n. 36, Warwick *Memoires* 298–9.

The remark about Fairfax leaving his physic too soon is from *Clarke Papers* I 101. The letter of 1 June about the 'greatest and newest newes' is in *Clarke Papers* preface XXV. Fairfax's recollections are from *SM*.

The alarm in the House is recorded in *Clarke Papers* I 117. For the officers who left the New Model in 1647 see Kishlansky *op. cit.* 219. The Derby House committee's demand and Fairfax's response are in Rushworth VI 129.

Fairfax's letter to the Speaker is in Cary *Memorials* I 224. For his conversation with Ireton see *Clarke Papers* preface XXVII. His own account is in *SM*. The soldiers' letter to the commissioners is in Cary *Memorials* I 223. Whalley's remark about the King being pleased to be a little merry is in his letter of 6 June to Fairfax in *Clarke Papers* I 122.

Fairfax and Cromwell 'kneeled not' — from Gibb *The Lord General* 166, quoting *Clarendon State Papers* II APP. p. xxxviii. The accounts of the discussion with the King are in *Clarke Papers* I 124–5 and Rushworth VI 147. Warwick's remark is in his

Memoires 299. Hobbes's *Behemoth* is in Maseres's *Tracts* II. Fairfax's quotations are from *SM*. Joyce's letter to Cromwell is quoted in Fraser *Cromwell* 194. The Clarendon quotation is from *Clar.* V 345.

CHAPTER 12   THE MARCH ON LONDON   pp. 111–112

Fairfax's letter about the minister at Otley is in Cary *Memorials* I 225.

Kentford rendezvous: Kishlansky *op. cit.* 231, Rushworth VI 135, *Gardiner HGCW* III 100, Whitelocke *Memorials* II 153. The Venetian quotation is from *CSP Venetian* 27 p. 320 (Gio. Battista Nani on 18 June 1647).

Triploe Heath: see *Gardiner HGCW* III 108–9. Fairfax's letter to the Speaker of 11 June is in Cary *Memorials* I 228. Rushworth's account of the drawing up of the *Declaration of the Army* is in a letter to Ferdinando in *FC* III 355. His letter to Ferdinando of 22 June is in *FC* III 357, and that of 27 June in *FC* III 359. The quotation about the army being unsatisfied is from a letter written to the commissioners by Rushworth on behalf of Fairfax and the council of war in Cary *Memorials* I 270.

Poyntz's letter is in *FC* III 359, the reply on p. 362. Fairfax's letter to the northern agitators is in the *Clarke Papers* I 146. The comment by the Venetian Ambassador (to France) (Gio. Battista Nani) dated 9 July 1647 is from *CSP Venetian* 28 p. 2. The Gardiner quotation is from *HGCW* III 134, Clarendon's from *Clar.* V 504.

Rushworth's remark to Ferdinando is in *FC* III 365. The Venetian comments are from *CSP Venetian* 28 p. 4 (11 July 1647).

Rushworth's remark about the Prince Elector's respect for Fairfax is in *FC* III 368.

Arrears. Fairfax's letter to the Speaker of 8 July is in Cary *Memorials* I 294–5, that of 16 July in *Clarke Papers* I 162. For the talks with Bellièvre: *Gardiner HGCW* III 144.

Fairfax's letter to the mayor and aldermen of York is in *Clarke Papers* I 166–7.

Charles I's suggestion that Fairfax and Cromwell should be bought off is in *Gardiner HGCW* III 172. Fairfax's letter of 17 July to Ferdinando is in *FC* III 371. His letter to the Speaker is in the Bodleian (Tanner MS 582).

Fairfax's letter to the commissioners is in Rushworth (23 July). Clarendon's remark is in *Clar.* V 464. Speaker Lenthall's letter to Fairfax is in *Clarke Papers* I 218–19. Fairfax's letter to the Lord Mayor is in Rushworth. Clarendon's remark is in *Clar.* V 463. The Venetian comment is from *CSP Venetian* 28 p. 11. (Gio. Battista Nani to the Doge and Senate 27 Aug 1647.) The Holles quotation is from his *Memoirs* 286; the Venetian comment from *CSP Venetian* 28 p. 12.

Fairfax's remark about Magna Carta is in *Gardiner HGCW* III 178. It comes originally from William Sanderson *A Compleat History of the Life and Raigne of King Charles* (1658) p. 1002.

Fairfax's retrospective note is in *SM*, Lucy Hutchinson's from the *Memoirs* 312.

Fairfax's letter to the Speaker about disabled soldiers is in Cary *Memorials* I 341–2. The surviving draft articles of agreement with the King are in *FC* III 394–6. His letter to the Lord Mayor is quoted in Rushworth VI 261.

For Anne's alleged leaking of information to the King see *Gardiner HGCW* III 203. The stories about the alleged robberies are in Capt. A. Smith's *A Complete History . . . of the most notorious Highwaymen . . .* 1933, reprint of 5th edition 1719, pages 285 and 323.

CHAPTER I3   THE LEVELLERS CRUSHED:
THE KING'S ESCAPE   pp. 123–130

For *The Case of the Army truly stated* see *Gardiner HGCW* III 214. Ireton's arguments at Putney are from Ramsay *Henry Ireton* p. 83 quoting *Clarke Papers* I. H. N. Brailsford's comment is from *The Levellers and the English Revolution* 292.

The allegation about Fairfax wearing the King's colours is in *Clarke Papers* I 410. His letter of 8 November to the Speaker is in Cary *Memorials* I 356.

The King's escape: see Fairfax's letter of 12 November to the Speaker in Cary *Memorials* I 358. That to a Commander in the North is in *Clarke Papers* I 418.

Fairfax's Remonstrance is in Maseres' *Select Tracts* Preface xxxiii–xxxix.

Corkbush Field, Ware: Fairfax's account is in Maseres' *Select Tracts* Preface xl as is William Clark's (lv–lviii). Ludlow's in his *Memoirs* I 192–3. The early nineteenth-century writer is Francis Maseres, in the Preface to his *Select Tracts*. This preface also has the declaration of Whalley's troops of horse (lxv). That by Okey's dragoons is in Rushworth (XV 318).

The Venetian comment is in *CSP Venetian* 28 p. 32. For the King's letter to Fairfax see Whitelocke *Memorials* II 243, and for Berkeley's mission to Fairfax *Gardiner HGCW* III 266.

For the negotiations with Parliament, see *Clarke Papers* I preface lvi. For Saltmarsh's talk with Fairfax see Whitelocke *Memorials* II 252. For Fairfax and Hammond see *FC* IV 7–9. The last meeting of the General Council of the Army is described in *Clarke Papers* preface lviii *et seq.* Its declaration is in Maseres' *Select Tracts* I 110–11, see also Brailsford *op. cit.* 302. Fairfax's letter about Jones is in Cary *Memorials* I 367.

The trouble with the lifeguards is in *Clarke Papers* I preface lviii note (a), Whitelocke *Memorials* II 275 (which also records the appointment of Cromwell and others to handle business) and Rushworth XV 350–51.

Ferdinando's death: see Whitelocke *Memorials* II 284 and *M* 302–3. For the April London riot see Rushworth VI 372–4.

CHAPTER I4   MAIDSTONE AND 'COLCHESTER'S TEARS'
pp. 131–141
('Colchester's Tears' was the title of a contemporary pamphlet.)

Fairfax's letter of 1 May to the Speaker is in Cary *Memorials* I 393 as is that of 7 May (p. 413). For the emotional Council of War see Brailsford *op. cit.* 332 and *Gardiner HGCW* III 365–6. Whitelocke's record of Fairfax being ordered north is in his *Memorials* II 310. See also *Gardiner HGCW* III 373. For the sending of Harrison north and Fairfax's concentrating his forces see Firth and Davies *Regimental History of Cromwell's Army* 119 *et seq.* Sir Anthony Weldon's letter is in *Clarke Papers* II (p. 15) as is the anonymous letter to Fairfax (p. 17), the letter from York (p. 20) and the letter from Barkstead (p. 22). Rushworth's letters of 30 May to the Speaker about Fairfax's advance up Shooter's Hill to Blackheath are in Cary *Memorials* I 437–9.

The doggerel Royalist rhyme about Fairfax is in a pamphlet in the possession of

Lady Fairfax — *A Case for Nol Cromwell's Nose, & the Cure of Tom Fairfax's Gout.* Fairfax's 'Proclamation against Plundering' of 31 May 1648 is in a pamphlet dated 2 June 1648 the main title of which is *The Lord General's Letter In Answer to the Message of the Kentish men* (London Library).

Fairfax at Blackheath: see Ludlow *Memoirs* I 193. *Gardiner HGCW* III 386–9, Fairfax's letter of 30 May to Sir Thomas Peyton and narrative (pamphlet cited above).

The quotation from Lucy Hutchinson is from the *Memoirs of Col. Hutchinson* 282.

Maidstone and after: Fairfax's own account (4 June to the Earl of Manchester) is in *FC* IV 32–4. See also Whitelocke *Memorials* II 323–4, Rushworth VI 407, *Gardiner HGCW* III 389–90, Hobbes's *Behemoth* in Maseres' *Select Tracts* II 599 (whence the quotation), *A Letter sent to the Honourable William Lenthall . . . of the Fight between His Excellency's The Lord Fairfax Forces at Maidstone And the Kentish Forces* (3 June 1648, written by Rushworth: London Library).

Whalley's reports to Fairfax are in *Clarke Papers* II 26–7.

For the siege see *M* 309–35, *SM*, Whitelocke *Memorials* II 330 et seq. Rushworth VI 416–75, *Gardiner HGCW* III 395–458, Warwick *Memoirs* 314, Firth *Cromwell's Army* 180–82, Firth & Davies *Regimental History of Cromwell's Army* 218, 353–4, 573.

Colchester 'not glad of their company' — *Clar.* VI 62.

Shooting of Lucas and Lyle. Fairfax's quotations are from *SM*, Clarendon's from *Clar.* VI 102. Fairfax's report to Parliament is in Rushworth VI 477. Lucas's memorial inscription is in his entry in the *DNB*. Fairfax's letter to the Speaker about what he understood by quarter is in *Clarke Papers* II preface xiii. See also Rushworth VI 499. An account of their death is in *Clarke Papers* II 31–9. See also *Gardiner HGCW* III 458–64 and a *True and Exact Relation of the Taking of Colchester . . .* (London Library).

The visit to Sir John Wentworth's is in Rushworth VI 487. Ludlow's talk with Fairfax at Colchester is recorded in his *Memoirs* 203–4

CHAPTER 15   THE KILLING OF THE KING
pp. 142–153

The story about Lord Auchinleck's remark to Dr Johnson is in J. W. Croker's *Correspondence and Diaries* (*The Croker Papers*) (1884) II 31. Doubt has been cast on its reliability. Boswell describes the row in his *Tour to the Hebrides*, but gives no details of what was said — only that both men were 'exceedingly warm and violent'.

Burnet's remark about Ireton is from the *History of his own Times* 48. See also *Gardiner HGCW* III 473–5 including, in note 1 on page 474, a rather dubious hypothesis of Sir Charles Firth's. For the St Albans meeting see Brailsford *op. cit.* 358–9 and *Gardiner HGCW* III 498–9.

Fairfax's declaration is printed in *The Representations and Consultations of the Generall Councell of the Armie at S. Albans* (London 1648) p. 5 (British Library E.472(3)).

'What happened next . . .' see *Gardiner HGCW* III 501 et seq. and Brailsford *op. cit.* 372–3. A different version, which I do not find wholly persuasive, is in David Underdown's *Pride's Purge* 120–22 (and note 34 on p. 120).

Cromwell's letter of 20 November to Fairfax is quoted in *Gardiner HGCW* III 515 and Gardiner's comment is on p. 518. Fairfax's letter to Cromwell of 28 November is in *Clarke Papers* II 62–3. Fairfax's comment is from *SM*.

Pride's Purge: see *Gardiner HGCW* III 531 *et seq.*, Ludlow *Memoirs* I 209–10, and Underdown *op. cit.* 143 *et seq.* The Clarendon quotation is from *Clar.* VI 205, Fairfax's from *SM*. Clement Walker's quotation is from his *History of Independency* Part II 31 quoted in Brailsford *op. cit.* 336.

The Yeats quotation is from his poem 'The Second Coming'.

For the General Council see the *Clarke Papers* II 73.

For Fairfax and the group of peers see *Gardiner HGCW* III 555 and for Cromwell's decision p. 558. The quotation from Burnet is from *History of his Own Times* 48. Contarini's remarks are in *CSP Venetian* 28 p. 84 (1 January 1649).

The Queen's letter is in Cary *Memorials* II 101 — Fairfax 'went away immediately': This is in Rushworth VI 566. His never appearing again — see *Gardiner HGCW* III 565 quoting *State Trials* iv 1052.

Anne's interruption: Rushworth VI 573 and *Clar.* VI 233. 'Sunday was se'nnight . . .' see Carte *Original Letters* 212 quoting a paper dated Rouen 10 February 1649 enclosed with letter from Sir E. Nicholas to the Marquess of Ormonde. 'Baited with fresh dogs . . .' — *Clarendon State Papers* II App. li. The description of the King is from the charge, printed in J. G. Muddiman *Trial of King Charles the First* 78.

Anne's second interruption is recorded — 'Here a Malignant Lady . . .' — in *The Proceedings of the High Court of Justice* (British Library 540 14). See also Rushworth VI 594 *note*. Elizabeth Fairfax's experience is in Underwood *op. cit.* 190 quoting British Library add. MS 36996 (Pontefract transcripts) fol. 143.

For Axtel's trial see Ludlow *Memoirs* II 318, and *Gardiner HGCW* III 572.

Pauw's report is in *CSP Venetian* 28 p. 90. For Fairfax's efforts to put off the execution see *The Kingdomes Faithfull Scout* Monday, 29 January 1649 (British Library 541 5). Brian Fairfax's story is in his *Memoirs of the Life of George Villiers, Second Duke of Buckingham* p. 7. The Dutch Ambassadors' second visit is in C. V. Wedgwood *Trial of Charles I* (1964) 186–7 . . . Herbert's account is in his *Memoirs* 135 and 194. The text of Buckingham's paper is in *FC* IV 253, and the report of Fairfax's funeral sermon (by Dr Stretton) in *FC* I cxviii note.

CHAPTER 16   THE END OF THE ROAD   pp. 154–162

For Fairfax's special 'engagement' see *Gardiner HCP* I 7.

The Levellers' challenge: see Brailsford *op. cit.* 474–5.

The Diggers: see Whitelocke *Memorials* III 18, Brailsford *op. cit.* Chap. XXXIV. The Council's letter to Fairfax is in the *Clarke Papers* II 209; Capt. Gladman's report is on p. 211 and the Diggers' appeal to Fairfax on p. 215.

The Leveller mutinies: see Brailsford *op. cit.* Chap. XXVI. Their objectives are from Whitelocke *Memorials* III 108.

Lockyer's revolt: Barry Coward *The Stuart Age* 213, *Gardiner HCP* I 46.

Scroope's mutiny, the march to Burford and suppression of the Levellers: Firth and Davies *Regimental History of Cromwell's Army* 109 *et seq.*, Whitelocke *Memorials* III

33–6, Fairfax's letter of 14 May to the Speaker in Cary *Memorials* II 136 and *Gardiner HCP* I Chap. II.

Fairfax at Oxford and Portsmouth: Whitelocke *Memorials* II 38–41 and *Gardiner HCP* I 54. See also Abbott *op. cit.* II 72–4.

Monk's letter is in the *Clarke Papers* II 213. 'to take off any reflection . . .' is from Whitelocke *Memorials* III 5. Fairfax's ordinances and his petition are from Whitelocke *op. cit.* pp. 58, 88, 98.

The Venetian report is in *CSP Venetian* 16 Aug. 1649. Fairfax's letter to Col. Cox is in the possession of the author.

The meeting with Cromwell: *Mercurius Politicus* for 6 June, 1650.

Whitelocke's account of Fairfax's resignation is in *Memorials* III 206–11, Ludlow's in *Memoirs* I 242–4. See also *Gardiner HCP* I. Chap. XI. Lucy Hutchinson's comments are in her *Memoirs of Col. Hutchinson* 314–16. Fairfax's letter, addressed to Speaker Lenthall, is in *Slingsby* 340–41. Gardiner's quotation of the preacher is in *HCP* I. 262. The granting of a pass to go abroad is in CSP Dom (1950) 232. The quotation from T. S. Eliot is from his essay on Andrew Marvell (1921) in his *Selected Essays*.

CHAPTER 17   MARVELL AND BUCKINGHAM
pp. 163–173

For Fairfax's omission from the new Council see Abbott *op. cit.* II 394 and note 48. Ludlow's note is from *Memoirs* I 254. '. . . Fairfax through infirmity of body . . .' This is from anonymous intelligence quoted in *FC* IV 132. The meeting with Cromwell at Ferrybridge was reported in *Mercurius Politicus* quoted in Abbott *op. cit.* II 450. The information about Fairfax's house in York is from Drake's *Eboracum* 269.

Marvell: Aubrey's description is from *Brief Lives* 73. The poems are quoted from *Andrew Marvell The Complete Poems* (1972). See also *Andrew Marvell* by John Press (British Council booklet, 1958) and the catalogue of the British Library exhibition of 1978, *Andrew Marvell, Poet & Politician*, 43–54. The miniature portrait, alleged to be of Mary Fairfax, in the Duke of Buccleuch's collection, signed by Samuel Cooper and dated 1650, which depicts a very plain young woman, cannot, I think, be of her, since it is manifestly not the portrait of a girl of twelve. Fairfax's poem is in the Bodleian (MS Fairfax 38). Another version is in the British Library (Add MS 11744, f. 48). Horace Walpole's comment is from his note on 'Thomas, Lord Fairfax' in *A Catalogue of the Royal and Noble Authors of England, Scotland and Ireland* (1806 Vol. 5 p. 112).

Fairfax's note on the breeding of horses is in York Minster Library MS Add. 47. Some of the Buckingham estates appear subsequently to have passed into Cromwell's hands — see Abbott *op. cit.* II 495.

'never accounted his own' — Brian Fairfax's remark is from his *Memoirs of the Life of George Villiers, Second Duke of Buckingham* 6. It is he who records that the rents from the Isle of Man were paid to Lady Derby. This statement is questioned by Abbott in *op. cit.* II 495 note 107, but no contrary evidence is produced, except that Lady Derby claimed to be destitute in 1657.

The report about the King's letter to Anne is in *Clarendon Papers* III 59. The Clarendon quotation is from *Clar.* VII 188–9. For Fairfax's rejection of a seat in the Council see Abbott *op. cit.* III 18 and for Fairfax's letter to Cromwell see Abbott *op. cit.* III 684. For the fears of the Independents see *Clarke Papers* III and for the agent's report see *Clarendon Papers* III 59.

Swift's description of Chesterfield is quoted in *Great Villiers* by Hester W. Chapman (1949) note p. 92. Clarendon's comment on the battle of Worcester is in *Clar.* VI 507–9. For Buckingham see *DNB*, Lady Burghclere's *George Villiers* and the *Life of George Villiers, Duke of Buckingham* by Brian Fairfax originally embedded in the catalogue of the Duke of Buckingham's pictures, published 1758; republished with Arbers' reprint of *The Rehearsal* 1868. The comments on him by Burnet, Horace Walpole (Lord Orford) and Brian Fairfax are quoted in the notes to Anthony Hamilton's *Memoirs of the Court of Charles the Second* (1846 edition) by Count Gramont. Dryden's lines are from *Absolom and Achitophel*. Brian Fairfax's remark is from his *Life of George Villiers*. Colonel Bampfylde's report is from *Clarendon Papers* III 736.

Hyde's comment is in *Clarendon State Papers* III 372. That by a member of the Council is in Chapman *op. cit.* 92. Mary as 'laide, intelligente et cultivée': this is from a note in Claire-Eliane Engel's edition (Monaco 1958) of Hamilton's *Mémoires du Chevalier de Gramont*. Her being 'transcendentally pensive' is from Burghclere *op. cit.*

Fairfax's meetings with Cromwell to secure Buckingham's release: see *Clarke Papers* III 123 and 129, and Abbott *op. cit.* IV 623, 656–7. The report to Hyde is in *Clarendon State Papers* IV 11. Brian Fairfax's description of the last meeting between Fairfax and Cromwell is in his *Life of George Villiers*. Fairfax's security for Buckingham — see *Cromwelliana* p. 182.

CHAPTER 18   FAIRFAX AND THE RESTORATION

pp. 174–183

For this chapter an important authority is an article in the *Yorkshire Archeological Journal* Vol. XXXIX (1958) p. 483 *et seq.* — 'Yorkshire and the Restoration' by A. H. Woolrych. See also Godfrey Davies *The Restoration of Charles II* (1955) Chap. VII. Brian Fairfax's quotation is from his *Iter Boreale* (I have used mainly the text of the manuscript version in the Edinburgh University Library MS. DK.5.25. — described by W. Ferguson in *The Bibliotheck* III (1960) as 'an excellent source that has never been properly utilised'.) Another, rather different, version is printed in *FC* IV 152 *et seq.* Thomas Gower's letter (to Sir Richard Leveson) is in *Hist. MSS Comm. 5th Report* Appendix p. 193. Clarendon's report is in *Clar.* VII 397. Brian Fairfax's ride is described by him in *Iter Boreale* (see above). Lilburne's march with Captain Turner: see the *Miscellanies of the Philobiblion Society* vol. 15 and *The Monckton Papers* p. 29. Dr Price's comment is from Maseres' *Tracts* II p. 748 — *The Mystery and Method of his Majesty's Happy Restauration* by John Price D.D. Brian Fairfax's quotations are from *Iter Boreale*, Burnet's from *History of his Own Times* 91. Strangeways' account is in *A Letter From a Captain of the Army*, Tadcaster 2 January 1659 (Bodleian Library). See also *A Declaration of the Rt. Hon. Thomas Lord Fairfax* (Leeds Reference Library).

The Letter to the Speaker from Fairfax, Cholmley and Arthington, sent from Poppleton on 1 January 1659 (1660), is in *A Register and Chronicle, Ecclesiastical and Civil* p. 13. Gower's remarks are in *Hist. MSS. Comm. 5th Report* Appendix p. 194.

Monk's letter to the Speaker is in *Clarke Papers* IV 239. The report of the House's reaction to Fairfax's letter is in *Clarendon Papers* IV 511. Brian Fairfax's claim is in one of the versions of *Iter Boreale*; Burnet's remark from *Own Times* 91. Monk's letter of 21 January (to John Weaver) is in *Clarke Papers* IV 251. For an account of his letter to the Devon gentry see Davies *op. cit.* 269.

For Fairfax and the meeting of the Yorkshire gentry I have relied on A. H. Woolrych's account in the *Yorkshire Archeological Journal* 501–3, and Davies *op. cit.* 286–7. Monk's letter of 18 February to Fairfax is in *FC* IV 208. Lady Willoughby's letter is in *Clarendon Papers* IV 567.

For the mission to the King in Holland see Davies *op. cit.* 350. For Jermyn and Langdale see their respective entries in the *DNB*. Fairfax's remarks in the House on the settling of old scores are in Ludlow *Memoirs* 268.

CHAPTER 19   DISILLUSION   pp. 184–189

The Waller lines are from 'Divine Poems'.

For Buckingham's carryings-on see A. Hamilton *Memoirs of the Court of Charles II*, Burghclere *op. cit.* and Chapman, *op. cit.*

Hamilton's quotation about Mary comes from the *Mémoires du Chevalier de Gramont*. The 'grand ballet' is noted in Burghclere *op. cit.* 243. The description of her by the Vicomtesse de Longueville is from the note on the Duchess of Buckingham (p. 404) from A. Hamilton's *Memoirs of the Court of Charles II* (1846 edition). The comments on Downing are quoted in H. G. Tibbutt's *Colonel John Okey*. Bowles's comment is quoted in *FC* IV 170.

Macaulay's verdict is from his review of *Hallam's Constitutional History*.

Fairfax's letter of 14 October 1663 to Buckingham is in *FC* IV 221.

The *Short Memorials* are printed in *The Antiquarian Repertory*, London 1808 Vol. III. Sir Charles Firth's edition of these, with his notes and a critical introduction, is in *Stuart Tracts 1603–1693: An English Garner*. Horace Walpole's remark is from *A Catalogue of Royal and Noble Authors* Vol. V 110. Fairfax's last letter is in *FC* IV 223.

Nikolaus Pevsner's remarks about the church at Bilbrough are in his *Yorkshire: The West Riding (the Buildings of England* (1959)) 100–101. It was built, at his own expense, by the then Lord of the Manor, Mr Thomas Fairfax. It cost him £2201 16s.

For the subsequent history of the Fairfaxes see *M* 403–14, 'The Fairfax Family' in *Old Yorkshire* new series Vol. III 196, *The Fairfaxes of Denton and Nun Appleton* by Lockwood Huntley (York 1906) and *Leeds Castle: A Brief History* by Lord Geoffrey-Lloyd and Peter Wilson (Leeds Castle Foundation, Maidstone).

Index